A MEMOIR BY

JOHN SCHNICK

Lightbulb Coffee

...or How I Survived the Sixties

Farm Boy Press
Berkeley, California

TO JOSIE,

who made a man of me.

Lightbulb Coffee

Copyright © 2020 by John Schnick

ISBN: 978-1-7343839-2-8 (paperback)
ISBN: 978-1-7343839-3-5 (eBook)

FarmBoyPress.net

John-Schnicks-Books-104139051170475
@SchnickJohn

Editorial development and creative design support by Ascent:
www.spreadyourfire.net

ALSO BY JOHN SCHNICK:

COLD 'COON & COLLARDS,
published by Farmboy Press

A Note To The Reader

———

THE EVENTS IN THIS BOOK took place from 1962 to 1977. All this stuff really happened. I've combined some days' happenings into one day, and placed some scenes out of sequence, both by accident and design. You need a story, not a hodgepodge of random memories.

Names of my immediate family are real, as are famous persons I've known over the years. The other names have been changed, both to protect the innocent, and because my memory fails me. Coming up with new names was a creative challenge and a pleasure. Sometimes I've combined two characters into one for dramatic reasons, but it's not a novel, honest. (I vastly prefer non-fiction, and stopped reading novels decades ago.)

Writing a memoir has turned out to be serious business. I was unprepared for the joy and the wonder I was in for. I hope you can experience some of the same feelings.

—JOHN SCHNICK, Berkley California 2020

PART ONE:
Delinquent Days

PART TWO:
Dirtbag Days

PART THREE:
Close Calls

John as a high school senior, 1968

PART
ONE

Delinquent
Days

Atomic Rockets and Tumbleweeds

MY THIRD PERIOD CLASS was Algebra I, with Mr. Royce. As the class snoozed through his explanation of integers, he was suddenly drowned out by a roaring like a hundred freight trains coming at us. The windows rattled, and the floor trembled. Mr. Royce stopped talking, and everyone in the room continued looking bored as they twiddled their pencils.

The roaring died down after a minute or so, and Mr. Royce continued as if nothing had happened. I wondered, *What in the world was that noise?* It was louder than a dozen Super Constellations warming up on the airfield back in Newfoundland. Everyone in the class ignored it. What exactly was going on here?

After the bell rang and the students filed out, I asked Joe, who sat behind me, "What was that noise?"

"It's the KIWI project on Sandia Base. They're testing atomic-powered rocket engines. Nobody ever talks about it. It's Top Secret."

My dad had just reported for duty at the base a couple of miles south of my new school. When I asked him that night about the noise, he looked uncomfortable. "I'm a chaplain. I don't have 'a need to know', and if I did, I couldn't tell you," was all that I could ever get out of him.

I understood then that only a select few really knew what was going on, and information of any sort was jealously guarded.

"Pay no attention to the man behind the curtain" was not just a line from *The Wizard of Oz*. It was a way of life on the military bases where I grew up.

A couple of weeks earlier, my family had arrived in New Mexico. Route 66 gradually descended as our big Plymouth wagon rolled into the Valley of the Rio Grande. Just beyond the river, the lights of the sprawling city of Albuquerque shone as darkness fell. The green oblongs of the Sandia range rose beyond the city.

Dad was assigned to the Defense Atomic Support Agency at Sandia Base. Our family rented a pink adobe house at the edge of town, on a desert mesa below the granite cliffs of Sandia Crest.

I started eighth grade a few days later and was allowed to ride my Phillips bicycle to Jackson Junior High. My dad had helped me mount new thorn-proof tires on the rims, because regular tires would be ruined almost immediately by the cactus and tumbleweed spines found all over the Mesa.

I could ride along one of the paved roads that skirted the Mesa, or cut straight across the packed adobe and sand and get to school twice as fast. A deep arroyo split the flat tableland. This forced me to dismount and carry the bike down one crumbling canyon wall, across the sandy bottom, and up the other bank.

Riding home on my bicycle after the first day of school, I dismounted at the edge of the arroyo. Instead of a crumbly dry gulch, I was faced with a rushing torrent of brown water. I could see that wading the flood would be impossible—the water too deep, wide, and fast to survive. If I were to be swept away in this, I would surely be drowned and carried off into the Rio Grande.

Having no choice, I pedaled back to the school and followed the paved road which crossed the arroyo on a viaduct about a mile downstream. As I rode, I puzzled where all that water had come from, since the sky was clear and blue in Albuquerque.

The riddle was solved when I turned east on Menaul Boulevard and faced the Sandias. A black cloud boiled in a box canyon up near the crest, which I knew was over 10,000 feet in altitude.

As I pumped the pedals up the grade to our house, I realized why twelve-year-olds could get motor scooter licenses, and fourteen-year-olds could get car licenses in New Mexico, like my mother did in the Thirties. The state was underpopulated, and schools were few and far between.

When I finally got home, sweaty and winded, I leaned my bike against the adobe wall and went in the kitchen door. I walked straight to the sink and poured a tall glass of water.

"How was the first day of school?" asked Mother, coming in from the parlor.

"Fine," I said, between gulps.

"Nothing interesting happened?"

"No, ma'am. May I watch TV?"

"Not until you've finished your homework."

"Yes, ma'am."

I write about this mundane exchange because it tells something about my life. From the time I had started first grade, my father required me to answer any question with "Yes, sir" or "No, sir", and "Yes, ma'am" or "No, ma'am" to my mother. If I was careless and forgot this honorific, I would get a belt-whipping for "being sassy". I think this was due to Dad's reverence for the Marine Corps. He wanted me to be prepared when I enlisted. It had become habit by the time I was in junior high. My mother, on the other hand, didn't really care about this stuff.

The only homework I had that first day was from Mr. Royce: a page of simple equations to be solved for X. I foundered immediately, being clueless as to how to solve any of the problems. Asking for help from my parents was out of the question. I had long been told that Dad's work was to preach the gospel, Mother's was to cook, wash, and sew, and mine was to do my lessons.

I decided to fill in random numbers. It would look like I had finished my homework, and I could watch TV.

The next day at school, Mr. Royce drew a big red zero over my work and kept me after class. Although Mr. Royce tried his best to drill some algebra into my head, as soon as I left the classroom everything he told me would drift away like smoke.

When I took a test, the numbers on the page became more meaningless the harder I stared at them. When I was given my report card at the end of six weeks, I got an A in English, A in Art, B in Science, C in PE, and an F in Algebra. When I saw the failing grade, I broke into a cold sweat.

I raced home on my bike across the Mesa, swerving around the cholla and prickly pear. If I hurried, Mother would not be home from picking up Polly at school and stopping at the store. Letting myself into the empty house, I rummaged in Dad's desk until I found a bottle of ink eradicator.

I carefully dabbed a bit of the clear fluid on the inked letter F, and it disappeared. Unfortunately, the area where the ink had been was now fuzzy with disturbed paper fibers. I realized that the ink for my new improved grade might bleed.

Mother's ironing board was already set up in the study, so I plugged in the iron and set the dial to "silk". I pressed the report card gently, and the fibers lay flat. I unplugged the iron, and carefully lettered "D" into the box with Dad's fountain pen. It looked okay, and it did fool my folks because I avoided a whipping.

It did not, however, fool the school. The next Monday I was called into the office. When I arrived, I was sent to the counselor. I knew I was in trouble.

"Hi John, come on in," said the blonde lady behind the desk. "Please close the door behind you." She rose from her seat, walked around the desk, and held out her hand. I shook it. "I'm Penny Prentiss. Please call me Penny."

"Yes, ma'am," I said.

"Penny," she said.

"Okay. . .Penny."

"Let's sit over here," she said, extending an open hand towards two office chairs beside her desk.

We sat. She crossed her legs.

"I just wanted to get to know you," she said.

"Is this about my grade in Algebra?"

"No, not really, I'm here to help you in any way I can. Are you having trouble in math?"

"I guess I just don't get it. I'm too stupid to do algebra," I mumbled.

"John, you're not stupid," she said. "I'm not supposed to tell you this, but on the Binet test, you got a very high score."

I remembered taking the Stanford-Binet test. Every new student in the school had to take it. I enjoyed it, because we got to skip third period and take the test in the cafeteria.

"Then why can't I pass Algebra?"

"Maybe we can find out together."

Penny invited me to join a discussion group, to meet once a week with her and a few other students.

A week later, instead of PE, I reported to the office. In a conference room, Penny waited at a round table with three other boys. I closed the door behind me.

"John, this is Carlos, Frankie, and Sam. Have a seat. Smoke 'em if you got 'em. It's okay in here," said Penny, smiling.

I noticed lit cigarettes in the glass ashtray in the center of the circle, and sat down.

Frankie, I knew from Art class; Carlos and Sam, everybody knew. They were the stars of the Jaguars football team. These were the biggest guys in the school, and I was probably the smallest. These guys had deep voices, and my voice had yet to change. Nobody spoke for a moment.

Sam picked his fag from the tray and took a drag.

"Well, I did it again," he said, blowing a cloud upward.

"What?" asked Frankie.

"Bought another Cushman scooter." Sam put the butt back in the ashtray. "That last one was a pain in the ass, but I gotta have wheels."

I was a lowly eighth grader, and these guys were all in ninth. I continued to attend the discussion group for the rest of the year. My Algebra marks did not improve, and I wondered what these Big Men On Campus thought about me.

I wanted to be like these guys: tall, muscular, and deep-voiced. Instead I was a genuine 98-pound weakling with a high, squeaky voice—a real disappointment to my father, who wanted a son like himself, tall, strong and athletic. I was used to being a "spazz", but it was getting old.

Frankie was in my art class, in the afternoon. The teacher, Mr. Renaud, taught us drawing, painting, and ceramics. One day Frankie came up to me while I was copying a Big Daddy Roth car monster on my drawing pad.

"John, if I brought in my dad's racing helmet, could you paint some flames on it?"

"Sure," I said. Frankie's dad was Jerry Samuels, who raced stock cars at Sandia Speedway, along with the famous Al Unser and his son Bobby.

Frankie brought the battered white fiberglass helmet to the next class. I sanded it lightly, then painted it deep blue with orange and yellow flames flowing back. Across the rear I lettered "Jerry". Frankie loved it and gave me a five-dollar bill.

Did this mean that Frankie thought I was okay? I hoped so, but at any rate, this was the first money I ever earned from artwork, and it gave me an idea.

Mr. Renaud liked my speedway art too. With his permission—and school paint—I started painting car doors with flames and competition numbers, as well as helmets for other father and son racing teams. I branched out into sweatshirts and tee shirts, with *Rat Fink* or *Wild Child* driving flaming dragsters across the front. Mr. Renaud told me where to buy aniline dyes to refill the magic markers I needed.

Soon, kids were coming up to me between classes and asking if I would paint a sweatshirt for them, or even two, so a girlfriend could wear a matching one. By the time I was in ninth grade, I made an oversize Jaguar head out of papier mâché and would clown around on the sidelines of the football games as a mascot. The head cheerleader, a tall blonde named Liska Pepper, would greet me by name when we passed in the hall.

I was still a runt who couldn't pass Algebra, but, maybe because people liked my art they were starting to recognize me. I realized that popular kids, like Liska, knew everybody's name, and used it whenever they could. Maybe I could do the same.

In eighth grade I didn't really understand why, but, when I forged my grades and spent my energy on art instead of math or sports, I was making a choice. Where that choice would lead me was something of a mystery.

Turquoise and Plutonium

AT HOME, WITH MY FAMILY, things were going along as usual: lots of prayers, church three days a week and twice on Sundays. If I came home and heard dreary organ music playing on the hi-fi, I knew Dad was writing a sermon and couldn't be disturbed. I pretty much toed the line, and, given that I had started faking my report cards, I hadn't had a licking since we had moved to Albuquerque.

The threat would still show in my father's eyes whenever he was displeased with a chore I'd neglected, such as shining my shoes on Saturday night. I knew that eventually something would set him off again.

I began to wonder if my parents' way of life was the only way to live, or even the best way.

I'd been to friends' houses and sometimes was taken aback by how differently other families ran things. At Wayne's house, his older sister was allowed to play Everly Brothers albums on the hi-fi in the living room and dance with her high school girlfriends. Tommy Gregg, my locker partner, had *Playboy* centerfolds tacked up on his bedroom wall, and his parents didn't seem to mind.

My parents would have flipped if they knew I had even glimpsed these voluptuous images. Part of me felt guilty, and part of me forgot everything my family stood for when faced with these images of feminine curves. In fact, it stood up and saluted. If the folks ever found out, I would be doomed to long prayer sessions and have to beg the Lord for forgiveness.

It wasn't that I didn't love my parents. I did. It was just that the atmosphere around their house was stifling.

I was getting restless and yearning for something different.

I was beginning to think that my parents were a little out of step with the world. Mom or Dad would have agreed with me. After all, one of their favorite gospel songs was *This World is Not My Home:*

This world is not my home I'm just a passing through...

I wasn't so sure about this. I knew there were some ugly and scary things on the earth, but I also knew there was transcendent beauty and delight. Heaven, with all its harps, robes, and angels, seemed like a big bore.

My mother was an art enthusiast. On road trips she delighted in stopping for art museums in the cities, or petroglyphs in the desert. She organized family excursions to Taos Pueblo, Shiprock, and Santo Domingo Pueblo. Indian culture had made a big impression on her as a girl growing up on horseback in New Mexico.

Mother heard that the Santo Domingo Indians would trade art and jewelry for second-hand clothes. She and I filled a couple of corrugated boxes with castoff hats, suits, and children's wear, and drove to the pueblo on the banks of the Rio Grande.

We passed unpaved streets and adobe houses on the way to the church square. We parked next to a long house with a ramada, or sunshade, in front. Silver jewelry was displayed on propped-up boards facing the street. We pulled our boxes from the back of the station wagon and set them on a table.

Two women came out of the adobe and started to pick through the boxes. Evidently they liked what they saw, because they picked up one of the boxes and started to carry it into the house.

"Hey, wait a minute," said my mom. "We want to trade..."

The two women paused then sat the container back down. The older one looked askance at Mother, then asked, "What you want?"

"Oh, anything," replied Mother, "silver jewelry, Kachina dolls..."

For the first box, Mother ended up with a trio of painted wooden Kachinas, and for the second I got a silver ring with a square blue turquoise set in the front. On the drive back to Albuquerque, Mother shook her head and laughed when we discussed our trading trip.

"I couldn't believe those gals thought we were just giving away all that stuff," she said. "I was hoping we could get a little more in trade than we did."

"It turned out all right," I said. "I like my ring."

"True," she said. "I've always wanted some Kachina dolls. They'll look great on the fireplace mantel."

Looking back, I wonder what my mom expected to get from our visit to the trading post. I thought at the time that we got a pretty good deal for our cartons of worn-out clothes. I knew my mother respected the Indians and wanted to help them, but I wonder if she had any real idea how hard their lives were. She wanted to help Alec Cooney's family, too, back in Arkansas, but perhaps the gap between the income of a Navy family and a sharecropper or Pueblo family was too large to bridge with good intentions.

The Defense Atomic Support Agency assigned Dad to "Temporary Additional Duty" for six weeks at the Tonopah Nevada Nuclear Test Range. He recounted his adventure when he returned to Albuquerque.

The test involved staking packs of dogs and herds of goats at varying distances from a tower. On the top, several pounds of pure Plutonium were contained in a dummy warhead. A charge of TNT was set off, blasting the radioactive materiel into the tethered beasts.

The object of the experiment was to predict the toxic effects of a "broken arrow" accident: if a nuclear device was lost or destroyed but not detonated. Army veterinarians slaughtered the exposed animals at intervals of hours, days, and weeks, and some were allowed to die or recover from radiation poisoning on their own.

The data generated by this abject cruelty was, of course, Top Secret. This shocked and depressed me at the time, and I worried about the veterinarians' coveralls that Dad had salvaged and brought back home to wear for yardwork or automotive repairs. These contaminated garments were supposed to be buried on the test site after the project had been completed, but as a child of the Great Depression, Dad couldn't bear to see what appeared to be perfectly good clothing go to waste. At least he didn't take them to the Santo Domingo trading post.

I knew that Dad considered the atomic bomb a blessing, since it ended World War II and prevented hundreds of thousands of deaths in an invasion of Japan. I was glad my Uncle George hadn't been forced to invade Honshu after the terrible fight in Okinawa, but I wondered, what was the point of developing bigger and better bombs year after year? Dad said it was because the communists were Satanic, and we had to fight them with everything we had.

This stuff was beginning to give me the creeps, but all the adults around me seemed to go along with it. Growing up on

Navy and Marine Corps bases, it was always assumed that I would follow in my father's footsteps, work my way up through the ranks, and become an officer.

The more I knew about the armed forces, the less I thought I wanted to enlist when I turned seventeen. Sure, that was still three years away, but a small doubt was growing. Was the Marine Corps really my pathway to manhood?

3

Orson and the Rattlesnakes

IN JUNE, SCHOOL LET OUT for the summer, and, because of my forgeries, my parents believed that I had passed Algebra. Instead of enrolling me in summer school, they sent me to a Presbyterian summer camp called Ghost Ranch. Georgia O'Keefe, the famous painter, lived there, and the picturesque old place had a wild history involving cattle rustling and gunfights.

My folks drove onto the ranch and dropped me off at headquarters, depositing me and my seabag. They waved as they drove off back to Santa Fe and Albuquerque. I looked around and saw the towering red sandstone cliffs above the place.

I knew that my parents thought it would be good for me to spend time with other young Christians and that the high desert air would be good for the asthma that had plagued me for years. They would turn out to be right, sort of.

"Hi! I'm Reverend Jerry," said a short, Spanish-looking man as he walked up to me. "I'll be your counselor for the next two weeks." He held out his hand.

I shook it. "Where do I sleep?"

"Follow me," Jerry said, and he walked up a path to a low mesa. I shouldered my bag and followed. The diminutive pastor led me to one of six canvas teepees pitched along one end of the small tableland. I saw a fire pit in the middle of the flat, and more conical tents beyond that.

"The girls' camp is off limits," Jerry said, "but everybody comes to the campfire at night."

Flipping back the oval canvas door of the teepee, the counselor stepped inside, and I followed. The tent smelled of cigarette smoke. Jerry introduced me to my roommates, Billy and Slick, then disappeared, closing the flap behind him.

Billy was stretched out on his cot reading a comic book, and Slick was sitting on another cot, hunched over, strumming a guitar. Slick looked up, took his fag from a rusty sardine can, and took a drag.

"Want to hear my version of *Traveling Man*?" he asked, blowing out a cloud of smoke.

"Sure," I replied, rolling my duffel under the remaining cot, and sitting on the edge.

He began playing an intro to the Ricky Nelson hit and got my attention. He could really play that guitar! When he started singing, he sounded just like the teen idol, except for one thing: he spiced the song with dirty words and explicit descriptions of sex.

Pretty Polynesian baby over the sea

I remember the night

When we fucked on the sands of Waikiki

And I held you, oh so tight. . .

My jaw dropped. Billy dropped his comic book, grinned, and started nodding his head to the beat.

After Slick finished singing, he gave us the lowdown on the girls' camp. In the next two weeks Billy and I were entertained by his lies nightly.

I'm sure Slick had a normal first and last name, but nobody ever used it. Even the counselors called him Slick.

The clangety-clangety-clang of a steel triangle sounded down at headquarters, and Pastor Jerry stuck his head into the teepee. "Chow time, Slick Gang, let's go."

So I'm in 'Slick Gang' now, I thought, as we walked to the mess hall. Girls were filing out of their camp and down the wide path to headquarters. The boys stuck together, as did the girls, but there were lots of sidelong glances.

After the meal of lasagna, green beans and Kool-Aid, the camp director led us in a couple of verses of *Down By The Riverside*.

I'm gonna lay down my sword and shield,

down by the riverside,

Ain't gonna study war no more. . .

I immediately thought of Sandia Base, and the research that went on there: bigger and better ways to kill more and more people. I was already aware that some Christians were pacifists, like Jesus had been. It seemed to be these kind of Christians that were running the summer camp, and I found out later that the staff this year were mostly Quakers. They were pacifists and told stories of the civil rights struggle in the South. Some of them were Negroes, but they never used that word. "Black" was the word now.

———

Pastor Jerry had a nice fire going in the pit when the campers returned, and Slick brought his guitar. One of the girls called: "Slick, play *Michael Row the Boat*."

Slick obliged, and we sang this and several other campfire specialties.

"Play *Traveling Man*," requested Wendy, who Slick seemed to hold in high regard.

This should be good, I snickered to myself.

I needn't have worried; he performed a letter-perfect cover of the song, with neither dirty words, nor salacious content. Slick knew when to let it out and when to reign it in. I think everybody liked him—girls, boys, and adults. He was obviously a delinquent, but his friendliness and good humor won everybody over. I didn't know the word back then, but he had *charisma*.

———

The next morning pastor Jerry walked around the teepees clanging on a triangle. I unzipped the side of my sleeping bag, sat up, and swung my feet to the ground.

"Everyone has to take a shower before breakfast," he called.

We all lined up in our pajamas at the boys' washhouse. The desert air felt cold.

"Stay away from the archery and the rifle range," Slick advised Billy and me as we waited in line.

"Why's that?" asked Billy.

"Chicks don't dig that stuff. Go for riding or wrangling. Chicks love horses and burros."

After breakfast, Slick and Billy went to the horse corral, and I went down to the burro barn. Sure enough, girls were clustered around the wooden fence, reaching through the slats and rubbing the noses of the burros.

I saw a girl I knew from the First Baptist Church youth choir in Albuquerque. She sat on the flat rail atop the fence, boot heels hooked over a slat beneath. She looked cute in her Levi's and cowboy hat. I knew her name was Jill. I'd always wanted to talk to her but had been too shy.

I was kind of a runt, but Jill was no taller than me.

Here goes, I thought.

"Hi, Jill," I said as I stepped up on the bottom rail.

She turned to face me, and I could see the strawberry birth mark on her smooth cheek.

"Hey, John," she said. "Are you going on the pack trip?"

"I think so. You?"

"I wouldn't miss it. I was here last summer, and the overnight trip was the best."

———

"Okay pilgrims, listen up," said the wrangler standing the middle of the corral. "If you want to go on the pack trip, you have to learn to take care of your burro. You will feed, water, and brush your burro every day, and teach it to follow you around the ranch.

"By the end of the week you will know how to throw a Diamond Hitch and pack your bedrolls and saddle bags."

I don't remember how it worked, but I ended up partnered with Jill, which suited me just fine. The wrangler, Fred Garcia, then assigned us to take care of Orson, a shaggy, spotted beast with long ears and a black nose.

Orson was a bit of a devil. He accepted the hackamore, and he followed us if we walked to the watering trough or the manger, but would sit on his haunches and bray loudly if we tried to lead him into the pasture or along a bridle path.

"Try coming in early, before breakfast," said Fred, when we came to him for advice. "If you feed and water him before the other burros, maybe he'll cotton to you."

The next morning at first light, I quietly dressed and grabbed my straw hat. As I pulled the tent flap open, Slick sat up.

"Where you going?" he asked.

"Jill and I are going to the barn to gentle that old burro," I whispered.

"Smooth move, Schnick," he said. "Go get her."

"It's not like that."

"Mm-hmm."

Closing the flap, I tiptoed past Jerry's tent and could hear the counselor snoring.

I met Jill at the cold fire pit. On the way to the barn we passed the darkened mess hall. The kitchen was already lit up and smelling of coffee as the cook rattled her pots and pans.

Orson stood in his stall, half asleep. He twitched his ears when Jill pulled the hackamore onto his big head, but made no objection. I snapped on the lead, and we led him into the corral. I opened a gate, and Jill led him into the pasture. This was a first; before today he had put up an awful fuss whenever we tried to lead him from the corral.

We walked a big loop through the pasture and returned to the corral. I pulled a flake of hay from an open bale and dropped it in the manger. Jill ran water into the trough from a spigot. After hanging Orson's tack outside his stall, we left the burro happily chomping alfalfa.

On the way back to camp, we met Fred coming from the cookhouse, a cup of steaming coffee in one hand.

"How's old Orson?" he asked, pushing back his Stetson.

"He was sweet as pie!" said Jill.

"I think we trained him," I added.

"Or maybe he trained you..." the cowboy winked, and continued along.

When we passed the mess hall, the lights were on and we could see a tall coffee urn just inside the screen doors.

I asked, "Do you drink coffee?"

"I've never tasted it," said Jill.

"Me neither," I said. "Let's try some."

We each drew a paper cup of black coffee and added sugar and milk.

As we walked back to the tent camp, Jill and I sipped coffee. The lodge poles of the teepees were catching golden light, and we could hear the counselors ringing their iron triangles.

"I think Orson will be fine on the pack-in next week," Jill said.

"I hope so," I said. I realized that Orson's new agreeability was due to Jill's calm manner and soft voice. I'd been scaring him by tugging on his lead and yelling at him.

We were holding hands as we came to the fire pit. As we parted ways, Jill said, "See you later, alligator."

"After while, crocodile," I answered.

I joined the line to the washhouse.

"How'd it go, Romeo?" asked Slick when he saw me.

"A-okay," I said. "We got that burro trained."

"Not the donkey, dimwit. . .the girl?"

"That went pretty good, too," I said.

———

Sneaking out to feed Orson before the camp awoke became a regular thing for Jill and me, as did drinking coffee on our way back to camp. My tent mate Slick, and Jill's tent mate Wendy, knew what we were up to, but didn't tease us much. They were sneaking out at night and meeting in the moonlight. Although Jill and I just held hands, I suspected that Wendy and Slick were making out hot and heavy during their trysts. At least that was the impression that Slick gave me.

I wasn't sure how much how much I believed Slick's stories, and I didn't feel that way about Jill anyway.

Well, maybe a little. I could hardly wait to go on the camping trip.

Later that week, Fred drilled his apprentices in cinching a wooden pack saddle to the burro's back, hanging panniers from the forks, and binding the tarp-covered bedrolls on top with a diamond hitch. We were as ready as we'd ever be.

The next morning, the junior wranglers reported to the corral with bedrolls, canteens, and straw hats. Each team saddled its mule. Lucy Garcia, Fred's assistant, came around and checked the tightness of the cinches, giving an extra tug on Orson's bindings. Lucy's dark pony tail bobbed through a hole in the back of her cowboy hat as she put her weight into the latigo straps. Lucy was tough as nails but cute as a bug's ear. She shod every horse on the ranch and was married to Fred.

Jill and I loaded the panniers so each side weighed the same. We hung them over the packsaddle. Next we draped bedrolls over the top, and last we wrapped the whole shebang with a tarpaulin. Fred checked our diamond hitch and gave the thumbs up. We untied Orson and led him into line with the other burros.

Fred opened the gate of the corral, and Lucy led the first burro onto the trail, the pack train following in single file. Fred brought up the rear and closed the gate. The dusty yellow trail rose steeply as it climbed out of the valley and switchbacked into the soaring, red rock cliffs.

Jill held Orson's lead for the first mile, then handed it to me. She ran up the line to talk with her tent mates. Orson and I trudged along in the sunlight. I wished I'd thought to soak my hat at the water trough. As we passed the red sandstone tower called Chimney Rock, Orson stopped and stared down.

The burro ahead disappeared around a boulder as I tugged on the lead. Orson stayed put and started braying to beat the band: "He-haw, he-haw, he-haw." I looked closer at the trail and saw two little rattlesnakes slither out of sight and into a patch of cactus.

Orson kept at it. "He-haw, he-haw, he-haw." I tried to calm him down by rubbing his nose, but he jerked his head away and rolled his eyes. "He-haw, he-haw, he-haw."

Oh great, now what? I thought.

"He-haw, he-haw, he-haw."

At this point, Jill came down the trail, went up to Orson, and put her hand on his nose. "Oh baby, what's wrong?" she cooed. Orson stopped braying and nuzzled up to her. I handed Jill the lead, and Orson followed her like a puppy.

I felt relieved but also embarrassed. I hadn't rescued the fair young maiden. She had rescued me.

That night, sitting at the campfire under the stars, I offered her my turquoise ring. She looked at it, looked me in the eyes, then back at the ring.

She hesitated a moment, then took the ring and slipped it on her finger.

<hr>

After the pack trip, after the civil rights workers had taught everyone to sing *We Shall Overcome*, it was departure day. Parents arrived at headquarters and collected their kids and drove back home to Albuquerque, Santa Fe, or Denver. Slick's parents drove him to the military academy in Kansas where he lived most of the year.

I didn't want to go home. I fantasized that maybe I could stay on the ranch forever, taking care of the burros and learning to paint from Georgia O'Keefe. When only Terry Atkins and I were left sitting on the veranda, I started to get my hopes up. Maybe my parents had forgotten about me, and I would be free!

My hopes were dashed when Terry's dad, a major at Sandia base, pulled up in his Buick and gruffly ordered me into the car with Terry.

Oh well, I thought. At least I'll get to see Jill at choir practice on Wednesday.

Things Fall Apart

FINALLY IT WAS WEDNESDAY NIGHT. Mom drove me the ten miles to the big downtown church we attended whenever Dad didn't have the duty at the base chapel. The Concord Choir was the youth choir, a farm team for the adult choir that performed every Sunday morning.

The director was rehearsing us in the Hallelujah Chorus, an exultant piece of music from *The Messiah* by Handel. I could see Jill's braids and sweet face in the soprano section, but I hadn't been able to catch her eye.

When we sang the last hallelujah, the director said, "I think we've got it." As the teenagers filed out, I met Jill in the corridor. The rest of the choir walked past us and down the stairs as we tarried on the landing. Jill hugged her sheet music against her chest with both forearms. I didn't see the turquoise ring.

"We have to talk," Jill said. "I can't keep your ring."

She fished in the watch pocket of her jeans and held it out to me. She looked at me with sad brown eyes. I looked away and stared at the wall.

"Was it your folks?" I asked, glancing back.

She nodded slightly, pushing the ring at me. "I can't keep your ring."

"I don't want it," I said, then turned and hurried down the stairs and into the parking lot.

I knew, as thirteen-year-olds, we were too young to be going steady. I had no idea if Jill's parents had talked to my parents, but it wouldn't have surprised me. Anyway, it looked like sports—or studying war—was what I was expected to do at this age.

An evangelist from England had come to the church in the spring for a special youth revival. He had lectured the teenagers about the dangers of kissing and "petting". I didn't really know what petting was, but I sure wanted to find out. I guessed I would have to wait a little longer.

———

Dad came back from another atomic test at the Tonopah Range. He sometimes took me to a baseball, football, or basketball game after an absence. These outings were preferable to the whippings I usually endured upon his return. This time, knowing my fascination with spaceflight, he took me to a lecture by Dr. Wernher Magnus Maximilian Freiherr von Braun, an ex-Nazi Sturmbannführer.

Johnson Gymnasium, home of the University of New Mexico Lobos, filled up quickly after we arrived. Dr. von Braun showed us slides of the rockets and landing modules he'd designed for the new Apollo program that was supposed to take Americans to the moon in the next ten years. The space race was dominating the newspaper headlines and the CBS Evening News.

The Soviets had gotten the lead in the race, with *Sputnik*, *Muttnik*, and the first orbit of the moon, but President Kennedy had promised that we Americans would land there first. After all, we couldn't have the Communists establish bases on the moon where they could lob hydrogen bombs down on our cities and our amber waves of grain.

The gym was packed with fathers and sons. The competitive atmosphere was excited, like a *Lobos* game, but there were almost no women or girls in the audience. Maybe it was like Slick said back at Ghost Ranch: *Chicks don't dig that stuff.*

At the end of the presentation, Dad steered me down to the podium where I shook hands with the genial scientist.

––––––––––

A friend and I were inspired by the exploits of Dr. Robert Goddard, an American inventor, and we set about building our own rockets. We wanted to fly to the moon ourselves, or, at least, to try.

We met in Wayne Watkins' garage, where he and his dad had built an enormous model train setup with mountains, trestles, and towns.

The garage was also equipped with woodworking and electrical tools. What we didn't have was rocket propellant. We had visions of building multistage rockets powered by kerosene and liquid oxygen, but we had to start at a more humble level. Wayne had a paper route, and I was making a few dollars per week painting car monsters on tee-shirts. We rode our bicycles to a supermarket, and came back with a brown grocery sack full of book matches.

We used an office paper cutter to chop the heads off thousands of matches until we had enough to fill a one-pound coffee can. By tacit agreement, our rocketry had devolved into bomb-making.

We pedaled our bikes to the middle of the mesa. We left our wheels and carried our experiment to the middle of an area of hardpan, clear of cactus or sage. Wayne set the alcohol burner from his chemistry set to the ground, a wire rack above it.

"Okay," said Wayne as he lit the burner, "put the can on top, then let's run..."

Blue flames came off the Sterno, and I clapped the taped-up can to the rack. We both ran to the bicycles and dropped flat.

We didn't wait long before a red flash, a loud bang, and a cloud of gray smoke went up.

Running back to ground zero, we found the Maxwell House can in smithereens, and the Sterno can flattened and extinguished. The wire stand was scorched but okay.

"We have to figure out how to slow down the reaction," announced Wayne. "Maybe we can grind up the match heads with some sugar or something..."

A week later we were back at our test site. This time we had a sleek cylinder made of three empty tomato paste cans soldered together, a cardboard nose cone and tail fins glued to the sides. In addition, Wayne had jury-rigged a flashlight: the batteries connected to the bulb with a thirty foot run of electric train wire. Wayne carefully popped the glass bulb with a hammer and inserted the bare filament into the base of the rocket packed with chopped match heads and sugar. Kids, don't try this at home.

We drew back about thirty feet, then sat on the sand. Wayne started a countdown, as I focused my dad's binoculars on the base of our vehicle.

"Five, four, three, two, one," he said, "ignition!" then flicked the flashlight switch.

Black smoke started to pour from the rocket nozzle, then *Bang!* it flipped over and started snaking across the sand towards us, white sparks and black smoke pouring out. We both jumped up and ran, as our rocket exploded just behind us sending smoking fragments past our ears.

———

President Kennedy came to visit Sandia Base about a month after the Cuban Missile Crisis. My family drove to the road leading to the base and parked. We waited at the edge of the pavement. A black convertible drove slowly past, just a few feet away. The young President stood in the backseat footwell waving. We all waved back.

When Jack Kennedy was running for president, my father had grumped about the fact that JFK was a Catholic and also wanted nuclear disarmament.

"We should have attacked Russia before they got the A-bomb, and gotten it over with," he had said.

I think Dad suspected that if the Western Allies disarmed, the Commies would only say they had, and we would be more vulnerable. He preached weekly about the Prince of Peace, but his faith did not apply to his political views.

I began collecting fallout shelter plans. I was reading lots of science fiction at the time, and fantasies of nuclear holocaust both tormented and tantalized me. On Armistice Day, Sandia Base held a big open house. I heard there would be lots of civil defense publications available to the public. Dad had the duty that day at the Base Hospital, and Mother was not interested in going, so she said, "Why don't you take the bus?"

It was good to be out on my own. I didn't really want to be with my family or Wayne, either, for that matter. I wanted to be with Jill, but that wasn't happening. I felt angry.

When I arrived at the base, I found plenty of instructions for do-it-yourself fallout shelters, but the best part of the show had to be the display of all the latest military hardware. Howitzers, missiles, tanks, and a tripod-mounted machine gun stood in a line along the edge of an overgrown runway.

The Marine Corps contribution to this arms expo was a

Model 1919 Browning .30 caliber medium machine gun, mounted in a nest of sandbags at the end of the runway. This was the type of shooting iron whose expended brass had contributed to my comics fund back in Newfoundland.

The gunnery sergeant in charge of the exhibit answered my questions about the linked ammo, then asked, "Would you like to shoot it?"

"Yes, sir!" I responded.

"Okay, hunker down here and hold on to the pistol grip."

I complied.

"The gun is bolted down so it won't move, and it's blank ammunition, so you can't hit anything."

"Yes, sir."

"Don't call me sir. I'm a sergeant."

"Yes, Sergeant."

The gunny flipped up a cover, then pushed the first cartridge of the belt into the open slot.

"Now pull back that lever on the starboard side. Pull it back 'til it clicks, then let it go."

After I cocked the bolt, the Marine said, "You're in battery now. Pull the trigger once and let it go."

"Bam!" the gun spoke.

That felt good! I thought. A whiff of cordite went up my nose.

"Good. Now hold the trigger down a little longer, try for three shots."

Bamity bamity bamity bam! Four shots rang out. Puffs of dust rose from the desert sand a few yards downrange.

"Not bad," said the gunny.

He let me fire several more bursts, then I had to move along. Another teenager wanted to try his hand.

I didn't feel so angry now, but Jill was still in the back of my mind. It was fun blowing stuff up in the desert, and shooting the machine gun was a kick, but I still missed my cowboy's sweetheart.

As I walked back through the base, I passed the movie theater. Some lurid horror movie was playing. The poster showed a pretty girl about to be devoured by a tiger. I paid my 15¢ and went in. This was the first and the last time I ever went to a movie alone.

The movie was corny and forgettable, and when I left, I realized that I was late: the family was supposed to go to a prayer meeting that evening at the First Baptist Church. I had been dreading this because Jill would likely be there, too. I was still hurting.

Dropping a dime into the pay phone outside the cinema, I called home. My mother answered, "Schnick residence."

"Hi Mom, I'm sorry I'm late."

"Where are you anyway?"

"On the road to the base," I answered. "I'm walking north."

"Your father will come to get you."

"I can walk."

"Your father will come to get you."

As I walked along the twilit highway, I felt trapped. I knew Dad was going to come roaring up the road in the big Plymouth. I knew I would climb in. I knew Mom would keep Polly distracted as Dad dragged me down the hallway. I knew Dad would throw me across my room onto the bed. Resistance was futile. Dad was six foot two. I was five foot two. He was thirty-five, I was fourteen.

I knew I was in for the beating of my life.

Dad didn't say a word as he watched me climb into the passenger seat. He said nothing as he drove to our adobe house.

The beating went down as expected. This time I refused to talk or cry. He told me about his beloved teacher who shed tears while beating children. I looked away. When he told me, "This hurts me more than it hurts you," I closed my eyes and gritted my teeth.

Dad left the room after he got tired of hitting me. I knew there would be no supper for me tonight. I didn't feel much like eating anyway.

I felt horrible. If he had machine-gunned me, it might have been better; at least I'd be dead. I decided that I'd had enough of military life, even as a dependent. Since astronauts had started out as naval aviators, that career seemed unattainable, especially since I couldn't pass Algebra.

I began to plot my escape.

Delinquent Communion

I HAD A FANTASY that my parents were not my real parents:
I was adopted. My real parents were elegant and worldly art
collectors who lived high in a Manhattan apartment. They drank
martinis, smoked cigarettes, and were Jewish.

———

After Sunday school, I started skipping the main service.
My father didn't care where I sat, as long as I was in the church
somewhere. If I grabbed the church bulletin before playing
hooky, I would know the pastor's Bible text and sermon title, and
could usually bluff my way through my father's interrogation
afterwards.

I usually hung out at the drugstore, kitty-corner from the big
downtown church. This Sunday, instead of thumbing through
Playboy to see nude photos of Mamie van Doren, I rotated the
paperback rack. I was looking for some science fiction title
that I hadn't read, but I picked up *On the Road* by Jack Kerouac.
After reading the first few pages, I knew I had to have it. Luckily

there was a fifty-cent piece in my pocket, so I wouldn't have to steal it.

I crossed the street and walked back into the church and sat in the back pew in the balcony. I had read the first twenty pages by the time the mournful organ chords of the altar call sounded. I slipped the paperback into the pocket of my sports coat.

Back home I excused myself after dinner, claiming I had some homework to do. At bedtime, I turned off my room light but continued to read with a flashlight under the covers.

Wayne Watkins, besides being my cohort in bomb-making and rocketry, was an acolyte at the chapel on the base. When my father had the duty on alternate Sundays, I was an acolyte, too. We each carried a shiny brass wand: a combination taper holder and bell snuffer. We had to wear a red robe with an abbreviated white surplice over it.

I liked wearing the robe; it made me feel a little bigger and more important—feelings that were in pretty short supply when I was at home. The U.S. Navy Protestant liturgy was more interesting than the Hard Shell Baptist services I was used to. We got to set the candles afire, then hide out in the vestry for most of the time, and if I didn't foul up the service, my father would leave me alone.

The chapel was shared with the Catholic Padre, so we also had to turn around the gold-plated altar cross. The Catholic side displayed a grisly and gruesome Christ nailed to the cross, and the Protestant side was empty except for a rosette with the letters "IHS", which was a Greek abbreviation for Jesus.

After lighting the altar candles, acolytes could hang out in the vestry during most of the service. A polished wood cabinet hung on the wall across from the bench where we sat.

"You know what's in there?" asked Wayne, pointing at the box.

"No."

"Wine."

"Let's drink it," I said.

When we unlatched the door, we found not only the red wine used for the sacrament but several bottles of Sauterne and Chablis, plus some boxes of communion wafers. We started on an opened bottle of Sauterne, passing it back and forth. The Protestant services only used Welch's grape juice for communion. We chomped down handfuls of communion wafers between pulls on the bottle.

When it was time to snuff the candles, after the benediction, I felt unsteady on my feet. Wayne grabbed his snuffer, went up the steps, and across the atrium. I hesitated but followed him. We were supposed to walk in front of the altar in step to the Bach recessional, solemnly snuffing each candle one by one. My long robe caught on the steps, and I almost fell.

That night, asleep in my bed, I had a nightmare. My robe caught on the carpet, and I pitched forward with my flaming taper, lighting the linty draperies. The flames flashed along the dusty curtains on the walls, closing off escape for the congregation who burned to death in agony. I writhed in hell, then I woke up.

I knew I had to get out of here. I knew I could never please my father for long, and I was getting tired of trying. Even so, it wasn't clear to me that a deeper, wider break was occurring between his world and mine.

––––––––––

Another night. . .

I woke to a faint tapping on my bedroom window. Moonlight shone on the face of my friend Tommy Gregg. He held up a shiny set of car keys and had a wide grin on his face. I threw back the sheet, swung my sneakers to the floor, and tiptoed to the window that I'd left open. My alarm clock's luminous dial showed three o'clock.

I had met Tommy in shop class at school. He had tried to sell me some small, black and white photos of a naked woman sprawled on a couch. It was only after I had been to his house that I realized that the woman in the pictures was his mother, Doris.

I climbed out the open window. At the curb stood a 1959 Oldsmobile Super 88, Tommy's parents' car. We got in, closed the doors as quietly as we could, and drove away. I think the plan was to go out to an unpopulated stretch of highway and "see what this baby can do".

Tommy couldn't see out his rear view mirror, so he pulled into a darkened gas station and set the parking brake. While he was wiping the dew off the back window, an Albuquerque Police prowl car parked behind us, and its searchlight lit the scene in shades of silver. I slumped down in my seat. I could hear the policeman questioning Tommy.

When Tommy could produce no license, the cop came up to the passenger side and shined his long, four-cell flashlight on me. I tried to shrink into the footwell.

"Get out," said the officer. I complied.

"Put your hands on the car, and don't move," he ordered.

Tommy and I assumed the position, and the patrolman frisked each of us. Leaving us leaning against the Oldsmobile, he walked back to his black and white car through the headlight glare. He reached into the open door and pulled out a microphone on a curly cord. He leaned on the door, keeping an eye on us.

"I have two juveniles out on Indian School Road," he called over his radio. "No license, no registration. Over."

Some unintelligible words came back. The officer said, "Ten four," and hung the mike back on his dashboard.

"Looks like you'll have to come downtown with me. Get in." He opened the back seat of the prowl car, and Tommy and I climbed in. When the officer closed the door, I noticed there were no handles inside.

"What's going to happen to us?" I asked as we sped down the deserted streets.

"Your parents will be called. If they don't come to get you, you'll go to Juvenile Hall."

The police car passed the First Baptist Church, then we arrived at the brick police station. The arresting officer escorted us up the stairs to the booking desk. As the jailer began to lead Tommy and me to the tank, the booking sergeant spoke up.

"Leave the little one here. He's only thirteen."

Tommy was only fourteen, but he was much taller and huskier than me. I watched as the turnkey unlocked the door to the tank and shoved my friend inside. I heard drunken groaning, cursing, and shouting before the door was slammed.

I sat on a tall stool in a corner and watched the sergeant book two more drunks before my father came up the stairs with a stricken look on his face.

After he signed me out, we drove home in silence. To my great relief, I was sent to bed without a whipping.

I had to attend a few counseling sessions later with a bored-looking probation officer, because of the curfew violation. Since Tommy's parents did not press charges, there was no mention of grand-theft-auto.

When we reported to the police station for our counseling sessions, I was dressed like I was going to church. My parents had insisted I wear a sport coat. They wore solemn expressions as we sat on the steel and vinyl chairs in the waiting room.

I picked up a copy of Sports Illustrated. On the cover was a color photo of Roger Staubach, the quarterback of the Naval Academy football team. When I started to read the article, my Dad snatched the magazine from my hands, threw it down, and glared at me. I was bored. I wanted out of here.

I guess my indifference to this whole visit was visible, signaling my father that I was no longer really concerned about his—or anyone in his world's—opinion of me.

The next Sunday, Dad had chapel duty. I suited up in the vestry, as did Wayne. We both noticed the new combination lock on the wine cabinet.

"I had a lousy week," said Wayne.

"Me, too," said I.

The organist started playing a processional. I lit both tapers with a kitchen match. We hurried across the altar, lighting all the candles.

Back in the dressing room, we retracted the waxy tapers into the brass tubes, and flames extinguished, we hung the lighters on their hooks.

"I'm going to Mexico," said the other acolyte.

"When? How?" I asked.

"I'm running away. In two weeks I'm quitting my paper route. I'll have six hundred dollars, and I'm taking a Greyhound to El Paso. Want to come?"

"You bet," I answered.

"Great! We can walk across the bridge to Juarez."

In the next two weeks we plotted our escape. We met the next Saturday and took a bus to the state fairgrounds. Wayne put a quarter into the slot of a cigarette machine, and a pack of Lucky Strikes fell into the tray. We already had the matches from our rocketry experiments, so we lit up and walked around inspecting the livestock on display.

After agreeing on what to pack in our bindles, we boarded an empty bus back to the base. Wayne lay on the back bench and wretched yellow bile onto the black rubber floorboards on the way home.

When D-day arrived, I was supposed to meet Wayne in his taxi at a strip mall a block away, at 2:00 AM. I had my bindle packed. After I climbed out the window, my father splintered the privacy lock on my door and stuck his head out the bedroom window.

"John Mark?" he shouted into the night. "Where are you?"

I was halfway to the street, but I knew the jig was up. I spent the next couple of hours hunkered down in the living room, with my parents crying and praying over me.

Wayne made it to El Paso, but was rousted by the fuzz while he was sleeping in Sand Hills Park. His parents had to drive down and pick him up. We were not allowed to see each other anymore.

I realized exactly what I was now: a juvenile delinquent. I knew that there were other kids like me. There were lots of them in the schools I'd attended which were overcrowded with baby boomers.

A few weeks later, on November 22nd, I stayed home from school with Rubella, or German measles, as it was called in those days. I was in my room, gluing together a plastic model of a P-38 Lightning. The local Top 40 station was playing *Please Please Me* by the Beatles. It was interrupted, and I heard an announcement over my transistor radio.

"We have an unconfirmed report from Dallas, Texas, that President Kennedy has been shot. He and Texas Governor John Connelly have been taken to a local hospital."

I had begun to realize that the government, the military, and the police didn't really know what they were doing. This would be proven beyond a shadow of a doubt in the next few years, as the U.S. tarnished its good name during a terrible war in Indochina.

6

North Beach

I CONTINUED TO FORGE my report cards, and when Dad got orders, my folks assumed I had passed ninth grade. Dad was miffed about his new assignment. Previously I had heard him say, "I would rather resign my commission than serve on a USNS ship."

Times had changed, however. My father's refusal to cooperate with Catholic chaplains had been noted over the years in his efficiency reports to BUPERS. With the amount of time he had been in uniform, he should have advanced to the rank of captain, or, at the least, commander. He was *age-in-grade,* and would probably be forced to retire at twenty years. His Naval career was toast.

Dad's stiff-necked Calvinism might have been acceptable in the Deep South in the Forties and Fifties, but by the Sixties, the rest of the country had changed, and he had not.

The *USNS Barrett* carried troops and Mobile Army Surgical Hospital units to the new war in Vietnam. It had a civilian crew, with a few naval personnel on board for appearances. Here's the part I liked: it sailed from Fort Mason Army Terminal in San Francisco.

After Mayflower Van Lines packed all the furniture, the chartreuse station wagon was loaded up, and the family headed West on Route 66. This time we left Needles at midnight and were passing Barstow by dawn. We had avoided sizzling in the Mojave.

Instead of following Route 66 all the way to Santa Monica, we turned North on US 395, which skirts just to the East of the granite peaks of the High Sierra.

When we came to Mono Lake, Dad drove over Tioga Pass and into Yosemite Valley. We set up our tent below Glacier Point. After the sun went down, most of the campers gathered in a meadow and stared up at the cliff and the stars above it.

A pinprick of fire flickered atop the cliff. From Camp Curry, a stentorian voice rang out:

"Hello, Glacier Point!"

"Hello, Camp Curry!" came back faintly from the top of the cliff.

"Is the fire ready?"

"The fire is ready!"

"Let the fire fall!" Camp Curry commanded.

"The fire falls!"

At this, the loud-voiced lad above started shoveling glowing coals over the precipice. A waterfall of fire tumbled three thousand feet down the granite face, and lasted a couple of minutes.

The temperature fell quickly after dark and, as we walked back to our campsite, Mother stopped and said, "There's a bear over there."

In the deep gloom, we saw not one but several bears filtering through the campground raiding the picnic tables. Frightened but fascinated, we dodged the marauders and arrived back at camp. Dad pumped up the gasoline lantern, and we ate a cold supper of shredded wheat, strawberries, and milk.

"Homer, let's get into the tent," said Mother. Dad shut down the Coleman lantern, and we adjourned to the eight-by-ten-foot canvas shelter smelling of kerosene and paraffin waterproofing.

We crawled into our sleeping bags, and, tired from the long drive during the day, the four of us fell asleep, but not for long.

"Git!" my father hissed. He lay prone on the tent floor, peering under the flap. In his left hand he held a flashlight, in his right he clutched the handle of an axe. I could see a big bear on top of our picnic table. As my father hissed and hollered, the bear grasped the aluminum ice chest between its furry paws, slammed it against the table once, twice, and on the third time the top flew back, and he was in.

He gulped down some peaches we'd bought from a farm stand near Bishop, then snagged a side of bacon lying on the ice.

"Git!" my father said.

"Whuff!" replied the bear. The slab of bacon hanging from his teeth, he moved away to the next campsite, where the neighbors were still away at a nature lecture. As we watched in the beam of Dad's flashlight, the bruin popped open their ice chest and pulled an aluminum six-pack of Schlitz beer from the melting ice.

One by one, the black bear shoved each can into his maw, chomped down, and foam shot out his nostrils and ran down the fur of his neck. After spitting out six shredded cans, the furry vandal reclined across the tabletop, gnawing the bacon in total contentment, grunting now and then. The neighbors returned from the campfire talk and woke the bruin by banging pots and pans; then he ambled off into the trees.

I think we all were frightened, but I also felt amused. After all, here was the powerful patriarch of our little family—yet utterly helpless, as a hairy beast stole the bacon. So much for Dad's mask of authority.

———

Fog swept through the girders of the Nimitz Freeway as we approached the Oakland-San Francisco bridge. Dad was driving in the fast lane, doing 60 and gripping the steering wheel tightly. Traffic whizzed by in the lanes to our right. A red light flashed behind us. Dad glanced up at the rear view mirror and muttered, "Himmel blitzen donnerwetter. . ."

As he steered into the middle lane, a Highway Patrol car drew abreast, and the patrolman pointed to the slow lane with a stern look on his face before zooming ahead. Dad moved over to the slow lane.

"They certainly drive fast around here!" said Mom.

We came to the toll booth plaza. Dad slowed down and

stopped. He gave the toll taker a quarter, and we drove over the soaring bridge into San Francisco. It was 1964.

Exiting the Embarcadero freeway, Dad drove us through North Beach to the Main Gate of Fort Mason. We would stay in the BOQ until the folks could find a house to buy. The fort was originally commissioned by Abe Lincoln, during the Civil War, on land confiscated from John C. Fremont, his political rival.

We ate lunch in the elegant Officer's Club, our corner table overlooking Aquatic Park. While I munched my sandwich, I noticed a procession of people in street clothes walking along the crescent of sand below.

Later, back in our quarters, I turned on the local TV news to see what had gone on down at the beach. As it turned out, a young dancer named Carol Doda had been modeling a topless swim suit as a publicity stunt.

I got the feeling that we weren't in Kansas anymore. This was great!

In the next few days, while Mom and Dad drove around the Bay Area shopping for a house, I was allowed to explore first Fort Mason, then Aquatic Park, and finally North Beach and Chinatown. I just had to be back in time for supper.

This may seem odd or reckless nowadays, but my parents had allowed me to roam snake-infested woods alone with my rifle, to skate on wilderness ponds, and to explore alligator swamps—all before I was twelve. What could go wrong in a beautiful seaside city like San Francisco?

As it turned out, nothing alarming ever happened to me, but I did wander into a quirky store called City Lights Books, and it changed my life. Here were more books by Jack Kerouac, and I didn't even have to buy them. I could hang out in the brick basement and read to my heart's content. I came to understood that Kerouac's novels were really *roman á clef*, memoirs with the names changed, and many of the Beat poets he had described were published by City Lights.

In a few weeks I had read the Pocket Poets series. Shig, the bearded clerk, never raised an eyebrow about my voracious reading but did look amused when I actually bought a copy of *Howl* by Allen Ginsberg, or *Gasoline* by Gregory Corso.

I recognized that the Beat poets and painters had broken free of the military-industrial complex, rejected organized religion, and seemed to be having great fun.

This is for me! I thought, knowing that my parents would have a fit if they could read my mind. I would have to keep the epiphany secret.

Vatos Locos

AFTER MOM AND DAD had narrowed the field to the East Bay, the whole family toured a tumble-down cliffside house in Oakland, a new but dreary ranch-style in San Ramon, then a small but comfy three bedroom tract home in Hayward, a prune-growing town turning into a bedroom community.

The folks bought the Hayward house because the price was right, and there was an elementary school for Polly just across the street. Tennyson High School, where I would be attending, was only a half mile away.

My report card forgeries had caught up with me, and I was enrolled in ninth grade, again. I planned on making the best of it. I had experienced a growth spurt over the summer and would no longer be the shortest boy in my class. Maybe I could start to "live up to my potential", as Penny Prentiss had put it back in Albuquerque.

On the first day of school, I lined up to get my Homeroom assignment. I also was assigned a locker and a locker partner, Fetu Talatonu. Fetu was a big, solid Polynesian kid whose family had just emigrated from Pago Pago, American Samoa. He lived a couple of blocks away from my house, and we quickly became friends.

The school had been built seven years earlier and was already over-enrolled, with more than a thousand baby boomers in the student body. About half the students were Hispanic, and the other half were a motley assortment of Anglos, Asians, and Pacific Islanders, but almost no Black students.

A gang of *Vatos Locos*—or "Vots", as everyone called them—swaggered down the halls with arms crossed on their chests, Pharaoh style. Any unsuspecting hispanic boy that neglected to "cover up" would be punched hard in the solar plexus, usually crumpling him to the tile floor. I supposed this had to be some kind of gang initiation. They never seemed to bother the Anglo guys, but it felt good to have Fetu beside me when the Vots walked past.

My science class yielded another friend, Alan Edwards, my shy but hilarious lab partner for both 9th and 10th grades. Our lab table stood in the second row: the middle of three. The enthusiastic Mr. Green, a student teacher, took over the class one day a week.

Mr. Green chalked the formula for nitrogen triiodide on the blackboard. The students dutifully copied this. He then proceeded to mix up a small batch of the explosive. The whole class, in their lab aprons, watched through their safety goggles as he fiddled with red iodine crystals, ammonia, and a clear glass flask. Don't *ever* try this at home.

Lifting a dark brown precipitate with a narrow paddle from the slanted flask, he deposited a mound the size of a pea on a white disc of filter paper. This he carried around the room, tapping the edge of the disk occasionally to drop few grains to the white linoleum floor.

"Okay," he said, "get up and walk around."

We all slipped off our stools, and as we stepped on the sprinkled areas, tiny explosions snapped and crackled under our shoes, and tiny puffs of red smoke spurted out. Giggles ensued as the teenagers shuffled around in green goggles, gloves, and lab coats, popping every last grain of the unstable explosive. This was way more fun than blowing up coffee cans on the mesa; there were girls here.

"Alright, class, back in your seats," said Mr. Green.

Everyone climbed back onto his or her stool and picked up a pencil.

"Want to try something really cool?"

A dozen crew cuts and ponytails nodded up and down.

"I'll formulate a larger amount of nitrogen triiodide, and we can sprinkle it up and down the hallway. When the bell rings, we can watch what happens during the change of classes."

My lab partner, Alan, and I looked at each other with raised eyebrows.

This time Mr. Green multiplied the iodine, ammonia, and so forth. He ended up with a heaping tablespoon of brown precipitate on the filter paper. As he walked towards the classroom door, for some reason he dropped the white disc, and it fell towards the floor.

In midair it disappeared in a white flash and thunder crack. A red ball of smoke hid the student teacher.

"Mr. Green, are you all right?" chorused several students.

"All right, class is over. Everyone can leave early," he said in a loud voice.

Alan raised one eyebrow and looked sideways at me.

All the students doffed their lab gear and filed out quietly.

The next day, Alan and I showed up to the science lab a few minutes early. Mr. Green was sitting at his small desk, across from the desk of the senior science teacher. I asked him how he was.

"Okay, now, but I couldn't hear for two hours yesterday. I'll never try that again," he said ruefully.

Dissecting a frog was almost as much fun as the nitrogen triiodide. Mr. Green issued Alan and me a frog and a dissection tray with scalpel, scissors, and clamps. The other five lab teams got the same. A pungent stench of formaldehyde rose from the preserved specimen.

Because of my previous experience in frog dismemberment, Alan graciously allowed me to make the incisions, while he did the clamping and pinning. I made the first cut.

The frog squealed, "No, no, aieee!"

Alan threw his voice without moving his lips or cracking a smile. As the dissection proceeded, the frog supplied a continuous lament of his crucifixion and martyrdom at the hands of two pimply adolescents. Alan kept his voice low, and neither teacher nor other students could hear. I was unable to keep a straight face, and drew a few looks when I snorted at some of Alan's better quips.

In Mrs. Leaf's freshman literature class, I made two friends for life: Skip Strobel sat at the desk just ahead of me, and Nick Albert sat behind me. For a Greek mythology report, Skip wrote a satiric musical entitled *Gods and Dolls*. He performed it for the class, singing the various parts in falsetto or bass as required. He took the melodies from Broadway numbers, but the outrageous lyrics were all his.

I drew a comic book with the various gods and goddesses depicted as grotesque car monsters. Nick Albert produced a written report. He also painted *Cronus Devouring his Children*, in oils, for the front cover. These guys were to be my friends for the next fifty years.

Nick played the five-stringed banjo, and Coleen Kilpatrick, who sat across from Nick and me, played a twelve-string guitar. Coleen organized a hootenanny at her parents's house after school, and Skip, Nick, and I were invited.

The girls wore peasant blouses, Levi's, and leather sandals; the boys favored chambray work shirts, Levi's, and desert boots. Ten teenagers lounged on the low, carpeted steps of the split-level living room. Coleen pulled a tuning fork from her guitar case.

"Pong. . ." She struck a note, then she and Nick bent over their instruments and twisted the tuning pegs until they were satisfied. Coleen strummed a measure on her guitar, then launched into *If I Had a Hammer*, her clear alto voice filling the space. Nick joined in, singing and strumming on his banjo, then all of us sang along.

It's a song about love between my brothers and my sisters. . .

My practice with the Concord Choir back in Albuquerque all came back to me, and I was delighted when I realized that I knew how to harmonize, not just sing in unison. We sang *Blowing in the Wind*, *Froggie went a Courtin'*, and of course, *Michael Row the Boat Ashore*.

Coleen concluded by singing *Kisses Sweeter than Wine*.

Although I thought about girls almost constantly, 1964 was a dry year for me in the romance department. Between my surf-side summer with Carol in Coronado, and my pack trip with Jill at Ghost Ranch, I'd had a taste of honey. I wanted more, but unfortunately Coleen was already going with my friend Jim.

Things were about to change for the better. In 10th grade, Alan was again my lab partner in Biology II. One Monday morning, he leaned over to me with a grin on his face.

"My sister smoked pot," he whispered.

I'd read about marijuana, both in *On the Road* and *The Cross and the Switchblade*. One book was all for it, and one was all about its dangers.

This felt like another very cool knife-edge to me. Fun and risk. It was an edge I wanted to walk. Anything to cut through the dull monotony of the rigidly conforming world in which I felt stuck.

"Can she get us some?" I whispered back.

"Maybe," he replied. "I'll ask her."

The next day Alan was back.

"Do you still want to smoke pot?" he whispered.

The Tunnel of Love

ON SATURDAY, Alan, who had just turned sixteen, drove us to Berkeley. I had told my mother I was spending the night at Alan's. He had told his parents he was staying at my house.

"Alice has two lesbian friends, Linda and Lucy," Alan said loudly over the blaring of the old Plymouth's radio. "They're going camping. They told her she could stay in their apartment for the weekend."

California Girls by The Beach Boys came on, Alan turned up the volume, the wind swept through the open windows, and we rolled along the Earl Warren Freeway through the Oakland hills. The freeway ended and we corkscrewed down twisty Tunnel Road into Berkeley.

We found the Durant Avenue address, and Alan parked on the gravel pad behind the old brown shingle quadraplex. As we climbed out of the car, the back door of an upper flat opened. Alice Edwards stood on the landing and waved, then ran down the steps. She wore a white peasant blouse, Levi's, and brown leather sandals. Her auburn hair shone where the sun hit it, and her braces glinted when she smiled.

"You made it!" she said, hugging her brother. Turning to me, she said, "Hi John, I know all about you. My best friend Gladys was in your art class last year."

Gladys Wong took an art class in her senior year at Tennyson; she had all the credits she needed to graduate, and had already been accepted to Mills College, a women's school in Oakland. I had developed a total crush on the cool, intellectual Miss Wong, and talked her ear off, which she had tolerated.

"Have you heard the new Bob Dylan album? I just bought it. I can't wait to listen," said Alice, her blue eyes and freckled cheeks just inches from my face.

Alan and I took our gym bags from the trunk and followed her up the steps. Anna's roommate, Ellen, had also checked out of their dorm for the weekend and was sitting in the tiny living room with her boyfriend, Greg, a big guy with a full, brown beard.

Alice carefully pulled the dust jacket from the cover, rolled out the new LP, and set the shining disc onto the spindle. The five of us sat cross-legged in a circle on the faded rug. Greg fished out a crinkled pack of Camels and produced a reefer rolled in yellow cigarette paper. He put it between his lips and sparked his Zippo lighter.

After taking a short puff, he handed the joint to Ellen on his left. As we passed it around the circle, the organ chords of *Like* a *Rolling Stone* rolled out of the stereo speakers, and the room filled with pungent smoke.

"I don't feel anything," said Alan.

"I don't think I do, either," I added.

Alice giggled, then Alan and I joined in laughing. I realized I felt. . .mellow.

We were stoned.

When the first side of *Highway 61 Revisited* finished playing, Alice got up to flip the record.

Greg and Ellen rose as well. "Greg and I are going to Big Sur, but Greg left you guys a present," she said.

The bearded boyfriend went into the kitchen and returned with a half-gallon jug of Thunderbird wine, which he set on the center of the rug. He then took a fresh joint from his Camel pack and laid it in the green ashtray, next to the roach of the first.

While Alice went to the kitchen for some glasses, I stood at the window and watched through the wiggly antique glass as Greg kick-started his Triumph motorcycle, then pulled it off its stand. Ellen climbed on the pillion and leaned against the sleeping bag strapped to the luggage rack. Through the antique glass, the scene became an Impressionist painting.

Alice poured three short tumblers of the yellowish wine, then dropped the needle on side two of her new Dylan album. By the time we heard *Desolation Row*, Alice was sitting on the carpet across from me, our knees touching. Her hands traced symmetrical arabesques in the air as she taught me a mirrored hand jive that she and Ellen had invented back in their dorm room. As her fingers wove through the air between us, I was mesmerized by the girl.

Her brother poured himself another glass of the sweet aperitif and held the bottle up towards Alice and me. I nodded, and Alice shook her head: she hadn't finished the first glass.

"Ooh, Alan, can you play that Sandy Bull record?" asked Alice.

Alan put the Dylan disc back in its cover and cued up *Fantasias for Guitar and Banjo*. I scraped a kitchen match across the dry hardwood floor and lit the second reefer. Each of us took a hit, then Alice snubbed it in the ashtray.

The psychedelic chamber music allowed us to talk easily. The poetry of Bob Dylan demanded close listening, but Sandy Bull's instrumental fantasies seemed to buoy conversation. Alice eagerly told me about her classes, especially her discovery of the metaphysical poets, such as John Donne.

Alan stretched out on the sagging couch, occasionally making an acerbic comment, but soon fell asleep. Alice and I kept talking animatedly. We had just met, but it felt like we were old friends. Alice was a National Merit Scholar, majoring in English, minoring in Russian, and fluent in French. I was far from her intellectual equal, but I couldn't get enough of her brilliant mind, her reddish brown hair, or her lightly freckled face. We talked on for another hour, and I finished my second tumbler full of Thunderbird. It was getting dark.

"John, do you feel okay?" she asked with a note of concern in her voice.

I felt dizzy and, when I opened my mouth to reply, I vomited all over myself.

The next thing I knew, I was sitting in a bathtub, naked, cold shower water spraying on my head. Alice had an arm around my wet shoulders, and Alan stood beside the shower nozzle, directing the frigid water at my face.

"Uh, yeah. . .I'm sorry," I muttered shamefully.

"Pish-tosh," said Alice. "The same thing happened to me when I moved into the dorm. I'll bet you never do *that* again. Here's a towel. Dry yourself off and lie down. I'll go to the basement and wash your clothes." She disappeared.

After I was dry, Alan led me into the bedroom, and I stretched out.

"I'm going to crash on the couch," Alan said. "Alice will be back pretty soon. I don't feel too good."

I pulled a quilt over myself and fell into a deep sleep.

When I awoke, the sun was rising. Alice was sleeping beside me, under the quilt but fully dressed. My cleaned clothes were folded on the foot of the bed. I slid from under the cover, pulled on my skivvies, and crept into the bathroom; I had to pee. While I was in there, I washed up. When I returned, Alice was sitting up and stretching, her auburn hair tousled about her head. Her blouse had slipped down, exposing a pale shoulder.

"What's the story, morning glory?" she asked, her voice husky from sleep. "Has Lazarus returned from the dead?"

"Hallelujah," I said.

"Let's get something to eat," she said. "Just give me a minute."

While Alice was in the bathroom, I pulled on my socks, Levi's, boots, and shirt. Going into the living room, I tried to rouse my lab partner snoring on the sofa.

Alan turned away, pulled a pillow around his head, and muttered, "You guys go without me. I want to sleep."

Alice came out of the bathroom, washed, brushed, and wearing pale pink lipstick and pale blue eyeshadow. The two of us tiptoed down the stairs and onto the street. Telegraph Avenue was deserted at seven o'clock on a Sunday morning. We walked several blocks, then Alice spoke up.

"I know a place that might be open." She took my hand, and we walked up Ashby Avenue to Dream Fluff Doughnuts. Over coffee and pastries, we caught up on our conversation from the night before. She maintained that Gregory Corso was a better poet than Allen Ginsberg, but neither of the Beats could hold a candle to John Donne or Andrew Marvell, her favorite metaphysical poets.

By the time that we got back to the borrowed apartment, Alan was up, showered, and listening to a John Fahey album on Linda and Lucy's stereo.

"If it's okay with you, I'd like to drive home now," he said.

Alice and I looked at each other.

"Sure," I said, "I can take the bus back to Hayward."

"I'll leave you lovebirds to do your worst." He nodded at his sister, and was gone down the rickety stairs.

Alice and I swept the place up, washed the tumblers, and

poured the rest of the jug down the drain.

The day ahead of us, Alice decided to take me on a tour of the Cal campus. Being Sunday, almost all the buildings were closed, but we wandered around the lawns, gardens, and redwood groves until we came to the immense Campanile. The elevator doors at the base of the granite tower were open, so we stepped inside and rode to the top, passing troves of college memorabilia visible through the steel mesh door.

On top, we walked around the viewing gallery, where we could see the entire San Francisco Bay, and stared upward at the huge bronze bells of the carillon.

"Put your hands over your ears," said Alice in a suddenly urgent voice. "Now!"

I followed orders, and we both pressed our palms to the sides of our heads as the biggest bell rang twelve times, struck by an automatic hammer. When it stopped, we dropped our hands and laughed in the vibrating air.

"How'd you know that was going to happen?" I asked.

She smirked and pointed at the wall clock inside the glassed-in control booth.

"Oh," I mumbled.

"Stick with me, kid," she said.

———

We walked downhill from the Campanile, across a foot-bridge, and came to Faculty Glade, a grass-covered slope with Strawberry Creek running below.

Alice pointed to a shady area beneath some redwoods at the bottom of the swale.

"The creek comes out of a tunnel down there. Linda and Lucy went through it all the way to Strawberry Canyon one time."

"Have you ever tried it?" I asked.

"I tried once, but I got scared and ran back out."

"Let's go," I said.

The entrance to the tunnel wasn't very scary. We saw two orange salamanders hunting insects in the clear water flowing over the rocks and pebbles. We walked into the round concrete culvert, the stream flowing on our left. As it got darker, Alice and I linked arms and leaned together as we advanced into the gloom. Our voices reverberated in a spooky way.

When we could no longer see our feet or the tunnel walls, we stopped and looked back. The sunlit entrance was now a tiny cameo of a forest glade with a rippling creek. We wrapped both arms around each other and stopped talking. When we kissed, it tasted slow, soft, and delicious.

"You want to go back?" I asked.

Both of us were breathing hard, and I could feel my heart thumping with hers as we hugged. I felt her head nod twice against my shoulder, and we went back towards the glowing cameo.

As we walked out of the cavern, our feet splashed through the water, soaking her sandals and my cowboy boots. Running up the green slope, we collapsed on the sunlit grass and laughed at the sky.

As boots and sandals dried, we lay in the sun. Alice told me about growing up in a small farming town in the San Joaquin Valley, and I related my adventures in Arkansas.

As shadows started to creep up the lawn, Alice sat cross-legged, and I lay on my back, head cradled in her lap. As I looked up, her auburn hair formed a curtain around our faces. I whispered, "I love you."

She kissed me beside my nose and said, "I love you, too."

———

Riding home on the AC Transit bus, I felt like I was dreaming. Cupid's arrow burned in my heart. Even though Alice had seen me at my worst, she loved me anyway. This brilliant, eighteen-year-old university scholar wanted me, a fifteen-year-old wimp who couldn't pass algebra. Kissing her had been nothing like the chaste pecks that Carol and I had exchanged back in Coronado. This was the real deal.

I wasn't tall, athletic, or particularly handsome, but this girl seemed to like me anyway. Maybe I didn't have to be good at sports to attract a female. Alice had never been to a football game. She did like riding horses and folk dancing, and I liked those pastimes just fine.

Later, I would realize how important those moments were—those times when my own dislikes and likes became clearer, and how they helped me begin to find my own way in the world.

The bus dumped me at the intersection of Tennyson Road, and I walked home. Mother was ironing in the brightly lit kitchen as I walked in. I was famished.

Tilting back the steam iron, she looked at me with a slight smile. "Your father has orders."

I stopped dead in my tracks, suddenly feeling numb.

"Where?" I said in a weak voice.

Mother crossed her arms over her apron.

"Beeville, Texas."

Summer Sunsets

MY HEART FELL into a dark, bottomless well. I grabbed the edge of the dinette and sank into a chrome and vinyl breakfast chair. Beeville was a tiny air base near the Gulf of Mexico, outside of Corpus Christi.

Mother's sly smile changed to a look of concern.

"I was just kidding," she said. "The orders are for Oak Knoll Naval Hospital, in the Oakland Hills."

My heart soared out of the depths and into the sky. I jumped up and hugged my mom. I think she was as happy as I was. Instead of her husband being at sea for months at a time, he would return home every night, and we could live beside the San Francisco Bay. I knew Oakland was much closer to Berkeley. This was great!

Meanwhile, back at the high school, I had passed algebra with a D-minus. This was the third time I had taken it, and the teacher probably just wanted to get rid of me. I was required to take a math class in tenth grade. I asked my councilor if I could take Business Math instead of Geometry.

"I don't think that that would advisable," Mr. Ross said. "All of your classes should be college-track. You want to go to college don't you?"

If he had asked the question a week earlier, before I met Alice, my answer would have surely been no, but instead I answered, "Yes sir!"

To my shock and delight, when I took Geometry, I consistently pulled down A's and B's.

Go figure.

————————

School was out for the summer, and Alan and I were sorting out sleeping bags, backpacks, and dried food packets in preparation for the John Muir Trail hike we'd been planning for months. All the supplies were laid out on the Edwards' garage floor. The door from the kitchen opened, and Alice walked in.

"I had to move out of the dorm until the fall semester," said my cute and brainy girlfriend. "I'll be living here until the end of August."

My heart started acting up again; she had told me this was a possibility, but here it was!

"I live in the next block!" I said.

Alice grinned, showing her braces.

"I *know* where you live," she said.

Alan rolled his eyes.

Alan and I finished packing the old Plymouth for the drive to the trail head, while Alice watched from a kitchen stool next to the workbench. Her mom invited me to stay for supper. Alice entertained the family with stories and descriptions of her first year at the university. I enjoyed seeing the family resemblance between Alice and each of her parents.

Alice's mom, like her daughter, was good with languages, but suffered from a gloomy disposition, unlike Alice's sunny outlook. Her Dad was friendly and enthusiastic, much like his daughter. Alan shared a lively sense of humor with his sister, although his was on the dark, sardonic side.

After dinner, Alice and I walked to the tule marsh that began at the end of the block. Hayward had not been fully developed yet; sheep still grazed in the hills, and steelhead spawned in the creeks. We held hands as we walked through tall grass along the edge of the rushes.

Suddenly a large bird exploded from the ground ahead of us, flapping its loud wings and cackling as it few off into the sunset.

"What in the world was that?" asked Alice.

"Ring-necked pheasant," I said, proud that I knew something a National Merit Scholar did not. We walked on, talking about poetry, art, journalism, and the Vietnam War—to which my dad's ship was sailing. We were exploring each other's minds before we explored each other's bodies. Evening or nighttime walks would become a regular routine after I returned from the High Sierra.

Being in love with Alice made the worlds of the church and the military seem empty and vapid. These institutions had no attraction to me anymore. Somehow the final, complete break with them had occurred.

10

High Sierra

THE BACKPACKING TRIP to Evolution Valley was a great adventure. Alan and I got blisters and sunburn. We crossed creeks rushing so fast and deep that we had to belay each other across with a rope. On the far bank we would drop our packs and pull off our soaked boots, wool socks, and britches. After wringing out as much water as we could, we put them back on, and they dried as we hiked. On the third day, after trudging up thousands of feet of sun-blasted granite switchbacks, we humped into Evolution Meadow.

At 9,500 feet of altitude, the wide rippling creek meandered through alpine grasses and massive granite boulders. A cool breeze flowed down from summer snowfields on the granite peaks above us. Most of our expensive, dried backpacking rations were exhausted by now.

We had already gobbled up the most easily prepared items, like bacon bars, powdered eggs, and pilot biscuits. Some of the backpacking foods such as cracked dried beans would simply not cook at high altitude. They remained rock-hard, even when simmered over the campfire for hours. After all the physical effort we'd expended climbing up here, we were hungry, all day and night. We tortured ourselves by describing fantasy meals we would eat when we returned to civilization.

I dropped a fishhook baited with a live grasshopper into a pool of the creek. Almost immediately, I felt a tug on the line and pulled out a trout! In a few minutes I had caught my legal limit of ten fish, and I still had grasshoppers left over in the Prince Albert can. I raced back to our camp with my full stringer to show Alan. He looked up from his Herman Hesse book with hungry eyes.

While I cleaned the fish downstream from our camp, Alan disappeared with his drop line in his hand. On my way back to our boulder-bordered camp, I picked a bouquet of miner's lettuce with tender round leaves like nasturtiums. I started a twig and stick fire in an old fire ring, several yards downwind of our tarp and bedrolls. I didn't want any cooking smells near our sleeping area. We had seen bear tracks and heard coyotes singing the past few days.

Alan arrived with ten more cleaned trout.

"I caught these on pickled salmon eggs," he announced.

I assembled our mess kits, salt and pepper canisters, and several tiny plastic bottles of *Vegelene*™ cooking oil left over from our depleted rations. Salting and peppering each fish, I fried them up, two by two, in the lid of my aluminum mess kit. I served the sizzling fish atop a bed of miner's lettuce which wilted from their heat. We made lemonade from an envelope of *Wyler's* powder and a quart of creek water. The meat of the golden trout was pink, like salmon. This was living: real food and plenty of it.

Just as we were tucking into our second round, a lone hiker came down the trail. He was humping a tall pack frame and moving right along. When he saw us, he veered off the narrow trail and into our granite and grass kitchen.

"How far is the cutoff to Florence Lake?" he asked, leaning his pack against a boulder.

"About twenty-five miles," said Alan.

"Great," said the bearded backpacker, "I have to be at Florence Lake by tomorrow night to meet my ride."

"Where did you come in?" I asked.

"I left Yosemite Valley two weeks ago."

"That's a hundred miles from here," said Alan.

"A hundred fifteen and four tenths, to be exact. I haven't seen another person since I picked up supplies at Mono Creek a week ago. I'm Adam, by the way."

"I'm John, and this is Alan," I said. "Would you like some fried golden trout?"

"Twist my arm," said Adam, sitting down.

Between the three of us, we ate twenty fish in less than an hour.

We all rose and stretched. Adam reached into his pack and pulled out a fat bag of gorp and an untouched Italian salami.

"I'll be at the road head tomorrow, so I'll leave this stuff with you guys. I'll never eat it," he said, handing Alan the foot-long

Molinari salami and two-pound sack of gorp: peanuts, raisins, dried apricots, and M&M's. He hoisted his pack, then disappeared down the narrow dirt trail.

Here was another awakening to the life that was mine to live. I had always thought I detested sports. I was usually picked last for a sandlot ball game, and was pretty dismal at throwing, catching, and hitting. Mountaineering was different. The freedom of the hills was intoxicating after my rigid upbringing. I felt independent, only responsible for myself and my partner. The vigorous exercise strengthened my body and cleared my mind of clutter—especially with no one barking orders or leveling criticisms.

The Trips Festival

ALICE HAD A PART-TIME JOB as a governess caring for the young daughter of two married doctors, the Zellers, in San Francisco.

I had found a part-time job picking up trash and weeding lawns and flower beds for the Hayward Parks Department. It paid less than minimum wage, but it included a pass to the Hayward Plunge, the antique, glassed-in pool in the main park.

Sometimes I would take the bus to the city and meet Alice when she got off work. We walked all over North Beach, Chinatown, and picnicked in Golden Gate Park. We ate dim sum at the Hang Ah Tearoom and spent hours poring over poetry in the basement of City Lights Books.

Dad and Mom were busy shopping for a house closer to the Naval Hospital, where Dad would be reporting for duty in a few weeks. One evening, when the folks were at Wednesday night prayer meeting, Alice came over to see me.

She and I were determined to lose our virginities together, and it looked like this might be the night. Just as things were heating up nicely, we both heard my folks' car drive up, and the squeaking of garage door springs. Alice grabbed her green sweater, pulled it on, and beat it out the side door of the kitchen. As my parents and sister came in, she tiptoed around the outside of the house to the sidewalk, walked around the block, then home.

———

The summer was over when my family moved to a modern three bedroom house in Castro Valley. Alice had moved back into the Berkeley dorm with her roommate, Ellen. I started eleventh grade at Canyon High School, nestled in the grassy hills and live oak glens of the unincorporated bedroom community.

The first day of the term, I walked up the sidewalk that climbed the steep hill to the campus. I was more than a little worried about fitting into this new school. Two teenaged boys stood to the side. When one saw me, he offered a rolled matchbook "crutch" with a fat roach burning at one end. I took a toke and made my first two friends at the suburban high school: Arthur and Dennis.

Later I was sitting by myself in the cafeteria eating lunch. Everyone around me seemed to know each other, and I was too timid to approach any of the groups of laughing teenagers. I sat alone, eating my peanut butter sandwich. Two girls sat down across from me.

"Hi, I'm Doris, and this is Nina," said the petite blonde.

The brunette beside her said, "We saw you sitting here and we're like, he looks cool."

I was wearing Levi's with old roper boots, a faded blue work shirt, and a Levi's jacket. Nina wore a fringed Davy Crockett jacket over a poorboy sweater, a wool skirt, and fringed squaw boots.

"I'm John," I managed to say. "You look cool, too."

Doris leaned across the narrow table conspiratorially, warm yellow curls framing blue eyes. Her Mexican blouse had bluebirds embroidered on the bodice.

"Do you turn on?" she asked in a soft voice.

I wasn't sure what she was talking about.

"Sure," I replied, nodding.

The world I was heading into opened wider—peopled by these two very nice-looking girls who judged me as "cool looking".

"Meet us in the parking lot after the final bell. Nina's car is the Studebaker RBR."

"What's an RBR?" I asked.

"Rusty But Runs," said Nina with a grin.

"We have to keep the windows open all the time," said Nina. "I think the exhaust manifold is cracked or something."

Nina was driving, I sat in the middle, and Doris sat on my right as the coupe barreled down Crow Canyon Road. Exhaust fumes boiled up from the floorboards, stinging eyes and nostrils. Doris tuned in the tube radio. *Telstar* by the Ventures came out of the speaker.

Pulling into a gravel driveway, Nina killed the smoky engine. We piled out and went into the den of a ranch house. Nina's folks weren't home, but her older brother Sean was there playing a Dave Brubeck album on the console stereo.

"Sean, did you get the lid?" asked Nina, plopping down next to him on the couch.

"Fuckin' A," he replied. "Have I ever let you down?"

He flipped a sandwich bag stuffed with a green ounce of marijuana to the coffee table.

Nina promptly took a pack of Zig-Zag papers from the pocket of her fringed jacket and pulled a three-finger pinch of pot from the baggie. She rubbed her thumb across her fingers and sprinkled the crumbled leaf and seeds onto the cover of *Time Out*.

After picking out the plump, shiny seeds and discarding them in a boomerang-shaped ashtray, she held a creased paper with her left fingers and sprinkled the cleaned weed along it with her right. Rolling a little cylinder with both thumbs, her pink tongue licked the edge and she held up a fresh joint.

The girl took a massive silver lighter from the coffee table, sparked it, and puffed the joint alight. Suppressing a cough, she handed it to me. I took a hit and passed it to Doris who eagerly inhaled the smoke. When she gave it to Sean he passed it on without partaking.

"I have a shoot scheduled in Oakland and I need to be straight," he said. He stood up and slung a leather camera bag over his shoulder.

"Thanks, Sean," said Nina.

"Anytime, baby sister," he patted the girl's head, nodded to Doris and me, and was out the glass door. He hopped into the seat of his open roadster.

Nina sucked hard on the smoldering reefer and handed it to me.

"That car of Sean's doesn't have a top," she said in a strained voice, exhaling blue smoke. "And the doors are jammed, so you have to sit on the trunk and drop into the seat."

"What does he do when it rains?" I asked.

"He wears a raincoat and a cowboy hat."

"Ooh, ooh!" spouted Doris. "Remember that cat who drove the Merry Pranksters' bus at the Trips Festival?"

"Sure," said Nina. "He was straaange." She spread her hands wide, wiggled her fingers, and swung her long straight hair back and forth, eyes gaping.

"That was Neal Cassidy!" said Doris.

"You mean Dean Moriarty, the guy in *On the Road?*"

"That was him!"

"Far out," said Nina.

"Wait," I said, "you went to the Trips Festival?"

"Fuckin' A," said Nina and Doris, in chorus.

The Trips Festival, held earlier that year, was at Long-shoreman's Hall, in San Francisco, the last two days that LSD was legal. The Grateful Dead had played. Ken Kesey, The Merry Pranksters, and Bill Graham had produced the event. I had been kicking myself that Alice and I had missed it.

"Can you get some acid?" I asked.

"Sure. I know Owsley," said Nina, a hint of pride in her voice.

Both of these girls were called *beatniks* by the other kids at the high school. Soon a columnist for the Chronicle popularized the word *hippie*, and that's what the long-haired, boots and sandals crowd were called from then on.

I wanted in. And as soon as I tried the hip drug of choice— LSD—my life would take a dizzying turn.

My parents had to attend a Southern Baptist Missions conference the next weekend. My mother told me if I didn't want to attend the mission conference, I would have to stay in the house alone.

"No problem," I said.

That Saturday, Alice checked out of her dorm and took the AC Transit bus to Castro Valley. I met her at the bus stop on Center Street. She carried a Guatemalan bag. We walked up the gentle hill to my house and went inside.

After I'd showed her the living room, kitchen, and patio, I showed her my room. Breathing hard, we slowly unbuttoned and removed each other's clothing, then climbed into bed.

We didn't really know what we were doing, but we kept trying. I fumbled awkwardly; Alice bit her lip and trembled.

Suddenly she cried, "Ouch!"

"Should I stop?" I asked.

"Oh, God no," she said, and we sank into a delicious, fleshy void.

A little later we caught our breath, talked for a bit, and raided the refrigerator. We sat up in bed eating fruit-flavored yogurt, giggling about the experience.

In a few minutes more, we staged a repeat performance.

Earlier, I had been convinced that I would die a virgin. *Who would be interested in a wimpy little punk like me?* As it turned out, I only had to wait until I was sixteen to find my place in the new, "hip" movement. A weight was lifted from my shoulders, and my confidence soared.

On Monday, back at the high school, Nina was as good as her word. At lunch, she and Doris sat on either side of me, and Nina handed me a matchbox with two small gelatin capsules nesting on a bed of cleaned weed.

"You can dump one of the caps in a glass of water," she murmured. "After it dissolves, you can drink half, and your old lady can drink the other."

Nina and Doris heartily approved of me going with a university student. After all, each of them had college-aged boyfriends.

"What happens if you drop a whole cap?" I asked.

"You'll see God," she said.

As it happened, it would be two weeks before Alice and

I could see each other again. I can't remember the particulars. We had to be content with long, soulful telephone calls, which caused me to be banned from using the family phone, since it ran up the bill when we talked for hours at a time. This meant I had to walk a few blocks to a pay phone and feed a quarter into the slot every three minutes. Alice had to talk on a dorm phone, on a third floor landing, with no real privacy.

Since I was always short of quarters, I figured out how to pay up front for a few minutes. After I finally hung up, the operator would call back to tell me what I owed. Now, whenever Alice and I went on and on, she would hang up first, and I would leave the black handset dangling by its armored cord in the florescent lit phone booth. The operator could not make the phone ring, and I would run away into the night.

After one especially longing phone session, I walked home. The lights were out; my parents and sister had turned in. I slipped into my room and closed the door.

I decided to take some LSD.

Since Alice wasn't there, I dropped a whole capsule.

For an hour nothing happened. I tried reading some poetry, sitting up in bed, but couldn't really enjoy it. I set the book to the nightstand. Glancing up, I was startled to see that the crumpled quilt on the foot of the bed had turned into a rugged mountain range, complete with peaks, glaciers, rivers, and forests.

I sensed a large animal in the room with me. I could hear it breathing and occasionally grunting lightly as I moved around my darkened chamber. Only after some time passed did I realize that the animal was me, or at least my body.

I wandered around my dimly-lit bedroom, absorbed and entertained. The commonplace objects around me took on a mystical significance, whether it was a crumpled tube of Naples Yellow oil paint, a carved dog whittled by my grandpa, or my old roper boots.

I undressed and managed to put on my pajamas. I turned out the reading lamp next to the bed and lay my head down. Staring up at the darkened ceiling, I was prepared to see God. As my head sank into the soft pillow, I could smell Alice, who had lain here last week, as we gleefully deflowered each other and made grandiose plans for our lives together.

All at once, I could see her—and all the times I had laid eyes on her—in vivid detail. The texture of her hair, the smoothness of her skin, and every inch of her body played through my mind in an instant that lasted forever. I didn't see God, but I saw a Hindu goddess.

After a few hours of various ecstatic visions, my brain started to cool down a bit, and I tried to sleep. Tomorrow was a school day, after all.

Sleep didn't come, and I began to have deep and profound thoughts about life, the universe, and everything. As I concentrated on these brilliant revelations, they appeared in yellow letters in the dark, like the news crawl above Times Square.

As I tried to memorize the illuminations, a cartoon gorilla came out of the void and ate the wisdom, stuffing the words into his mouth as fast as I could think them. I stifled my laughter into my pillow. After all, my parents might think something was amiss if they heard me laughing crazily before dawn.

When my alarm went off, I sprang up and took a quick shower in the Jack and Jill bathroom between my sister's and my room. At breakfast, the raisin bran tasted wonderful, and I set off to school. As I walked up the curved street to the high school, the dry yellow grasses on the hill looked like snowfields to my dilated eyes.

As usual, I met the two senior girls, Doris and Nina, for lunch. We tucked in to our Sloppy Joes and mixed vegetables.

"I dropped acid last night," I said.

Doris giggled, and Nina dropped her fork.

"Did you see God?" inquired Nina, with a mischievous grin.

"No, but I saw a goddess..."

"Far out," said Nina.

———

Later that month, in one of our late night telephone marathons, Alice dropped a bombshell.

"I think I'm pregnant," she said.

Her voice sounded like her hand was cupped over the mouthpiece of the receiver.

We should have known better than to depend on withdrawal as a contraceptive. Since I was only sixteen, the druggist at the local pharmacy had refused to sell me rubbers, and Alice was not eligible to get birth control pills from Cowell Hospital without her parents' consent, an impossibility.

Abortion was a felony back then. Alice knew that giving birth would bring a screeching halt to her promising academic career, perhaps permanently.

"Let's get married," I suggested, ignoring the fact that I wouldn't be 21 for five more years.

"Don't be silly," said the goddess. "We couldn't support ourselves and our baby. Besides, I would still have to drop out."

Having no answer to the dilemma, I said, "I love you."

"I'm going to see an intern at Cowell," she said. "I heard that he has helped girls with this before. Call me tomorrow."

"Okay," I said.

"I love you," she said, then the line went dead.

I walked away from the phone booth, leaving the the receiver dangling, as usual.

The next morning, I was like a zombie at school. I went through the motions, but even in my favorite classes, like English Literature, I didn't really participate, but sat like a lump at my desk.

When the bell rang, I turned down an invitation from Arthur and Dennis to go smoke weed in the grove behind the football field. I walked home.

At eight o'clock, I was at the phone booth, and I pumped in three quarters.

"Channing Hall, Ellen here," came a girl's voice on the other end.

"Hi Ellen, it's John. Is Alice there?"

"Hey, John, she's here, hang on."

I heard Alice's laughter as she came to the phone.

"When I was walking to Cowell today, I got my period," she said. "I went inside and canceled my appointment."

"That's great," I said.

"We have to be more careful next time," she said.

"I have a friend who's 21," I said, thinking of Nina's brother Sean. "I'll ask him to buy some rubbers."

"I'll tell the doctor that I have painful periods, and maybe I can get the pill without my parents' signature."

"Or I could forge it," I suggested.

"Why Johnny, that would be illegal," she said, then laughed, and I laughed too.

———

Meanwhile, back at the high school, I was enrolled in Journalism I. Alice had advised me that editing my high school paper would look great on a college application. If I could get into Cal, maybe we could live together while she pursued a master's in English, French or Russian.

———

As a reporter for the Canyon Courier, I covered student events, clubs, and rallies. I talked to all kinds of students—not just the hip crowd, but the jocks, cheerleaders, ranch kids, and surfers.

Mr. Solito told us we could publish anything we wanted, but we had to make sure it was true, and and we couldn't use dirty words. When I submitted a story about the dean of students suspending Nina, Doris, and Caroline for dress code violations, the faculty advisor shook his head and handed it back to me.

"Kill it," he said. "We can't comment on matters of student discipline."

I tried to reason with him. The student dress code said that boys had to wear slacks and a shirt with a collar; girls had to wear dresses or skirts, hems at the knee or below. There was no mention of bras being required for girls, or boys.

Mr. Solito rolled his eyes and repeated, "Kill it."

When the delinquent girls returned to school the following Monday, they were wearing bras but seemed amused by the whole thing.

"Mrs. Harris never said a word about it last year when I didn't wear a bra," said Caroline. "I think it's because of the new dean, Mr. Pratt."

"He's creepy alright," said Nina. "I've noticed him staring at me when I walk past."

She, Doris, and Caroline nodded, and said, "Creepy!" in unison. They were good at that.

"John," said Nina, "I have to drive to Telegraph Avenue after school, want to come? I'll be back by five or so."

"Sure," I replied.

At three o'clock, I met Nina in the student parking lot, and we drove away in the rickety Studebaker. "Look in the glove compartment," she said. "I think there's a doobie in there."

I lit it from the dashboard lighter, and we passed it back and forth as we drove down the tree-shaded Earl Warren Freeway into Berkeley. By the time we parked at the curb in front of Shakespeare and Company, we were totally wasted, giggling, and leaning into each other as we entered the beat bookstore.

This shop specialized in poetry and, like City Lights, only sold paperbacks. It also sold tickets to the Fillmore Auditorium.

"Do you have tickets to the Saturday show at the Fillmore?" Nina asked the clerk.

He looked up from his book and said, "Um, yeah, I have four left."

"I'll take two," she said. Then she turned to me, "Johnny, you *have* to get the other two. Alice would love it."

I looked at the swirly psychedelic poster behind the clerk.

"The Young Rascals? Sopwith Camel?" I said, "I don't know...."

"Yeah, right," Nina acknowledged, "but the opening act is The Doors. They're from Venice Beach, and they just cut their first album."

I had ten dollars in my pocket, earned from the yard work and housecleaning chores I did for Mrs. Roth back in Castro Valley.

I shelled out six dollars to the clerk, and he handed me two tickets.

On Saturday, I caught the AC Transit bus to the city and met Alice outside the Zeller's Victorian house, when she got off work. We hadn't seen each other for two weeks. She ran down the steps and threw her arms around me.

"I got tickets to The Doors tonight," I said, once we finished squeezing each other.

"You're kidding!" she said, drawing back and looking in my eyes.

"Nope. Seven o'clock at the Fillmore."

We walked down the hill into Chinatown. We ordered fried rice with bean curd, the cheapest thing on the menu at Sam Wo.

"Ellen saw The Doors at the Whisky a Go Go, when she was in LA with Greg," said Alice. "She says Jim Morrison is the new Rimbaud."

Alice had read the poems of Baudelaire and Rimbaud to me, in French, then English. I knew what she was talking about.

We caught a MUNI bus out Geary Boulevard, past St. Mary's screwdriver-shaped Cathedral, and got off at Fillmore. Neither Alice nor I had ever been inside the hulking, brick building with the famous dance hall upstairs. We were both minors, and were excluded from The Matrix, the city's rock nightclub. The Fillmore did not serve booze, so baby boomers were welcome.

We walked in through open doors on the street, and up the wooden stairs. On the first landing we surrendered our tickets, and our hands were stamped with ultraviolet ink. In the lobby stood a bin of apples. The hand-lettered sign above the fruit said, "Have One . . . or Two."

We each took an apple. Holding hands and munching, we walked into the auditorium. Colored lights splayed around the ceiling, and recorded music was playing. We sat Indian style on the floor, with hundreds of others. The house lights dimmed and a spotlight hit the stage, revealing a craggy-featured Bill Graham standing at a microphone.

"Here's a band from Venice, California. I think you're going to dig them: The Doors."

Four hip-looking guys walked out. One sat at an electric organ, another at the drums, one held an electric guitar, and a handsome jock of a guy strode up to the microphone.

The drummer started banging out a rhythm with rim shots and bass drum. The organist played a deep *Bom bom bom, bom-bom ba-da bom*. The jock grabbed the mike stand like he was going to strangle it.

Bom bom bom, bom-bom ba-da bom...

———

The words and music flowed over us. Someone handed Alice a joint. She took a puff, coughed, and handed it to me. When The Doors started playing *Light My Fire,* we were up and dancing under a strobe light. Alice twirled her necklace like a jumprope and, under the strobe, the beads' motion was arrested at the top of the arc. We started to jump in synch, and our bodies were frozen in mid-air, in various goofy positions. The amplified music allowed no conversation.

I loved the way the instruments would stretch out, syncopating the rhythm, making sweet and thunderous hard rock jazz.

Pulsating amoebas of color danced on the walls of the ballroom, and I was fascinated by the light show. I realized, with satisfaction, this was *not* the kind of place in which my Baptist parents would want me to be.

Nina danced up to us under the strobe light, hugged me, hugged Alice, then disappeared into the dark ballroom.

During a lull in the music, Alice put her lips next to my ear and asked, "Was that Nina?"

"That was her," I answered.

We might have stayed for The Young Rascals and Sopwith Camel, or not—I can't remember. Riding the 38 Geary bus back to the Transbay Terminal, we raved about the music and poetry we'd heard. Standing on the departure platform, we hugged and pressed our bodies together but didn't talk.

Alice climbed onto the "F" Berkeley bus. It pulled away, while she watched me through the scratched and clouded window. I rode home on the "N" Castro Valley bus alone, a throbbing pain in my nuts. I had heard of *blueballs* before, and now I knew what that meant.

—

On Monday morning, back at Canyon High, I told my friends about the amazing show we'd heard at the Fillmore on the weekend. I went on and on about The Doors' soaring, syncopated, and jazzy music, the light show, and Jim Morrison's American Symbolist poetry.

When I sat down for lunch with Nina, she was beaming, looking at me under her bangs.

"Was I right? Was that the best concert ever?"

"Fuckin' A!" I answered.

"I liked Alice, she's cool."

I laughed. "You barely saw her."

"*Au contraire, mon ami,*" she said. "I was dancing under the strobe light forever, and you two didn't take your eyes off each other."

I blushed and said, "Thanks for telling me to buy the tickets."

"Well, if you liked that, you'll love this," she said, shoving a copy of *The San Francisco Oracle* across the table. On the front page was an announcement for *A Gathering of the Tribes for a Human Be-In.*

When I called Alice at her dorm that night, I told her about the big event in Golden Gate Park coming up on the weekend.

"Let's go!" she said. "I don't have to work on Saturday. Meet me at the dorm in the morning, and we'll make a day of it."

Saturday morning, I took an early bus to Berkeley, and Alice met me in front of her dorm on Channing Way. Her Guatemalan bag held a loaf of Baroni's sourdough and a good-sized hunk of cheese. I had a wineskin of Burgundy hung from my shoulder, and a rolled up Mexican serape under my arm. We were ready for anything.

We got off the MUNI bus on Fulton Street—the northern border of the park. The bus disgorged baby boomers. Some of the girls wore Indian print shifts or skirts; some of the boys wore headbands over longish hair. The dress code for this event seemed more liberal than that of the high school; none of the girls, including Alice, seemed to be wearing bras.

Walking south to the Polo Grounds, the sun shone down on everyone. On January 14th, the air felt like summer, not a bit like the usual "forty-nine degrees and foggy" this time of year. As we wound along the paths through the trees and shrubbery, more and more pilgrims joined the procession.

Rounding a grassy berm, we could see the Polo Field before us. Twenty or thirty thousand people were spread out across the equestrian arena.

Alice and I stopped short, then a couple bumped into us from behind.

"I don't want to go out there," said Alice.

"Me neither," I said. "Let's split."

We walked away from the Human Be-In, crossed a low rise, and found a little glen—a leaf-strewn clearing in the trees. A small pond sparkled at the bottom of the gentle slope.

"How's this?" asked Alice.

"Perfect."

I threw out the serape on a bed of leaves between gnarled oak roots where they kneeled into the ground. Alice sat on the woven wool and leaned back against the tree trunk. I joined her, and we looked up at the dappled light coming through the leaves.

"We have a light show and everything," she said, with a grin that showed her braces.

The sound of Buddhist chanting came over loudspeakers from the Polo Grounds, echoing off the oaks and poplars around us.

"That was the most people I've ever seen at one time," said Alice.

"Yeah, me too," I said. "I saw the altar call at the Billy Graham crusade in Madison Square Garden, and this was worse."

Alice pulled the block of Port d'Salut from her sack and laid the loaf of sourdough beside it. I pared slices from the cheese with my jackknife and tore the bread into chunks. We swallowed squirts from the Basque wineskin, a red drop or two landing on Alice's peasant blouse. The poetry and music from the gathering over the hill echoed off the oaks around us.

A loaf of bread, a jug of wine, and thou beside me singing in the wilderness, wrote Omar Khayyam.

After we ate and drank, we rolled up our jeans and waded in the pond, splashing each other and laughing. As it turned out, we saw no one during our picnic. We could have gone skinny dipping, but were too shy.

As the sun went down that day, we gathered our kit and joined the throngs streaming out of the Polo Grounds. Nina and her boyfriend came bounding down the berm, and Nina—wearing her oversized straw hat, jacket fringes flapping—threw her arms around Alice and me and smiled a dreamy smile, eyes dilated.

And that was how Alice and I played hooky from the Human Be-In.

The next day, The San Francisco Chronicle proclaimed *The Hippie Movement*. The columnist Herb Caen had coined the word *beatnik* nine or ten years earlier, and now he pushed the noun *hippie*.

I wasn't in "Slick Gang" any more. I wasn't a beatnik, so I must be a hippie. . ..

The Summer of Love was just around the corner.

Lines were being drawn. On one side was Lyndon Johnson, Robert McNamara, and the military-industrial complex, who were busily cooking up reasons to send American troops to Vietnam. Opposing them was the boots and sandals crowd, a few Quakers, and other pacifists.

In my English Literature class I read *The Second Coming*, a poem by William Butler Yates:

Things fall apart; the centre cannot hold. . .

In 1967, we could feel the electricity in the air. We knew that something was happening here, but we didn't know what it was. It was as if the secret baby boomers club had grown so large that it wasn't a secret anymore.

And what rough beast, its hour come round at last, slouches towards Bethlehem to be born?

I was about to find out.

Teenage Wasteland

ARTHUR AND DENNIS, the first two friends I'd made at Canyon, were constant companions after school. Arthur was a tall, blond, and laconic musician. Dennis spent hours tinkering with crank-start English roadsters. His stocky form was often hidden under the bonnet of a Triumph or MG when Arthur and I would come over to his house. He owned three sets of socket wrenches: English, Metric, and Wentworth.

One beautiful spring day, the three of us piled into his tiny TR 10 and drove to the Nike missile base in the hills off Lake Chabot Road. We parked along the shoulder, walked through the tall green grass, and sat outside the chain link fence.

We each swallowed a cap of White Lightning acid, then we shared a bomber joint.

"You know," said Dennis, "sometimes they test the gantries. If you're around here you can see the nose cones come up just beyond that grass hill."

We didn't see them test the nuclear tipped missiles that day, but we had a fine time imagining World War Three, as mushroom columns of flame and fallout blossomed around the San Francisco Bay spread out below us. We ran down the grassy hills, laughing and making explosion and machine gun sounds. I recited what I could remember of *Bomb* by Gregory Corso.

When the manic portion of the trip was over, I lay prone in the lush fescue, feeling real grief for the fates of the ants, grubs, and doodlebugs moving through the jungle of roots, inches from my eyes, unaware of the looming holocaust.

Another time, I remember my mother coming home early when I was flying high on acid. She sat on the Japanese *Obi* chair, across from me on the couch. She failed to notice my altered state. We talked for two hours about philosophy, art, history, and nature.

"John, I'm so glad we had this conversation," she said as the evening wound down. "We should do this more often."

The whole family went to the movies a few weeks later. My folks had heard of *The Endless Summer,* and they knew of my fascination with surfing—both back in Coronado and now at Santa Cruz and Stinson Beach, in Northern California. Since I didn't willingly go to church with them anymore, they probably thought this would be a nice thing to do as a family.

It sounded good to me too. In fact it sounded so good that I dropped a half-tab of acid just before we left for the drive through the hills to San Ramon. I figured that I would start to come on just after after the movie started, and would peak before the film ended, and be in the quieter, contemplative portion of the trip for the ride home.

How wrong I was.

The acid did start coming on after we'd sat down in the theater. *The Endless Summer* captivated all of us with its good-hearted vision of perfect waves, carefree youth, and tropical travel.

When the credits rolled, we all clapped, inspired and happy. As we stood up and filed out, however, I realized that my trip was just beginning to peak, and I was hallucinating vividly. My family and the other moviegoers had animal heads and bodies wearing middle-class clothing: warthogs, cobras, giraffes, and so on. The walk across the parking lot became a fearful safari across the nighttime veldt.

When we got to the car, a blue '65 Ford Fairlane, Dad stopped and tossed me the keys.

"John, why don't you drive us home?" he asked. "You've never driven at night, and it would be good practice for you."

I caught the keys, gulped, and said, "Thanks Dad." Mother and Polly sat in the back.

The drive through Crow Canyon was harrowing. The headlights of the Ford blazed out like twin blowtorches, melting the undulating asphalt and setting the writhing trees afire beside the winding road.

When I pulled into the driveway of the tract home on New Haven Way, Dad said, "Well done son, you should take the test and get your license next week."

I, however, was seriously traumatized. It would be twenty more years before I worked up the courage to get my first driver's license.

———

Another time my experimentation landed me in the madhouse for a week.

I had stayed in touch with my friends from Tennyson High School: Nick the precocious artist, Skip the campy performer, Coleen the talented folksinger, and Alan, Alice's brother.

Alan and I went backpacking again, the summer following our first adventure. This time we packed better, bringing gorp, salami, biscuit flour, and marijuana. I had invited Alice, but she demurred, in no uncertain terms.

"I would never sleep on the ground or in a tent," she proclaimed. "Forget it!"

The trip went well. We learned how to use our new ice axes, and we covered more territory. A month after we had returned, Alan drove over to my house in Castro Valley.

"Got any weed?" he asked, as he slammed the door of his old Plymouth.

"Negative," I said. "No acid either."

Faced with the prospect of a weekend with nothing to do

besides watch TV or wander the muddy spring hillsides, I came up with a bright idea.

"The drugstore on Center Street sells Asthmador cigarettes," I offered, "and they're made of Belladonna and Datura." (The common names of these plants are deadly nightshade and locoweed, both known to kill the cattle that ate them.)

"Let's get some," said Adam.

We walked over to the drugstore—the same one that refused to sell me condoms—and picked a pack of the old asthma remedy from a shelf of patent medicines.

In my back yard we tried smoking one of the cardboard-tipped cigarettes. After waiting a few minutes, we agreed that the only noticeable effect was a slight numbness in the chest.

"I think we should try eating it," I said.

I dumped the contents of several of the medicinal cigarettes into a cereal bowl, and we ate the dry, crumbly herbs with spoons, washing it down with water.

Please, don't ever try this at home.

An hour later, Alan was curled up on the couch, laughing like a hyena, and I was sitting in the Obi chair, a colorful geography book on my lap. My cheeks had turned to wings, and my disembodied head was flying across a map of Asia.

"John! John! Are you alright?" I could hear my mother's voice and felt her arm around my shoulder.

I dimly thought, "That's silly, why would I answer her?" After all, I was happily soaring over the Gobi desert at the time.

Then I blacked out.

The next thing I knew, I was seated in a wheelchair, as an angry Navy petty officer—an MP evidently—roughly jerked my shirtsleeves back, inspecting my forearms for needle tracks. Finding none, he put his face close to mine.

"Where'd you get the LSD, son?" he asked.

I didn't answer. After all, I wasn't on acid.

I was wheeled away to an examining room. A corpsman sat across from me and asked what day is it, who is the president, what year is it, and so on. Although I understood his questions and knew the correct answers, I couldn't seem to open my mouth. I realized I was in the ER at Oak Knoll Naval Hospital.

A doctor came into the room, a white smock thrown over his khaki uniform.

"How's our patient?" he asked the corpsman.

"Completely unresponsive, sir."

"Vital signs?"

"Pulse and blood pressure both normal, sir."

"I'm admitting him to the neuropsychiatric ward overnight, for observation."

"The locked ward?"

"No, he doesn't seem too dangerous. The country club ward will be fine. Give him 25 milligrams of Thorazine, sub-cu, before you take him up."

"Aye-aye, sir."

The doctor left the room and the corpsman prepared the injection. After he gave me the shot, I swooned and fell asleep.

I awoke between white starched sheets, in a white painted brass bed, in a white room with white sunlight flooding through a window. A brunette in a white nurse's cap stuck her head through the doorway. Her cap had two blue stripes across the top: a lieutenant.

"Chow call," she said brightly, "in the day room in ten minutes."

"Yes, ma'am," I responded, and knew I'd recovered the power of speech. Out of bed, walking toward the tiny bathroom, I realized that I had evacuated my bowels into my skivvies sometime during the night. Dumping the curiously firm and dry turds into the commode, I flushed them away and wadded my shorts into the trash bin.

I washed up, found my clothes in a brown paper sack, and got dressed, sans underwear.

I found the day room down the hall and joined the other crazies. Taking a tray from the mess cart, I sat down to eat my oatmeal and fruit cocktail. None of the other inmates looked particularly insane: all eating, joking, and laughing.

Across the table, a young man with a crew cut, wearing a Hawaiian shirt over khaki slacks, held up a coffee pot and asked me if I cared for a cup. "Yes, please," I answered.

While we drank our coffee, Crew Cut asked me, "What're you in here for?"

"Drugs, I guess," I muttered, staring down at my plate. "I ate Belladonna and Datura. My parents came home and I was really out of it." Looking up, I asked, "How 'bout you?"

"I drank three bottles of wine on my birthday, and when I was supposed to report for duty the next morning, the officer of the deck came looking for me. He found me in my quarters, passed out, and puke everywhere."

"Then what happened?" I asked.

"They took me to sick bay, pumped my stomach, and brought me here. They think I'm suicidal. After a week they'll release me, and I'll be court-martialed. They might revoke my commission, or they might send me to the fleet." He looked glum.

He described the daily routine in the NP ward. After breakfast, patients were called in to the doctor's office for individual sessions. After that, group therapy sessions took up another hour, then came lunch. The afternoon was open for arts and crafts, or sports, for those so inclined.

"Schnick," came over the PA speaker. "Report to the nurses' station." I stood and returned my breakfast tray to the rack of the mess cart. A female corpsman in blue scrubs stepped out of the nurses' station and beckoned me to follow her down a hall and into the doctor's office. Commander Barlow, in crisply pressed khaki uniform, sat behind a heavy oak desk. Corpsman Riggs handed him a chart, then left the room, her service oxfords squeaking on the polished linoleum.

Looking up from the chart, the officer said, "Have a seat, please."

Obediently, I sat. At the time, I didn't think about the psychic gravity that was dragging me back into the world of barked orders and conformity. I just knew I'd crossed a line in my drug use.

"I see you gave your parents quite a scare," he looked over his glasses, directly at me.

Ashamed, I looked at the floor.

"What exactly did you do to end up here?"

I couldn't speak for a moment.

"You must have some idea," he said, speaking softly.

"I ate Belladonna and Datura," I said.

"Why?"

"Bored, I guess."

"What do you want to do now?"

I looked through the window behind the doctor. A line of gnarled live oaks followed a grassy hill along the rim of the knoll, like a Maxfield Parrish painting.

"I'd like to go walking up on that ridge," I said.

"Okay, we'll talk again tomorrow," said the doctor. "Would you like to stay here for a week? It's voluntary."

"Sure," I said. I was in no way eager to deal with my parents.

Group therapy was interesting, if not particularly fun.

Ensign Macintosh, the crew cut suicide attempt was there, along with a glowering young woman with cropped blonde hair, wearing navy dungarees. There was also a grizzled warrior with a shaved head riddled with scars, and a mustachioed guy.

I completed the quintet. We sat on folding chairs arranged in a circle, along with Dr. Barlow.

"We have a new member today, so let's each introduce ourselves," the doctor announced. "Sandy, would you start us off please?"

The blond girl leaned forward, elbows on her knees and head down. "I'm Sandy. I broke up with my girlfriend and tried to kill myself."

"I'm Tom," said the bald guy, gnarled hands grasping his knees. "I got hit in the head in an accident on the flight deck. This hospital is bullshit."

Next the bushy-haired guy with the mustache spoke up. "I had nothing else to do today, so why not hang out in the asylum with the other crazies."

"Ernie. . ." warned the doctor.

"Sorry, Doc," he said. "I'm a manic-depressive, and I won't take my meds."

"Hi, I'm Ed," said the crew cut guy. "I drank way too much Château d'Yquem, and blacked out."

Now it was my turn. "I'm John. I ate Belladonna and almost died."

Tom Bailly, the flight deck accident, said, "You're full of shit."

Later, in the afternoon, I left the ward and walked down a sidewalk to the arts and crafts building. The woman attendant asked me what I'd like to do. "Oil painting," I said. She handed me a shoebox of crumpled tubes of oil paint, a few brushes, and a square of canvas-covered cardboard.

I set up a folding easel on the porch of the old frame building. I sketched the outlines of the hill and fringe of oak trees in charcoal. Next I squeezed blobs of color around the edge of the wooden palette. I mashed some of the colors together with a palette knife, added a dribble of linseed oil, a few drops of turpentine, and started painting.

I was enjoying myself. I thought about Vincent van Gogh recovering from his shaving accident at the monastery. When I decided the picture was more or less done, I asked the docent if I could leave it there overnight.

She said, "Sure, just rinse your brushes in turpentine, scrape off your pallet, and put the picture on the shelf over there."

After I put everything away, I thanked the lady and walked back to the NP ward.

Ernie was sitting on the whitewashed wooden steps, grinning when I arrived.

"What's up?" I asked.

He held a finger to his lips. I sat down next to him.

"There's going to be a fight tonight," he whispered.

"A smoker?" I asked, using sailor slang for a boxing match.

"No, a real fight. Sandy and Corpsman Riggs are going to duke it out, bare knuckles."

"You're kidding," I said.

Ernie shook his head.

"You know how Sandy said that she broke up with her girl-friend before she tried to kill herself?"

"Yeah." I said.

"Well, Corpsman Riggs was the girlfriend." I raised my eye-brows, and he continued, "Sandy went out drinking last night with a couple of dudes, and Riggs found out about it."

After dinner, after the stewards had rolled their cart back to the mess hall, and after the doctor and nurse had gone home for the night, Corpsman Riggs was in charge of the ward. All the patients went out to sit on the steps to watch the show, except Tom, who grumped off to watch TV.

The women squared off on the sidewalk below the steps. The sun was low, the light was golden, and the streetlights were flicking on, one by one, across the hospital campus.

"You sure you want to do this?" asked Riggs, as they raised their fists.

"Fuckin' A," said Sandy, throwing a left jab.

Riggs parried the jab and landed a solid punch on Sandy's shoulder. Then they went at it hammer and tongs. Ernie kept up a humorous running commentary as the other inmates moaned, whistled, or shouted encouragement.

I had never seen a girl fight like this one. Back at Tennyson High, a girl fight consisted of name-calling, hair-pulling, and blouse-tearing: two *Cholas* quarreling over the affections of some *Vato Loco*.

These girls were trying to pound each other into hamburg-er—breathing hard and grunting now and then. After a few minutes, Sandy had a nosebleed, Riggs had blood in her mouth, and both were crying and hugging each other. The spectators moved aside as the reconciled couple climbed the steps and into the nurse's station to patch each other up.

The week in the NP ward was an eye-opener. Gay Annapolis graduates, lesbian corpsmen, and manic-depressive comedians were living under one roof, and I got an earful. I had known for years that the Navy was well-supplied with homosexuals, but nobody talked about it. Decades later, when gay people were officially accepted in the armed forces, I was amazed that it had taken so long.

I learned another lesson from my stay in the looney bin. I could handle cannabis and LSD just fine, but I will avoid loco-weed, junk, crank, and coke for the rest of my life.

My week of insanity was soon over, and my mother came to collect me when I was discharged. My father had turned my discipline over to her after that last beating in Albuquerque. He was probably embarrassed by his shouting and violence, which wasn't working anyway. Whenever I misbehaved these days, I could hear my parents praying in their room late at night, beseeching the Lord on my behalf.

When I was able to see Alan again, after another week, we met at a donut shop, and he told me what had happened to him.

"My parents were out to dinner when your folks tried to phone, so they called the Alameda County Sheriff's Department," he started chuckling. "A deputy came, picked me up in a prowl car, and took me to an office in Hayward."

Now my friend was laughing harder. "They put me in a room with a detective, and he asked," (more laughter) "he asked, 'Where did you get the LSD son?'"

Alan was breathless for a moment, then wheezed, "I told him I got it at Trader Vic's!" and collapsed in helpless guffaws. I laughed too. Trader Vic's was a tiki bar and restaurant on San Pablo Avenue in Oakland that claimed to have originated the Mai Tai.

"When my Dad finally came to get me, the detective told him they were going to investigate the restaurant tomorrow."

Teenage Editor

WHEN ALICE AND I next saw each other, we sat in the Caffè Mediterraneum, or "the Med", as most people called it. We shared a 65-cent bowl of minestrone, and talked in low voices.

"I'm not angry, exactly, but a little sad that you and Alan could be so reckless," she said, her blue eyes looking into mine.

"I will never, *ever*, try anything like that again," I said. "It was horrible."

She took my hand.

"You know," she said, "you have a good chance of being editor of the school paper this fall. With that, plus your high scores on the SAT, the college boards won't care so much about your grades."

When I had received my results from the Scholastic Aptitude Test, I had been startled. In two of the three categories, I had scored in the 97th percentile. In the Math category, however, I was in the 40th percentile, which was not so startling.

The first meeting of the Journalism II class was the next Monday.

Mr. Solito handed out a list of all the jobs available on the paper, like Typist, Sports Editor, Social Editor, or Editor.

"I want you each to write a paragraph about the job you want," he said, "and why you would be good at it. Tomorrow I'll announce your place on the staff."

The next day I saw a list on the blackboard. At the top of the list was my name, the word "Editor" beside it. This turned out to be one of the best things that ever happened to me. I never did get into Cal, but the skills I learned as a high school editor set me up to earn a living for the rest of my life.

The first thing I did was call a staff meeting and find out what each editor was planning for the next issue—due out in two weeks. The business manager and I brainstormed about finding new advertisers.

I visited the printshop in contract with the school and selected a 120-point, black-letter font for the new masthead. The printer showed me how to set the letters on a "stick", then lock them into a form. I rolled a rubber brayer first across a flat square of glass, spreading out the sticky ink, then across the type.

We pulled a dozen or so proofs, and the sharp, oily smell of printer's ink went up my nose and into my brain. Much like how the smell of gun smoke or marijuana had taken hold of me earlier, I was hooked. I would be an ink-stained wretch the rest of my life. The only jobs I would ever hold down involved designing, editing, and printing.

I started drawing a comic strip for the paper. I called it *The Adventures of Mongoose Man.* The main character, a clueless nebbish in a herringbone tweed suit, was plagiarized from Dick Raley, a talented artist I knew back at Tennyson High. We had both drawn the character on notes passed in class, then he had been whisked away to Beaverton, Oregon, when his father found a new job.

It was my job to edit all the copy, spec the type, select and size photos and line art, and order engravings. When the long galley proofs came back from the typesetter, I had to proofread each story and mark it up for correction. When the corrected galleys arrived, I would cut out the columns of type, headlines, and engraving proofs, and paste up layouts for the pages. The printer would lock up the type, then pull page proofs; after I approved them, he would print the issue.

The spiffed-up Canyon Courier came out on time. Stacks of the six-paged tabloid were quickly depleted from the library, cafeteria, and office. The other high schoolers seemed to like the new format; we got some letters to the editor, and students began to greet me by name.

Two students seemed to resent me, however. A tall guy with buck teeth and a short dude with a perpetual smirk began to show up whenever I visited my locker. They would close in and start to call me names like "wimp", "hippie", or "faggot".

I had no idea why these two had it in for me, nor what their names were. They did know who I was. When I tried to ask their names, they laughed, and the tall one said, "Fuck you, Schnick."

I thought of them as "Mutt and Jeff", two comic page idiots who blundered through life.

I didn't know how to handle these goons, so I tried to avoid them. Most of my best friends at the school, like Nina and Doris, had graduated the year before, and Arthur had moved to San Francisco, where he attended Washington High.

One time when when I entered the boy's room, I stepped up to the urinal to pee. Before I got my pants unbuttoned, I felt the hairs on the back of my neck stand up. I spun around and saw Mutt and Jeff leaning against the white-tiled wall behind me. They dropped their cigarettes to the floor and went for me.

Before either could grab me, I was out the restroom door and into the covered breezeway, which was full of students walking to their next classes. I walked across the open quad to the boy's gym, where there was always a coach in the glassed-in office. For the rest of the school year, I used the toilets there.

A few days later, in home room, I received a summons to the office of Mr. Pratt, the Dean of Students. I knew who he was but had never spoken to him. When I arrived at his office, he barked, "Sit down."

I sat. He came around his desk and leaned against it, his beefy frame and bald head looming over me.

"I want you to tell me what happened yesterday afternoon."

"Uh, I proofread the galleys for the school paper," I said, "sir."

"Don't give me that. You know what I'm talking about. Don't lie to me."

I had no idea what to say, so I said nothing.

"I happen to know," he said, leaning in close, "that you were seen crawling around the Senior Patio on all fours and barking like a dog." I could smell the cigarettes on his breath.

I suppressed a laugh.

"No sir," I said. "That didn't happen. Who told you that?"

"I can't tell you, but it was a very reliable source."

"I think someone's pulling your leg, sir."

Dean Pratt scowled and went back behind his desk, clenching and unclenching his fists.

"Since you insist on denying it," he said in a low, constrained voice, "here's what's going to happen. The next time I hear of any of this bizarre behavior, I'm taking you down to the Sheriff's Department so fast it will make your head spin." He leered grotesquely. "They will test your blood for LSD and you will be expelled from this school. Now get out of my office."

I got up and went out the door. As I walked to my next class, I puzzled over what was really going on. Why was Pratt making empty threats? I knew, and he should have known, that there was no blood test for LSD intoxication. The minute amount of drug was gone before any of the effects were apparent, and I never dropped acid at school anyway.

Suddenly I realized who put the dean up to this. It had to be Mutt and Jeff. No one else at the school had ever expressed any ill will towards me.

The next Friday, after my last class, I was in the boys' locker room, packing my gym suit to take home and wash. As I was putting my sneakers in my bag, I saw a shadow appear on the floor. I glanced up, and there they were, big as life: Mutt and Jeff.

I was trapped. The two said nothing but smiled as they slowly closed in. Their arms hung at their sides, fists clenched. As the tall one leaned over me, he drew back his arm, and the short one chuckled.

I was holding a sneaker in my right hand. I bolted to my feet and swatted the sole of the shoe into his face as hard as I could. Mutt screamed, threw his hands over his face, and stepped back. Jeff turned away from me to check on his pal. I shoved him aside and ran past the two of them, out of the locker room, through the gymnasium, and into the empty quad.

I had hold of the gym bag in my left hand and a sneaker in my right as I reached the parking lot. I was apprehensive that the two goons might still come after me, until I saw my friend Dennis, with the bonnet up on his Triumph. I helped him push-start the car; we both hopped in, and he gave me a ride home.

The dean's two informants never bothered me again. They avoided me, and I seldom saw them the rest of my time at Canyon. Dean Pratt, however, wasn't quite through with me.

I loved working on the paper every week. I had never done anything so challenging or so rewarding. I probably let my other classes slide, but I was so digging this.

I worked for two weeks, perfecting an op-ed piece on the need to review the ban on marijuana. I wanted to get it right, so I read the fifty-year study of Jamaican laborers that showed no ill effects on their health from massive daily intakes of ganja. I read about the crusade of the avowed racist, Harry J. Anslinger, against marijuana, which resulted in the banning of the weed in the United States in 1939, ten years before I was born.

I wrote a calm and reasoned editorial which concluded that the ban on cannabis was ill-considered, and that Congress should review the law. Mr. Solito carefully read the copy, marked a couple of typos, and approved it for the next issue. We went to press as usual. The students read it. I got a few winks and thumbs up from my friends—and even compliments from two of my teachers.

The next Monday, during the staff meeting, Mr. Solito called me into his office. He looked tired.

"I don't like telling you this, but the next issue will be taken over by the dean of students," he said, not meeting my eyes.

"The whole paper? Why? Couldn't Mr. Pratt just write an op-ed piece?"

"I suggested that in a meeting with him and the principal. Pratt wanted to expel you, and Principal Gancher said that wasn't happening, that Pratt and I had to work it out between the two of us."

"So what happens now?" I asked.

"Go start working on the following issue."

The dean's issue came out pretty lame. The Courier masthead was still on top, but there was no student content, no headlines, sports, ads, or graphics. The six tabloid pages were were covered with gray type. The copy was obviously culled from other sources, cobbled together in a mishmash of dire warnings about "Marijuana, the Assassin of Youth" and so on.

The few students who picked up a copy soon discarded it when they realized that there was nothing in it about them, their friends, or the school. Most of the edition sat unwanted at the distribution points and lingered until they were replaced by the real Courier, two weeks later.

I was struck anew at the bumbling incompetence of the establishment. The dean spent his time inspecting the girls' chests, then suspending the best students in the school. He eagerly swallowed the stories that his goon squad fed him, and made empty threats at the students falsely accused.

He had probably just glanced at my op-ed, then went to the principal and asked to have me expelled. When he hijacked an edition of the Courier, the ad income was missing and the next issue had to come out late and in a reduced size. Of course nobody read his propaganda paper.

His angry behavior made me proud to be a journalist. I began to understand that the establishment would not give up power easily, even when they were in the wrong.

14

Foxy Lady

ALICE AND I huddled against the brick wall of the Fillmore. Rain pounded down. She wore a blue trench coat and a soggy beret. I wore an army poncho. We'd heard that even for a sold-out show, a few tickets would go on sale when the doors opened an hour from now. A poster, locked behind a glass frame, displayed a flying eyeball surrounded by spermatozoa, or flames, or something.

Along with the two of us, perhaps a dozen hippies waited in the downpour. One long-haired dude in a cowboy hat pulled his mouth harp from a dirty red bandana and started playing blues riffs. A bedraggled blonde started singing a lament:

". . .my baby done left me at the drive-in movies. . ."

Her voice and phrasing sounded identical to Janis Joplin, the lead singer for Big Brother and the Holding Company, but it couldn't have been, could it?

The ordeal by water ended when Bill Graham walked up wearing a dripping fedora.

"What are you guys doing out in the rain?" he asked. He unlocked the door and swung it aside.

"You might as well wait in the stairwell. The box office will open in an hour." Dripping hippies filed inside and sat along the side of the stairway. The promoter looked up and down the sidewalk, pulled the bar latch, and locked the door.

Happy to be out of the rain, everyone shook out their coats and hats, leaving puddles along the steps. An excited buzz filled the air, and someone lit up a joint. As it was passed around, Alice hit it and passed it on to me. I passed it to a dude with a Jewish afro wearing bell bottoms sewn from an American flag. The stairwell already smelled of wet wool, like the inside of a bus on a rainy morning. Now it smelled like pot smoke, as well.

The door below us swung open, and a gust of wind and rain swept in. A young dude strode up the stairway, pocketing his key ring. He was followed by Noel Redding, Mitch Mitchell, and Jimi Hendrix. As the diminutive guitarist came up to my level, he stopped as if transfixed, gaping at the stars-and-stripes britches of the guy beside me.

"Oh wow, man," he said, "USA!" The ex-paratrooper held his fingers in front of his face, as if to shield his eyes from Old Glory.

The band continued up the steps into the auditorium. We heard the street door below us slamming and locking.

"The band just flew in from London," said the last guy up the stairs, as he disappeared into the lobby. The people strewn along the steps nodded, stoned-like, excited, but still trying to act cool. We heard the sound of a hammer echoing from the ballroom, through the lobby, and down the stairs.

"They're nailing down the drums," pronounced the cat with the flag pants. Alice pulled off her beret and wrung out the water. A moment later, a drum set boomed from the ballroom.

Bomba-dom-bam, bomba-dom-boom....

Sound check time.

Soon we heard the *whoomph!* of big amplifiers booting up, then a click and a hum, and a voice: "testing, testing."

Without warning, the rhythmic notes of *Purple Haze* blasted down the stairwell.

The band played complete songs, all the way through, every song letter perfect, like the LP, *Are You Experienced?*—except this was bigger, louder, and live. This was less a sound check and more a rehearsal.

The damp youngsters along the stairs stood up and started dancing the Frug, boogaloo, or whatever occurred to them. Alice and I joined in. Everyone was warm by the time a girl removed the CLOSED sign from the box office window and called, "Come on up."

Alice and I paid $3.50 apiece, got our hands stamped with fluorescent ink, and entered the lobby. We each took an apple from the bin, walked into the ballroom, and sat cross-legged on the floor in front of the stage.

Albert King, BB's brother, opened the show. His sweet and piercing electric guitar filled the room as he launched into his first song, *Born Under a Bad Sign.*

The Chicago blues woke everyone. I had expected a college course in the blues tonight, and it was happening now.

After the band left the stage, Alice and I got up and walked around. We returned to the lobby and took two more apples, because we were both short of cash and couldn't afford the snack bar plus bus fares back to the East Bay.

John Mayall & the Bluesbreakers played next, with a young Mick Taylor playing astounding electric guitar behind John Mayall's electric organ.

Alice grabbed my hand and pulled me onto the dance floor. We danced to every number in the set. Liquid lights poured down the walls and across our undulating bodies. We were winded and sweating by the time the Bluesbreakers were done.

I saw a patch of space close to the stage, and we stepped a twisty path through the huddled masses, people making way and offering hands for balance. We sat down, Indian style, and caught our breath.

Hendrix and his two sidemen took the stage. They set up a symphonic storm and launched into their first song, *Foxy Lady*.

I looked at Alice next to me, bobbing her head to the beat.

She turned to me and smiled.

Her braces were gone!

After the show, we both caught the "F" Berkeley bus. I had told my mother that I was spending the night at Skip's house in Hayward. Alice now shared an apartment with Ellen, her old roommate from the dorm. I was eighteen, and Alice was twenty one. She was also on the pill.

Ellen and her boyfriend were gone for the weekend, so we had the house to ourselves. The foxy lady and I took full advantage of the situation. No blueballs tonight.

Alice and I loved experimental films, foreign films, and documentaries. A month after the best date ever, we saw *Chushingura*, by Kurosawa, at the Berkeley Cinema Guild. The film ran for four and three-quarter hours, with two intermissions.

As we left the theater, Alice stopped in mid motion as she pulled on her peacoat. She stared at a news rack. I followed her eyes and read the headline on the Berkeley Gazette.

DR. KING MURDERED

Alice said, "God damn fucking shit." I felt a pain in my throat, and tears blurring my eyes. I dropped a coin into the slot, and we read the story as we lock-stepped back to her apartment. Inside, we listened to the radio. We hardly talked.

I had school the next morning, and so did Alice. I left a little after dark. Riding the bus down East Fourteenth Street through Oakland, I thought about Dr. King. I thought about the Cooneys, the sharecropper family back in Wattensaw, and my nickname at Carlisle Elementary, *Nigger Lover*. I thought about the colored drinking fountain in Brunswick, Georgia, and the angry clerk who had threatened to tell my mother that I had drunk from it.

I thought about how my father had approved of Dr. King until he denounced the Vietnam War. "I think he's a communist," Dad had said.

The bus shuddered to a stop, and I looked up and out the glass windows. Hundreds of black people milled in the street, shouting and carrying on. As the driver eased the big vehicle forward, a few people slapped and banged their fists against the sides.

As we crept through the melee, I saw, under a streetlight, a white policeman with a twelve-gauge shotgun hoisted in his right fist, his left arm around a shirtless man covered with blood from his head to his stained trousers. I couldn't tell if the bleeding man was white or black. Nobody said a word inside the bus. I was the only white person on board.

As the driver eased the coach past the angry crowd, a stone hit the back window, hard. I looked back and saw a spider web of cracks radiating from the edge of the window. The driver started to accelerate, and soon the ghastly tableau was blocks behind us. Nobody said a word for the duration of the ride.

The next morning I rummaged through my mother's sewing scraps until I found a strip of black fabric. This I wrapped around my upper right arm, over my shirt, and secured with a safety pin. I was in mourning.

At school, I went to the library and read *The San Francisco*

Chronicle. It reported that the bleeding man was an Italian-American grocer, beaten severely by a gang of youths while tending his store.

I wore the black armband for seven days. Kids came up to me during the week. "What's with that thing on your arm?"

"It's in honor of Dr. King," I would answer. They would shrug and walk away, assuming it was another of my eccentricities, like how I smelled of patchouli oil, or wore temple bells tied above my calf under my Levi's. In other words—a weirdo.

Not everyone thought me a weirdo. A tall, popular surfer named Sergio was always cordial with me, and we had become friends. He enjoyed my Mongoose Man comic strip, and his surfing exploits were fascinating to me.

He came up to me in the breezeway that week while I was stacking a book in my locker.

"Hey John, could you use a job flipping burgers?"

"You bet," I said. "Where?"

"I'm quitting my job at McDonald's. If you go down there today, talk to Rick and you'll get the job. Tell him I sent you."

Sure enough, the manager of the drive-in hired me on the spot, for minimum wage: $1.25 an hour. I filled out an application, then reported to duty the next afternoon.

I knocked on the steel back door, and Rick opened it. He led me down the steel ladder-stairs to the basement and gestured towards a clothes rack. He handed me a slim employee's manual, and told me to change my shirt and put on a paper hat.

"Bring up a sack of potatoes, and I'll show you how to make french fries," said the manager as he disappeared up the steel steps.

I pulled off my blue shirt and hung it on a hanger, then pulled on a starched white short-sleeved shirt with the McDonald's logo on the breast. Tilting the overseas-style hat at a rakish angle, I glanced at my reflection in a mirror, and I was ready to go.

Stacked on a pallet against a cinder block wall were six burlap sacks, each stenciled IDAHO RUSSET POTATOES 100 LBS. I walked over and gave the ears of one sack a mighty tug. It didn't budge.

I found that if I lifted the end of the unwieldy mass as I tugged, I could get the sack to hang over the edge of the stack.Then I could squat and get my shoulders underneath. Once I straightened my legs, I took the weight on my shoulders and back, then walked stiff-legged to the bottom of the steps.

Taking each stair slowly one at a time, I carried the spuds up into the kitchen and set the sack next to the potato peeler. I only weighed 120 pounds, but the years of compulsory physical education, particularly the weightlifting and wrestling, seemed to be paying off.

Dick showed me how to dump 25 pounds at a time into the rotating abrasive drum of the potato peeler and squirt water over the tumbling spuds. The perfectly peeled potatoes were then tipped into the left side of a deep stand sink. I sprayed them again from the nozzle suspended overhead and filled the other sink with cold water.

One by one, I placed each potato atop a grid of blades, pulled down a long lever, and the slim slices shot into the water. Plunging my arms into it, I stirred the raw potatoes for a minute, then pulled the rubber plug from the bottom of the basin, letting the water run out, along with an inch or so of starch.

Next, I had to fill fry baskets with handfuls of cut potatoes and hang the baskets on a rack above the sink to dry. After the water had drained off the potatoes, I plunged the baskets two by two into a three hundred degree fryer filled with pure beef tallow. They fried slowly for a few minutes, and, when an alarm sounded, I pulled the baskets out and hung them on a rack beside the high temperature fryer, ready to be plunged into the seething cauldron of suet to brown as needed.

I learned how make milkshakes, how to grill and assemble twenty burgers at a time, and how to handle the counter when we sold a thousand dollars' worth of the 15-cent burgers in an hour. Rick, the manager, would stick his head out of his tiny office whenever we were particularly busy and ask in a loud voice, "What kind of place is McDonald's?"

"McDonald's is my kind of place!" every crewman was required to shout, in unison.

This was okay, except when my friends were at the window ordering. Then it was embarrassing.

I got two things from working at the hustling drive-in: a work ethic, and enough money to buy a white gold ring with a tiny yellow diamond.

———————

I knew that radical hippies condemned marriage and materialism as bourgeois delusions. Some said that the Eastern religions, like Hinduism or Zoroastrianism, held the key to life, the universe, and spiritual happiness. I wasn't sure I was onboard with all that. Spirituality of any sort was beginning to seem like a scam.

I *was* sure that I felt happy when I was with Alice, and I wanted be with her forever. *A loaf of bread, a jug of wine, and thou beside me, singing in the wilderness*, was what I was after.

Heartbreak Hotel

DURING HER SPRING BREAK from the university, Alice stayed in Hayward with her family. I took a bus from Castro Valley and met her in a park. We walked across green lawns in the fading light. We sat on a bench overlooking a pond. As usual we talked about everything: poetry, politics, and art.

The setting sun turned the sky and the water pink, and I took the little jewelry box from my jacket pocket and flipped back the lid.

"Alice, will you marry me?" I said.

She took the ring from the box, slipped it on her finger, and said, "Yes I will, but not until I graduate, and we both have good jobs."

We were both elated as I walked her home, but there were storm clouds just beyond the horizon.

―――――――

Alice wasn't interested in trying LSD.

"I think pot is fun, but I like my brain just the way it is, thank you," was her first and last comment on the subject.

I could see her point; she had one of the finest minds of our generation and was not about to see it destroyed by madness.

I, on the other hand, was determined to roll the dice. I loved the way things looked when I was tripping. I loved how the world turned into a flowing liquid painting. Sometimes the LSD experience was reflected in everyday life, like when tall grasses on a hillside rippled in the wind, or a northwest swell blew in from the Gulf of Alaska, turning the Pacific into endless sets of rolling waves.

Another thing that Alice had no interest in trying was mountaineering or camping. Starting on the granite boulders of the Sandia range above Albuquerque, my appetite for adventure was whetted by the burro packing trip with Orson and Jill at Ghost Ranch. By the time Alan and I started trekking into the High Sierra, I had accumulated some climbing gear.

I was on fire to climb mountains, ski glaciers, and slide my tongue down the inside thigh of lusting Mother Nature. I had always hated sports in high school, but this was different.

One time, Alice and I were happily holed up in her bedroom—quilts, pillows, and poetry books around us, rain pelting the window. I fantasized how much fun it might be to hike the John Muir Trail for our honeymoon.

Alice recoiled instantly.

"I'll never sleep on the ground," she said. "That sounds horrible."

I never brought it up again.

———

I continued to drop acid on a weekly basis in the spring of 1968. Whenever I tried to take it more often, I found that the stuff had little or no effect. My old pals from Tennyson all had cars now, and we would drive over the hills of San Francisco loaded on Blue Cheer or Orange Sunshine.

Sometimes I would go on a three-way date with Alice and Skip Strobel. This would consist of Skippy driving all over the Bay Area, with Alice and I smooching in the back seat of his Citroen. This couldn't have been much fun for poor Skip.

———

The Vietnam War was heating up. Friends were starting to enlist, be drafted, or go to Canada. The CBS Evening News showed video of burnt Vietnamese children and bleeding GIs regularly.

The day I turned 18, my father insisted on driving me down to the Selective Service office in Hayward, California. He wore his undress khaki U.S. Navy uniform. He knew that, left to my own devices, I would probably neglect to register for the draft.

The clerk at the draft board took down my name and Social Security number, and handed me a stapled, multi-page form to fill out and return. Among the questions I had to answer was a real stumper: *Please list all prior addresses where you have lived, by year.*

With Mom's help, and her meticulous record keeping, we determined that I had lived in twenty-one different houses in my first eighteen years. It didn't seem possible, but bundles of saved letters from my grandmother proved it. The postmarks on the envelopes were dated from 1949 to 1967.

There was the beachside barracks in San Clemente, the trailer in a swamp near Camp Lejeune, and the house on the hill in Freshwater, Newfoundland; they were all there, as well as places even my mother could barely remember.

I would rather have gone to prison or Canada than participate in Lyndon Johnson's bogus war on the Vietnamese. "Vinegar Joe" Stilwell, the American commander in China during World War II, had known in the 1930s that American forces could never prevail in an Asian land war. I'd read a biography of him, and it seemed obvious to me as well.

The next question on the form offered a glimmer of hope.

Please list any physical ailments that might interfere with your ability to perform your duty in the armed forces. Please attach relevant medical records.

As a Naval dependent for eighteen years, every visit to the dispensary—for vaccinations, flu, asthma, broken bones, or chicken pox—had added pages to my medical record. This file had followed me from duty station to duty station all my life. I wrote a letter to the records office at Oakland Naval Hospital, and a few days later, a top-bound stack of copies arrived in my mailbox. It was two inches thick.

On the Selective Service form I claimed allergies, asthma, and hay fever. I signed it, and mailed it, along with the phone-book-sized U.S. Navy medical record. In another week, I received my draft card in the mail.

It classified me as 4-F, "unsuitable for military service under any circumstances".

This was fine by me. If I had been drafted, I would have hitchhiked to Canada. If I had been captured, I would have gone to prison for five to ten years. I could never be part of this stupid war. I had no beef with my friends who were drafted or enlisted, I just knew I couldn't do it.

———

As Alice's graduation from Cal approached, the political situation in the country got worse. She and I marched in anti-war demonstrations, and once we were tear-gassed by the Berkeley Police Department for failing to disperse. By May, Alice had decided to join a walkout planned for her graduation in the Greek Theater.

One night at the apartment on Derby Street, we were arranging pillows and candles on the floor. Maybe because Ellen had recently adopted a cat, I came down with a ferocious asthma attack.

I had suffered these off and on for years, occasionally ending up in the dispensary or hospital. After a couple of hours of desperate wheezing and coughing, the paroxysms settled down so I could breathe normally. I was exhausted.

Alice came over to me as I hunched on a chair, palms braced against my knees. She put one hand on my shoulder and held out the engagement ring in the other.

"John, I can't marry you," she said firmly. "Please take your ring."

Her words hit me like an executioner's axe.

She continued, "I know you love mountain climbing. I could never sleep in a tent. We're not right for each other. It would never work."

I stood up quickly, shrugging her hand from my shoulder.

"Keep the ring," I said. "I don't want it."

I turned, grabbed my jacket from the back of the sofa, and was out the door. Before I closed it, I looked back and saw her standing in the candlelight. One arm was extended, holding up the ring, and she was biting her lower lip. I ran down the stoop and into the night.

Walking down Derby Street to the bus stop, my eyes were flooded. Alice was right, and I knew it. I was a sickly, asthmatic acidhead with no prospects whatsoever. On the hour-long bus ride back to Castro Valley, I curled up on the back bench, writhing in mental agony.

———

I went to Dennis's house. His parents allowed him to live in the garage with his English roadster. He had already been accepted at San Francisco State and was waiting out his high school graduation. He planned to drive to Alaska in June and work at a salmon cannery until he started college in the fall.

When I told him about my heartbreak, he commiserated, then pulled out a half pint of bourbon and handed it to me.

Over the next hour, I drank the whiskey diluted with tap water. It didn't do any good. Instead of being miserable, I was now drunk and miserable. The next morning I called my mother and told her the sad news.

"I'm sorry to hear that," she said. "I know Alice meant the world to you. Will you come home now?"

I thanked Dennis for putting up with me and trudged to my parents' house, slumped over and dejected.

When I sat on the bed in my room
the depression and anguish crashed over me
like giant breakers when you're caught inside the surf,
unable to paddle out to the smooth swells beyond.

I knew I couldn't bear living in my parents' house anymore, and going back to the high school seemed utterly dismal, too. Being in love with Alice had given me a strength and confidence that felt superhuman at times, but now I felt like an empty shell: deflated, feeble, and unfit to associate with normal people.

I was eighteen now. I decided I would drop out of school, leave home, and go on the road. I gathered some camping gear and stowed it in my rucksack along with an extra shirt, socks, and soap and towel. I threw in an old campaign hat and a sketchbook with a small tin of watercolors. I didn't exactly feel good about this, but at least it gave me something to do.

My father had gotten wind of what I was up to. He came into my room to talk with me—something he rarely did anymore. He sat on my bed, elbows on his knees, and hands clasped.

"John Mark," he said with a catch in his voice, "I would rather you had been killed fighting with the Marines in Vietnam than be involved with this bizarre life you've chosen." He had tears in his eyes.

With a sarcastic edge to my voice I said, "Thanks, Dad." I hitched up my pack and walked out.

I hiked up the steep hill to the high school and into the office. Mrs. Fein, the attendance clerk, looked up and said, "Hi John, so why are you late today?"

I swung the rucksack to the floor.

"I'm dropping out."

Mrs. Fein put her hand to her mouth.

"But why? In two weeks you'll graduate."

"I've been in high school for five years. I'm done."

She sighed and shrugged. "You'll have to get a signature from each of your teachers and the dean of students."

"But I'm eighteen," I said.

She shrugged again and handed me a form.

Mr. Pratt's office was right down the hall. I walked to his door. He looked up from his desk. When I told him I was dropping out, he held up his hand for the form. He signed it and handed it back without a word. At least he didn't gloat about it.

Mr. Pratt was easy, but my favorite teachers turned out to be more difficult.

Mrs. Moscovich, my literature teacher for two years, got angry.

"John, you can't do this. You have a lot to contribute to the world. Stay with it." I knew she had been one of my defenders when Dean Price had tried to get me expelled.

"I'm going on the road. I want to climb mountains."

She finally signed the form.

Mr. Solito, the journalism advisor, grilled me quickly about my reasons for leaving, then signed the paper. He shook my hand. "Good Luck."

My American History teacher, Mr. Collins, laughed when I told him.

"You can't wait two more weeks?"

I liked Mr. Collins, and he had given me an A-minus each quarter. This class was the last I needed to graduate, but I wasn't interested.

"No, I'm leaving today," I insisted.

After I turned in the withdrawal form at the office, I walked to the Senior Patio and dropped my rucksack to the grass. A few of my friends had heard what I was up to and came up to me to ask if it was true. I kept up a good front, cheerfully telling about all the mountains I was going to climb, the freights I was going to hop, and the paintings I would produce.

I fired up my tiny white gas stove and set a small aluminum teapot on top, filled from a canteen. When the water boiled, I shut down the flame and dropped some black tea into the pot. As I served tea to my chums, we talked and even laughed a few times. Perhaps I only imagined the questioning look in Susan's, Ruth's, and Michael's eyes.

I packed up my cook bag, hoisted my sack, and waved good-bye to the high school. On my way out of town, I stopped by McDonald's and picked up my last check. It was for seventeen dollars and eighty cents. I hitchhiked to Berkeley.

My last ride let me off on Telegraph Avenue in front of Ashby Flowers. I went in and bought eighteen yellow roses. I wanted to make a gallant gesture to Alice, to tell her thanks for the memories, no hard feelings, or something...

Ellen answered the door and said, "Alice isn't here, John."

I held out the bouquet. "Can you please give these to her?"

She glanced at the flowers, then took them. "Are you okay?"

"Never better. I lost Alice, dropped out of high school, left home, and quit my job."

"Do you have a place to stay?"

"No."

"I have a friend with a house down in the flatlands—maybe you can camp in his back yard for a few days," she said. "I'll call him." She turned back into the apartment, taking the roses with her. I waited numbly on the porch.

She returned a few minutes later with a slip of paper in her hand. "Here's Harvey's address. He said you could crash in his back yard for a week, but no more."

"Thanks, Ellen," I said, and walked down to the street.

I didn't go directly to the address on Ninth Street in the flatlands; instead I walked through the Cal campus, through Faculty Glade, and dropped my pack on the bank of Strawberry Creek. I walked into the tunnel where Alice and I had first kissed, and paused, looking back at the cameo of light at the entrance.

I took my Barlow knife from my pocket and my sharpening stone. I began to stroke the blade in flat circles on the abrasive Arkansas rock. I wanted it to be razor sharp. I pressed the fresh edge against the artery in my left wrist until I could feel my pulse through the handle of the knife.

PART TWO

Dirtbag Days

On Ralph and Louise's Farm

16

Home on the Range

I STOOD IN THE DARKNESS with a knife against my wrist. I had expected a crescendo of emotion during my big suicide scene, but I just felt silly. What the hell was I doing? After a moment of strain, trying to summon up some passion, I folded the pocket knife and dropped it into my back pocket.

I retrieved my rucksack and wandered around Berkeley for days, sleeping fitfully at night under hedges or in Ellen's friend's backyard. Her gruff ex-boyfriend wasn't interested in a roommate and wouldn't allow me to enter the house or use the bathroom. I went to the gas station on the corner or along the railroad tracks for such. I didn't speak to another person. I didn't remember to eat.

My clothes became stained and rumpled from sleeping in the dirt, and my hair curled greasy and matted down my neck. I could sense people averting their glances as I passed on the sidewalk. I had become invisible. In shrink talk, I was having a nervous breakdown.

I spent a dreadful afternoon bent over in the sun on a patch of yellow grass, in Harvey's back yard. I cried convulsively until I threw up. I hadn't cried since I was in grade school. I understood why: it hurts way too much.

I took a bus back to Castro Valley. Mom, Dad, and Polly were glad to see me. The prodigal son returned. I felt like a schmuck.

Mom cooked Swiss steaks smothered in gravy, with biscuits, and greens with salt pork. I hadn't eaten in days. I ate my fill. I was still glum and depressed, but I fell asleep early that night.

In the morning I heard Mom on the phone as I walked into the kitchen.

"That's wonderful, Louise. Thank you. . . I love you too. . . Goodbye."

I sat down at the dinette, and Mom poured us each a cup of tea.

"That was Aunt Louise on the phone. She and Uncle Ralph want you to stay on their farm for the summer. Ralph could use some help around the place, and Louise would just be tickled to see you." Mom looked at me over her cup. "Would you like that?"

"Sure," I replied.

"Then it's set," she said.

The next morning, the family all drove to the Richmond station of the Atchison, Topeka, and Santa Fe Railway. I went up to the ticket counter while the family waited next to my foot-locker. Dad had given me enough money for a one-way ticket to Fort Worth, where I would have to transfer to the Missouri Pacific Railway—better known as MoPac or "The Mop"—then continue on to Little Rock.

I found the car listed on my ticket by number; the name *Kiva* was lettered beside the door. A porter took my footlocker and grip, stowing them at the end of the car. Dad shook my hand; I hugged my mother and my 13-year-old sister. I stood in the entryway, my mom giving me some last minute advice about train travel.

"All aboard!" called the conductor as he walked down the platform. When he came to my car, I climbed the steps and found my seat. I saw my family outside on the platform, and we waved at each other through the thick glass window as the locomotive began to take up slack, the couplings clanking one by one down the length of the train as each car was jolted into motion.

The San Francisco Chief pulled out of the station and was on its way.

———

The Chief ran down the San Joaquin Valley, with the snowy peaks of the High Sierra to the left. I read a paperback copy of *The Catcher in the Rye*. Skip and I had found it in a trash bin behind Sears, Roebuck, and Company, at a shopping mall in Hayward. The front cover had been torn off, as were the covers of several other Salinger books that had been remaindered.

I read about the adventures of Holden Caulfield in his boarding school, and his flirtation with madness on his train journey. Darkness fell as the streamlined train headed east through the mountains. I slept.

During the night we must have passed through Arizona. Soon after I awoke, we were in New Mexico. Later, as the train neared the Texas border, I walked forward towards the lounge car.

"I'm eighteen," I told the Fred Harvey steward at the end of the domed car.

"I'm forty two," said the black man, as he polished a glass. "So what?"

"May I have an extra dry Martini, please?" I asked.

He laughed, put the shiny glass in a rack, and leaned over the bar. "When we cross the Texas line, you can have all the dry you want."

When a *Welcome to Texas* billboard flashed past the window, he asked me, "Can I see your ID?"

I pulled out my wallet and handed him my U.S. Navy dependent's card. He looked at the card, looked at me, and shrugged. I must have looked like I was fourteen.

He slid a tumbler of ice across the bar and followed it with a four-ounce can labelled "Martini."

"That'll be one dollar and fifty cents," he said.

I paid, then took glass and can up a stair to the glass-domed observation car. I pulled off the aluminum tab, dumped the canned booze over the ice, and drank the watery stuff as the train rocked *clickity-clack* over the Texas plains. I had been hoping for something more elegant—like a catchy rhythm with a silver shaker, a cute martini glass, and an olive on a toothpick. This was my first legal drink.

I tried not to think about Alice. I had mooned and carried a torch over both Carol and Jill after I could no longer see them, but that had just been adolescent infatuation. Alice and I had even planned what to name our children: Vera, Chuck, and Dave. I put the cute little heartbreaker into a mental box. I didn't think about her much for fifty years, until I started this memoir.

I slept again, and dawn was breaking as the train slowed and stopped at the Fort Worth Santa Fe station. I stepped onto the platform and claimed my luggage. Inside the station I saw a luggage cart with *Missouri Pacific Lines* in a red starburst mounted overhead. I showed my ticket to the porter and he tagged my footlocker and grip, placing them on his cart.

"I'll haul your bags down to the Mop station in a few minutes. The Little Rock train don't leave 'til 4:39. You can claim 'em and board the train after four PM."

This left me eight hours to cover the eight blocks between the Santa Fe station and the Mop. I decided I might as well explore the old cattle town in the meantime. On the sidewalk, just outside the station, I saw a painted showcard in the window of a diner.

Grits, Two Eggs,

Ham, Orange Juice,

Toast and Coffee—53¢

Never one to pass up a bargain, I went in and sat down. Besides, I was starving. The food was hot, the orange juice was cold, and the coffee was okay.

Fort Worth seemed quiet, if not deserted, as I walked along the downtown streets. The stores were closed: Woolworth's, Merle Norman cosmetics, Justin Boots and Saddles. With a shiver, I thought of the rapture.

The Worth Theater, however, was open. The letters on the lighted marquee proclaimed "INDY 500 - Live". It was Thursday, May 30th, Memorial Day, 1968.

———

The Little Rock train rumbled up to the platform in the afternoon heat, looking old and scuffed compared with the streamlined Santa Fe Chief. I stowed my footlocker on a shelf in the front of my coach, and the grip in the rack over my seat.

I settled down in my sagging seat and started reading a second-hand paperback of *The Grapes of Wrath*. The conductor shuffled down the aisle and punched my ticket.

"I'll wake you up before we get to Little Rock," he said.

As I read about the Joad family's journey from Oklahoma to California, I was struck by the fact that I was headed the opposite direction, from California to a farm at the edge of the old Dust Bowl.

The Joad family had finally reached California before I fell fast asleep, rocked by the rhythm of the rails.

"Next stop Little Rock, next stop Little Rock," the conductor called as he strode down the aisle.

As I lugged my footlocker and grip across the sidewalk in front of Union Station, I spotted Uncle Ralph leaning against his Chevrolet sedan parked along the curb. He wore a denim chore coat and a crumpled fedora. When he saw me, he dropped his cigarette to the street and stepped on it with his boot. He waved at me and opened the Chevy's trunk.

According to the clock on the brick tower, it was 12:30 AM, *oh dark thirty.*

Ralph didn't talk much on the drive to Beebe, except to comment on the new but empty freeway leading away from the station.

"Waste of taxpayer dollars, if you ask me," he said. He glanced over at me. "How you doin' anyhow, Mark?"

"Fair to middlin', Uncle Ralph, fair to middlin'," I answered. He nodded and nothing else was said for the next hour.

Aunt Louise came to the door in her nightgown and robe, as the sedan crunched gravel next to the farmhouse. Sure enough, she branded my face with her red lipstick, as I carried my bags up the porch steps.

"Marky! How you've grown. . ." she exclaimed. "I'm so tickled you came to visit. You must be starved. Sit down."

Uncle Ralph disappeared into the bedroom.

Louise opened the tin breadbox on the counter and took out a wedge of cornbread. From the Frigidaire she pulled a stoneware pitcher of buttermilk. Crumbling the cornbread into a tall water glass, she filled it with buttermilk and stuck in a long, iced-tea spoon.

How did she know I'd been craving this for years? I shook pepper on top, then dug in.

———————

The next morning I awoke to a rooster's call, but it was still dark, and I fell back asleep. The next time it crowed, sunlight was hitting my window, and I popped out of bed. I discovered that the house now sported indoor plumbing and a butane range. Louise sent me to the henhouse for eggs, and, when I brought back four, she made fried egg sandwiches with a slice of ham and *Velveeta* cheese dripping out of the *Colonial* white bread. I ate one, Louise ate one, and Uncle Ralph ate two.

Louise poured three cups of coffee from a blue enamel percolator, and Ralph spoke up. "Mark, I've got to fence off a two-acre weaning pen this week, but after we get that done you can saddle Betty and ride and patch fences."

Uncle Ralph ran white-face beef cattle these days. That and raised his coon hounds.

"No more of that *Milk 'em in the Mornin' Blues* for us anymore," he said. Louise laughed and squeezed his hand. We all knew the old Tennessee Ernie Ford song.

The next few days, Ralph showed me how to pound sharpened cedar fence poles into the moist spring earth with a wide iron pipe, rebar handles welded along the sides. It took Ralph five or six licks with the driver to sink a post to shoulder high. It took me about twenty licks.

"You have to pound it down like you're stabbing the devil," he said. "We need to get a rod of fencing across before Sunday."

"How much is a rod?" I asked.

He looked at me, rolled his eyes, then looked away. "Sixty-six feet," he said, got back in his truck, and drove away. The fence posts lay next to stakes that marked the spots to sink the poles. My work was cut out for me.

Stabbing the devil or not, I struggled to get all those posts in the ground. My shoulders burned and my back ached by the end of the morning. While I was pounding one more post into the turf, I saw Uncle Ralph walking across the field towards me in a hurry.

"They killed Bobby Kennedy," he said as he came up to me.

I broke for dinner, and back at the farmhouse we watched a news report on the television. Louise looked like she had been crying. I felt sick and disgusted. First John Kennedy, then Dr. King. Now the only man who had a real chance of stopping the murder in Vietnam was dead.

———————

In the days that followed, I don't think my work was quite up to snuff. Ralph didn't say much, but then he seldom did. He patiently showed me how to string and tighten barb wire on the new posts with fencing pliers, but it became obvious that he needed no help from me.

Ralph and Louise didn't quite know what to make of me. The last time they'd seen me I was a ten-year-old with a crew cut. Now they see a rail-thin hippie with long, unruly hair and a prominent Adam's apple. They were puzzled, but they put up with me without judging.

To keep me busy, Ralph showed me how to saddle his roan mare, Betty Boop.

"Make sure Bill can't get loose when you take Betty out to ride," he said. "He gets crazy when she's out of his sight."

Bill was a paint stallion that Ralph kept for breeding, and, like most stallions, he was high-strung and jealous. Bill had to stay in his own corral with electrified wire whenever Betty was taken out.

Ralph and Louise farmed about 160 acres, most of it open pasture for the whiteface beef cattle they raised. I rode around the whole place almost every day, looking for breaks in the fences and for sick or injured cattle.

Bill hated it when I took Betty out for a ride. I could hear him stomp and whinny behind the shock wire until I was out of earshot.

I had brought a matchbox of marijuana seeds with me from

California, and I lost no time in planting them in an untrodden corner of the pasture.

I checked on them a week later. There had been a thunderstorm that week, and new grass had sprouted along the fence line. I dismounted and laid the reins on the ground. Unlike many saddle horses, Betty would stand quietly, never trying to run back to the barn.

I walked over to the fence and saw maybe a dozen tiny shoots with serrated leaves coming up beneath the bottom strand of barbed wire.

"This is great," I told Betty as I mounted. We headed back to the corral at a walk. As we came into view of Bill, behind the electric fence, the stallion whinnied, and the mare whinnied back. Bill started galloping around his pen in a circle, then burst through the wire with a twang, a crash, and a clatter—and made straight for us.

The thought occurred that he might bite and pull me from the saddle, but as soon as he got near us, he fell into step and followed us into the the main corral. I got down quick, hitched Betty's hackamore to a post, and swung the corral gate closed.

Uncle Ralph had heard the commotion, and he came out of the barn. He went to the tack shed and turned off the fence transformer.

"I reckon Betty Boop's fixin' to go into heat," he said, "and Bill knows it. I'm going to breed her this year, so I think your riding days are done for a while."

While I pulled off Betty's riding tack and brushed her down, Ralph doctored a wire cut on the point of Bill's shoulder with purple ointment.

Two weeks later, I walked to the far corner of the far pasture to check on my pot plantation. The cattle had eaten every plant.

The summer passed. There were no young people close to my age at any of the surrounding farms, and my shirttail cousin Nancy had married and moved to Fayetteville.

Uncle Ralph showed me his collection of Colt .45 "Peacemaker" revolvers, and let me shoot one a few times. When he needed salt licks or fence wire, he took me along to the feed store in Beebe. In the Western Auto Hardware store I saw a Stevens single shot .22 rifle hung on the wall behind the counter. The price tag said "$19.99".

I bought it out of the cash Dad had given me and took it back to the farm. There wasn't much to shoot at anymore at Ralph and Louise's place. The woods that once grew between the farms were gone, to make way for more pastures. Whiteface Herefords filled the fields. Not much room was left for cottontails, squirrels, or raccoons.

After plinking at tin cans a few times, I cleaned the gun, removed the barrel from the hardwood stock, and put it away in the bottom of my footlocker.

American agriculture had changed drastically in the decade I'd been away from the farm. Big corporations like Monsanto, Con Agra, and Tyson Poultry were calling the shots in the farming business, and family farms were failing and being bought by corporations.

My grandparents' old dairy farm had been leveled by a Rome plow. The pond, orchards, and woodlot were gone, replaced by endless rows of soybeans—nothing else. The old farmhouse was spared, but was now used as a bunkhouse for migrant laborers.

A Slow Boat to China

DAD WAS NOW RETIRED from the Navy. He had applied to the Southern Baptist Foreign Mission Board and had been hired to establish a "Christian Servicemen's Center" in the British Crown Colony of Hong Kong. Huge numbers of American servicemen were arriving there on "rest and recreation" (R&R), a respite from combat in the Vietnam War.

The idea was to steer the young men away from the prostitutes, saloons, and opium dens of the wide-open colonial city. Instead they could come to the servicemen's center for fellowship, prayer, and non-alcoholic beverages.

Dad called me on the party line telephone at the Beebe farm. He made an offer that was hard to refuse. If I were to enroll in junior college in the fall, he and mother would pay the rent at a Christian rooming house for the school year. They would fund a small checking account meant to tide me over until I could find part-time work.

Time was short. A registered letter arrived in the mailbox with an airline ticket back to San Francisco. I packed my footlocker and grip. I thanked Aunt Louise for putting up with me. I thanked Uncle Ralph for teaching me how to build a good fence, and apologized for Bill busting down the electric fence. My aunt and uncle drove me to the Little Rock airport.

My gloom had lifted in the time I'd been on their farm. I could carry on a conversation again, I had put on some weight, and my broken heart was starting to mend. I loved my lipstick aunt and my taciturn uncle for their kindness and generosity.

Before I boarded the Western Airlines prop jet, Louise looked sad as she stamped me with bright red. You could tell she missed those days when her niece Nancy and I would go frogging in Bull Creek, or she and my mother would cut and sew dresses for each other.

I missed those days too.

Arthur and I hurried south along the San Francisco Embarcadero. The SS President Wilson would depart in an hour from Pier 28, and my family was already on board. Arthur's strides were longer than mine and I was hard pressed to keep up.

We arrived at the pier, with the immense white ocean liner looming over, and walked up the gangplank. The purser checked our names on a list and directed us to the folks' stateroom.

Along with Mom, Dad, and Polly, several other missionary families were sailing to the Orient on the Wilson, and they were all standing around a table in the dining saloon. My folks introduced my pal and me, then one of the Missionaries lead everybody in an a cappella chorus:

Bringing in the sheaves,
bringing in the sheaves,
We shall come rejoicing,
bringing in the sheaves. . .

I joined in, because I knew the words to the old hymn—a metaphor about saving souls. Arthur joined in too, because he was a musician and liked to sing. After the hymn we all held hands, bowed our heads, and my father prayed fervently for the safety and success of this missionary voyage.

After the prayer meeting broke up, Arthur and I raided the *Bon Voyage* fruit basket in my family's stateroom, then went off to explore the ship. We climbed the laddered stairway to the bridge deck and peered up at the red and blue smokestacks.

We bumped into some kids about our own age: two guys and a girl. They were also there to see family members off on the voyage. One of the guys raised his eyebrows and pantomimed smoking weed. The five of us ducked behind the aft smokestack and shared a fat joint.

"All ashore that's going ashore," came the announcement over the ship's PA system. The impromptu pot party broke up. Stoned, Arthur and I ran back to the folks' cabin in time for last goodbyes. He and I walked down the gangway and stood along the quay as the plank rolled back, and the hawsers were cast off.

My family stood on the deck of the ship above and across from us, leaning against a white rope-covered rail, waving. Colorful streamers were flying from the ship to the wharf, and my mother threw a red one that spiraled down and landed across my outstretched hand. I held one end and she held the other, our eyes locked. We both knew it might be ten years before we saw each other again.

After one long blast of the ship's horn, the ribbon first drew taut, then began to stretch, and finally broke as the Wilson pulled away. The curly ends fluttered down to the bay water. I stood on the quay and watched as the liner receded, growing smaller as it steamed towards the open Pacific.

Now I'm finally on my own, I thought happily. I couldn't know the hardships or happiness I was in for. I'd long fantasized about being an orphan, and now I was one, sort of.

18

Life on the Homefront

CANTERBURY HOUSE stood across the street from Edwards Field, the track and field venue for the university. My room was in the rear of the badly worn Victorian building, with a south window facing an unpainted fence. The building was owned by the Episcopal church next door, which was likely the reason my parents had selected it for me.

There were no religious requirements for residents, however, and the other tenants were an eclectic mix of foreign grad students, under-employed musicians, dirtbag climbers, and one sweet old queen—always willing to brew some tea and show us photos of him and his late boyfriend exploring Egypt in the thirties. My backpacking partner Alan left Hayward and rented the room across the hall from me, relieved that I was no longer obsessed with his sister. It was good to have a friend nearby.

I attended Merritt College, just across the Berkeley line in Oakland. The lightly crumbling Spanish Colonial style buildings were crawling with baby boomers eager for a free education, to avoid the draft, or both. I didn't know anybody but was used to starting a new school, like any other Navy brat.

In an effort to make friends, I took a flyer from a girl standing on the front steps. She wore what I thought of as the Berkeley radical uniform: long, dark hair drawn back by a leather clasp at the nape of the neck, a ribbed poorboy sweater, brown plain skirt, black tights, and loafers—more beatnik than hippie.

The flyer announced the first meeting of the Merritt College chapter of Students for a Democratic Society. I showed up at four o'clock to the room designated. The dark-haired girl that had given me the flyer stood up in front of maybe a dozen students and announced the principles of the society.

"We in the SDS are working to increase Americans' involvement in democracy. We register voters and support students' rights." A young blonde woman beside her passed around a sheet of paper.

"If everyone writes their name and address on this list, the college administration will allow us to meet in a room on campus."

I signed, and at least ten of the other students did as well.

Sometime later, during the Nixon administration, the FBI forced all US colleges to turn over membership records of "subversive" student organizations. Merritt College complied. My name was doubtless on the list.

The Vietnam War was tearing the country apart, just as it had torn apart my family. My father and I had argued constantly about the war. He maintained that communism was Satanic and was poised to take over the world—that America must stop this cancer in Vietnam or all the Asian countries would fall like dominoes, to be followed by Europe and the Americas.

I insisted that it was a war of liberation. Their war against Japanese, French, and American colonialism was the same as the United States' revolution against the British Empire.

Dad had made it perfectly clear that he would rather have a dead Marine than a live peacenik for a son. This saddened me but made me determined to do what I could to end the war.

Marches and demonstrations were happening weekly all over the country, steadily becoming larger. I went to all the rallies that I could. I saw Muhammed Ali give a speech at the San Francisco Civic Center Plaza, after his title had been revoked and he had been sentenced to five years in Federal Prison for refusing induction.

"I ain't got no quarrel with them Viet Cong," he said.

My friend Arthur was living in San Francisco, and on weekends we hung out together, went to rock concerts, and tried to meet girls.

One Saturday, as we were walking past the San Francisco Public Library, Arthur spun on his heel and faced me. "My dad has a job for you; it's only for a few days, though."

Arthur's father was a major contributor to the California Democratic Party and had run for statewide office.

"What kind of work?" I asked.

"He's researching the history of the Vietnam War. He needs a copy of every news story about Vietnam since 1949."

"How could I do that?" I wondered out loud.

"It's easy," said Arthur. "Follow me."

We went into the library and climbed two flights of stairs to the reference room. Arthur showed me how to check out microfilms with issues of the New York Times arranged by year and date. The next Monday, I showed up early and checked out a few reels and was assigned one of the viewers lined up on a long table. The room was dimly lit so that the back-lit screens would be visible. I flipped the light switch on my viewer.

Threading the film into the left side of the machine, the gear teeth meshed with the sprocket holes in the film. By turning the cranks below the screen, I could scroll through page after page projected full-size on the screen above. I could magnify any section and move around on the page. I was driving a time machine. There was something romantic and mysterious about this pursuit of truth. I loved it and felt happier than any time since Alice dumped me.

Whenever I came across a Vietnam-oriented headline, I would zoom in, read the story, and write the frame number on an order form. After several hours of hunting, I would take a reel and an order form to the facsimile room. If I ordered the prints early enough, I could get them back before the reference room closed.

As I read, over the next few days, the aims of the military and the Defense Department became apparent. The brass needed a war to advance their military careers and grow their brand. It wasn't hard to see how a false radar contact in the Gulf of Tonkin could be exaggerated into an excuse to bomb, strafe, and burn. An Admiral Morrison had sent his ships into sorties with the imaginary gunboats and expended millions of dollars worth of ordnance shooting at the non-existent attackers in the dark. He had claimed, with no evidence, that his ships had sunk two communist gunboats. LBJ had seized on the incident to promote his war to Congress.

The military had been locked, loaded, and ready to rock and roll. . .

———————

By the end of the week, I had assembled a substantial sheaf of the smelly sepia photostats. I took them on the bus to Arthur's family home. Pete Daniels, Arthur's dad, answered the door, took the roll of prints, and told me to sit down in the front room. He unrolled the stack of facsimiles on a coffee table and flipped back a few.

"Thanks, John," he said, "this is just what I was looking for." He rolled the sheaf up and replaced the rubber band. He went into another room and returned with a check for me.

"Arthur's on his way, he'll be home by six," Mr. Daniels said, sitting down on the sofa. "I know you guys like rock music, but let me play some of the music that I love."

He went to the big console stereo and slid back a door. He pulled out an album and set it on the turntable. He returned to the couch.

"This man is a genius—listen."

Miles Davis' *Sketches of Spain* started playing, and we both listened raptly to the first cut. Pete Daniels told me about the sidemen that had recorded with Miles, and how the cuts on the album told a musical story. I was hooked. From that day forward, I still dug folk and rock, but jazz was *it* for me.

Dennis, the sports car enthusiast from Canyon High, was attending San Francisco State. The college seethed with political protest, and the students went on strike against the college administration. The strike was about racism and the war.

One Sunday evening, Dennis heard a commotion on a street below his apartment. He climbed out the window of his apartment and crossed the roof of an adjacent building so he could see the street. Down below, a boat on a trailer was tangled with a Muni Bus. While he watched, he saw a white man in a sports shirt pull a handgun from his belt and shoot a black man.

Dennis recoiled in horror, hurried back into his apartment and called the police. When he heard sirens approaching, he braved the roof again and was startled to see the policemen gather around the shooter and start talking with him—ignoring the inert body of the bus driver.

Dennis called Arthur that night to tell him about it. Arthur came over the next morning and Dennis showed him where he'd seen the shooting. As the two longhairs peered down over the parapet, the policemen investigating below spotted them and sent officers up the stairs to Dennis's apartment, where they frisked the two hippies and questioned them aggressively.

Weeks later, a trial was held in Superior Court, City and County of San Francisco. The shooter, an off-duty San Francisco police officer, had been charged with Manslaughter in the First Degree. The victim was a black truck driver. Dennis was called as the first witness for the prosecution.

I started cutting my civics classes at Merritt and sat in the gallery every day, as did Arthur. When it came time for Dennis to testify, we paid rapt attention, as did the family of the deceased. The young district attorney asked Dennis to describe what he had seen that Sunday, occasionally asking for clarification on one point or another.

Next came the cross-examination from the shooter's attorney, Jake Erlich, a legendary defense lawyer hired by the Police Officer's Association. It was rumored that his courtroom theatrics were the inspiration for the fictional Perry Mason. Every eye in the room was on the celebrity lawyer as he strutted past the bar, approached the bench, and exchanged a few pleasantries with the judge.

He started asking Dennis questions about the strike at San Francisco State and about whether he was a communist—obviously trying to paint him as a dangerous radical.

"Is it true, Mr. McCully, that you are currently enrolled at San Francisco State?"

"I am," answered Dennis.

"Is it true also that you participated in the student strike recently?"

"Yes sir."

The dapper lawyer turned to the judge.

"Your Honor," he said, "I'd like to introduce Defense Exhibit A."

The judge nodded, "You may proceed."

The Defense team quickly set up a viewing screen and switched on a slide projector.

Slides of scenes from the student strike flashed onto the screen, one after the other: shots of long-haired students carrying protest signs, students being handcuffed by the police, and the walls of jail cells after their incarceration.

Turning back to Dennis in the witness stand, the lawyer said, "Mr. McCully, please read to all of us what the strikers wrote on the wall of the county jail while they were being held."

The DA shot to his feet. "Objection, Your Honor, this has nothing to do with the case."

The judge, without looking at the prosecutor, said, "Overruled," then looked at Dennis. "Go ahead, read it."

"But Your Honor," protested Dennis, "I've never been arrested for anything, and I don't agree with that stuff."

"Read it," said the judge.

Dennis shook his head, then began reading the graffiti projected on the screen.

"Kill the Pigs," he read in a monotone. He then proceeded to read all the slogans that the prisoners had allegedly scrawled on the walls of their cells.

The superstar lawyer hung his jacket on the back of his chair and strutted around in front of the jury box, his thumbs stuck into the armholes of his pinstriped vest. He looked for all the world like a bantam rooster preening in front of his hens, flapping his elbows like wings.

Arthur was also called to the stand. The rooster set about demeaning him too, even though he was not a witness to the killing. I think the defense just wanted the jury to see Arthur's long, blond hair and scraggly beard.

The off-duty cop ended up being exonerated, largely because the only eyewitness testimony had been impeached by the bantam rooster.

After the jury was dismissed, Dennis and I walked from the courthouse to his Mission district apartment.

"Can you believe that verdict?" Dennis said, shaking his head.

"I can't believe that judge," I said. "It was like he had a crush on Perry Mason."

Both of us were appalled by this miscarriage of justice.

A white dude who had been drinking beer all day smashes his boat trailer into a MUNI bus when he attempts to park the rig. In a drunken rage, he ends up shooting an unarmed black man to death, leaving a widow and children.

After sitting in the courtroom every day and seeing the shenanigans of the policeman's attorney, I am convinced that many among the police and those running the courts are racists masquerading as public servants. It's best to have as little to do as possible with these jokers.

"I'm leaving," Dennis said. "I've got to hit the road; I'm going to Mexico."

At this I looked up. "You're dropping out of State?"

"The strike pretty much did that," he said.

"What about Marcia?" I asked.

"I already broke it off with her. She's married, and when we get together, we screw, and then she goes away. I want a real girlfriend: someone to take to the movies, or go camping with. . ."

I thought about how I had asked out several girls at my junior college, for lunch or such, and had received no takers. I had also missed too many classes to get any credits for my semester at the school. I was pretty lonely. I had bumped into my former girlfriend, Alice, on the steps of the Student Union, and she had told me that her new boyfriend had taken her camping, and she loved it.

I had joined a sensitivity group. In two weeks of sessions and an overnight retreat, I was the only member who didn't get laid.

"Can I go, too?" I asked spontaneously.

Smuggler's Run

DENNIS AND I pulled our rucksacks from the side of a VW bus, on a downtown street in San Diego. Our last ride had taken us from the San Fernando Valley, near Los Angeles, to this city near the Mexican border. Streetlights and neon signs glowed above the dark streets. We walked with all our possessions on our backs.

"Okay you two, hold it right there," came a deep voice behind us.

We both turned and saw two white-hatted sailors standing behind us, truncheons and handcuffs hung from their pistol belts. Each wore a white armband with the black letters "SP" stenciled thereon: Shore Patrol.

"Let's see your draft cards," the taller one said.

We both pulled out our billfolds. Dennis produced his 1-Y student deferment, and I handed over my 4-F card. After checking the cards in the beam of a flashlight, they gave them back and told us to move along.

Hundreds of uniformed sailors and marines milled around the downtown sidewalks on a Saturday night, looking for women or a fight—whichever came first.

"We should get off the street," said Dennis.

"We can't hitch a ride after dark," I said. "Let's duck in here."

We each paid $1.50 and went into the all-night theater.

We slept the night in there, fitfully waking to glimpses of one of the three movies that repeated over and over: *The True Story of Adam and Eve, Jayne Mansfield in Las Vegas*, and a Western called *Revenge on Boot Hill*.

Emerging from the grind house with stiff necks on Sunday morning, we caught a city bus to San Ysidro and the border crossing. Sailors, couples, and families were walking along the broad viaduct that crossed the international border. Occasionally a U.S. Border Patrol agent would ask to see someone's ID, but mostly he just waved everyone through.

He stopped us and checked our names against an alphabetical list of wanted criminals and draft dodgers. Finding everything in order, he gave back our papers and waved us through.

On the Mexican side, a Mexican federal officer was welcoming everyone that approached, saying *"Bienvenidos a Mexico"* to each group of people. As we approached, he stepped from the shade of his gatehouse and stood square in front of us, legs spread and arms folded above his substantial belly.

"Alto," he said in a loud voice, holding up the palm of one hand. "No hippie in Mexico."

We both pulled out our U.S. passports and our 90-day visas issued the week before by the Mexican consulate in San Francisco. He refused to even look at them.

"No hippie in Mexico," he repeated, pointing us back toward San Ysidro.

"*Vamos.*"

With no alternative, we turned around and trudged back.

When we got to the American side, the Border Patrol agent looked amused.

"Pancho wouldn't let you in, huh?"

Dennis shook his head.

"You can wait in here for a few minutes," the American said. "The fat guy has been there all morning, and he has to take a break sometime."

Dennis and I dropped our backpacks to the floor and sat on a bench inside the gatehouse.

The patrol agent ducked inside a few minutes later. "Pancho's gone; another guy's there now."

We hoisted our packs and walked the stretch of sidewalk again. Now there was a younger *Federale* at the post. He smiled and said, "*Bienvenidos a Mexico,*" as we walked past. We had not gone ten feet when we heard Pancho's voice behind us.

"*Alto!*" he shouted. We stopped, turned, and saw him coming out of the guardhouse, fastening his belt and scowling. He shoved the younger officer into the kiosk.

"No hippie in Mexico!" he sputtered. He was really mad now.

We walked back into the United States. The American guard grinned and shrugged as we walked past. "Welcome home," he said.

I was beginning to wonder if there was a place for me anymore. JFK, Dr. King, and Bobby Kennedy were gunned down in the U.S., then hundreds of students were machine-gunned by the Mexican army in *Tlatelolco* square in 1968. The culture that had raised me now rejected me, and now Mexico wouldn't honor our visas.

"Let's hitch to Arizona and try to cross the border there," said David. "Maybe the *Federales* will look at our visas there."

Dennis and I waited, thumbs out, at an on-ramp to Interstate 8. We stood next to a sign that read "Yuma 170 mi". A full-sized pickup with an extended camper shell lurched over to the shoulder. It had Colorado plates.

The driver leaned across the cab to the open passenger side window. "Where you fellows headed?" he asked.

"Mexico," I said.

He opened his door, came around the back of the camper, and opened a rear door. "Throw your gear back here, and you can ride in front," he said. In a moment we were sitting three across in the cab, headed east on the freeway.

"You know why I stopped for you guys?" the driver said as he merged into the fast lane.

"Why?" Dennis asked.

"Because you had all your stuff together. No suitcases or garbage bags."

The driver, Glenn, regaled us with tales of his adventures for the next few hours. It was long after dark when he stopped on a gravel road between two low adobe buildings.

"*Donde vas*?" asked a *Federale* beside the driver's window.

"*San Luis*," replied Glenn, "*para las cantinas!*"

The officer smiled and pointed down the dirt road.

The rig rolled along the dark desert road until we saw colored lights and scraps of neon on the corners of a few adobe buildings ahead. Glenn steered the rig off the rough road and came to a stop in an even rougher vacant lot.

"It's party time, boys." he said happily. "The *chicas* await!"

That sounded okay to Dennis and me, so we followed him into the biggest of the three cantinas, *La Gloriosa*. We walked under an archway and through a pair of swinging doors. As soon as we were inside, a woman in a yellow cocktail dress ran up to Glenn and threw her arms around his neck. He looked in my direction and winked.

"I'll check with you boys before I go back to the rig," he said. "Happy hunting."

The driver and his friend curled up in a booth along a wall. Dennis and I went to a table along the edge of the cracked tile dance floor. As soon as we were seated, two girls in wrinkled dresses sat down in the remaining two chairs. They looked friendly but bored—and maybe 16 years old.

It became apparent that neither spoke English, but Dennis had taken high school Spanish.

"*¿Quieres una bebida?*" he said, in a Castro Valley accent.

Both girls shrugged, then said,"*Si.*"

A waitress appeared and Dennis said, "*Quatros cervesas, por favor.*"

When the drinks came, I noticed that the girls' glasses contained water. Dennis and I sipped our beers while the girls fidgeted and glanced around the room, each sipping water through a straw. *Oh Blah Dee, Oh Blah Dah* by the Beatles came on over a loudspeaker, except it was a Spanish language cover version.

Dennis had taught me a few Spanish phrases while we were thumbing our way down the coast highway back in California.

"*¿Te gusta bailar?*" I asked the girl beside me.

She looked up, surprised that I had opened my mouth, then shrugged. She took my hand, and we went out on the tile dance floor. I tried shuffling around to the music with her, but I was as inept at dancing as I was at Algebra.

As we returned to the table, the other girl stood up, then both of them walked over to the bar where two truck drivers were standing. Obviously they sensed that the two long-haired gringos had no money to spend on their services.

Dennis and I paid for four beers, and we left through the swinging doors. Out on the dirt street an old man had set up a charcoal burner and was selling steak tacos, a peso apiece. As we ate our tacos, a three man Mariachi band walked up and sang a song about lost love, accompanied by guitar, trumpet, and *guitarrón*.

Glenn and the lady in the yellow dress came out of the cantina.

"There you guys are," he called. "Where's the girls?"

"Uhh, I guess we struck out," said Dennis.

"No money, huh?" said Glenn.

"We gotta save it if we're gonna make it to Guatemala," said Dennis.

"Well, I hope Ramona and I don't drive you crazy tonight," said Glenn.

The four of us walked back to the camper in the parking lot; Glenn and Ramona climbed into the bunk over the cab and drew the curtain on their festivities. Dennis and I unrolled our serapes on the bunk in the back.

Before we fell asleep, we heard some Spanish conversation and laughter, then some earthy sounds. It was hard not to laugh, but Dennis and I kept it down, because Glenn had given us a place to sleep.

The next morning, I was awakened by the door of the camper opening and closing as Ramona slipped out.

"Alright boys, drop your cocks and grab your socks," called Glenn, as he climbed down from his berth. "Ramona's going to cook us breakfast."

Taking turns, the three of us washed up in the narrow bathroom and were combed and presentable when the courtesan returned. She chatted away in Spanish as she made a pot of coffee and a skillet of chorizo and eggs in the tiny galley. The eggs were dyed red from the chili in the sausage. I'd never tasted real Mexican food before, and I mopped up every last bit with warm and tender tortillas.

Ramona washed the dishes, the coffee pot, and the skillet. Dennis and I both said, "Gracias, Señora."

She was out the door with a wave of her hand and "*de nada*" on her lips.

"I've got something to show you," said Glenn, after she left. He lifted the mattress of the forward bunk, and underneath was a compartment holding six small Sony black and white television and maybe a dozen new Iver-Johnson .22 revolvers.

"There's a big import duty in Mexico on manufactured items, and this stuff pays for my whole trip," said Glenn with a grin. "We still have to pass customs in a few miles, but it's never been a problem."

The giant Saguaro cacti cast striped shadows across the road as we drove in the early morning sunlight. The camper rig pulled up and stopped next to a painted sign that read *Aduanas Fronteriza Norte*.

Glenn set the handbrake and grabbed an aerosol can and a gray rag from a cabinet.

"You guys stay in here; I got this," said the smuggler as he went out the door. Dennis and I watched through the camper window as Glenn walked across the gravel towards a square white building.

A man wearing a khaki uniform, a black mustache, and a peaked cap emerged. Glenn shook his hand, then held up his other hand with the aerosol can and rag. The customs agent nodded, then Glenn pulled the officer's revolver from the holster, sprayed it with gun polish, and buffed it with the gray flannel rag.

Handing the gleaming gun back to the *Federale*, Glenn put an arm around his shoulders, and they walked back towards the rig together. Glenn talked a blue streak in Spanish.

"Uh, oh," I said. "Here's where they tell us 'no hippie in Mexico'."

The door opened, and the guard stuck his head into the camper. Dennis and I held out our passports and 90-day visas. The officer smiled, said, "*Bienvenidos a Mexico*," and waved off our papers without a glance. The smuggler and the *aduana* walked back to the white cinder block building and disappeared inside.

"Now what?" said Dennis.

Glenn reappeared, hopped into the driver's seat, and started up the engine. Two inspectors waved as we drove away, and Glenn waved back.

"What happened inside the office?" asked Dennis.

"I polished the *jefe's* pistol for him," replied Glenn.

"Why didn't your friend ask for our papers?" I asked.

"Arturo and I go way back," he said. "He asked me if you guys were hippies, and I said definitely not; you were '*vagabundos*'." He laughed.

As we drove south through the Sonoran Desert, the land flattened out to hardpan glaring in white sunlight to the horizon. Thousand-foot black granite pyramids lay scattered about as if they were playing pieces tossed onto a colossal game board. Our truck and the road seemed microscopic as we moved through the stark and immense landscape.

Glenn spoke up. "If you guys finally decide to dip into your grubstake to hire some girls, I have a little advice for you."

"I'll bite," I said. "What?"

"You guys are young, and you can get away with it. Tell the girl you're cherry, all shy, like. They love that. She'll be extra sweet and maybe give you a discount. You ever have a girl go down on you?"

"Yeah," said Dennis.

I had no idea what Glenn was talking about, but said, "Sure."

"Well, if you tell her you're cherry, she might go down on you for no extra charge," he said.

"Mmm... mmm," he hummed, lost in thoughts of past glory.

Blasting across the blazing desert, the truck's tires sizzled on the asphalt. Since all the windows were open, we had to shout to be heard over the road noise, so mostly we kept quiet.

I am on the road for real now, I thought to myself, or maybe I'm on the lam. Dennis and I had dropped out of college, and the military machine and the San Francisco Police Department seemed miles away. I knew that Dennis would stay in Mexico, or go to Canada, rather than be inducted into the army. We were both excited by this new vagabond life and couldn't wait to see where it led.

One thing was for sure. The life of conformity to middle America's "dream" was in my rearview mirror now.

Although neither of us were interested in paying girls to have sex, I was curious as to what "going down" was. I was pretty innocent in those days. Later, when I asked Dennis what it meant, he rolled his eyes. "It's a blowjob, dimwit."

Alice and I had done that once, and it had made her throw up. I felt bad about it and never tried it again.

———

The setting sun was painting the Sea of Cortez pink, as we rolled into Guymas. I knew that NASA had tracked orbiting spacecraft from a radar station here, but that was all I knew about the town. We pulled up to a ramshackle *carneceria*, and we went in and Glenn bought thin beefsteaks, green chilis, and onions. Next door, at the *tortillaria*, I bought a kilo of fresh corn tortillas, hot off the *plancha*, wrapped in brown paper.

Back in the camper, Glenn chopped up chilis and onions, threw them in a pan with a lump of lard, and set it on a propane burner. Another skillet was laid on the second burner to heat up. As the peppers and onions sautéed, they gave off a fine aroma. When the empty skillet started smoking, he slapped the first red beefsteak into the pan where it began to sizzle furiously.

Glenn gave the aromatic vegetables a quick shake and a stir, then turned over the searing steak. After a moment, he picked it up with a spatula and laid it atop the chilis in the other pan. The two other steaks were seared and stacked in quick succession. With the skillet still hot, Glenn heated a dozen tortillas, one by one, and placed them atop the steaming mound of peppers and steak keeping warm on the back burner.

"Dennis, there's forks and steak knives in the drawer, and John, you can open three beers from the icebox." Our guide set the food on an aluminum hot pad in the middle of the small table, pulled out three tin plates, and sat down.

We each took a few tortillas, one beefsteak, and a mound of steaming chilis and onions.

"Be sure to use plenty of this stuff," said Glenn, handing me a bottle of *salsa picante*. "It sinks the amoeba, so you won't get dysentery." Dennis and I dutifully shook lots of the chili sauce onto our steaks. The hot sauce came in a pop bottle with a nail hole through the cap, crusty with dried red.

We devoured the steak and pepper tacos, washing them down with *Dos Equis*.

"You know, this is our last night together," said our smuggler friend. "I can drop you off on the highway in the morning. You sure I can't sell you a pistol? It might come in handy if you're camping in *bandito* country. I'll give it to you for fifty dollars, my cost. . ."

"Thanks Glenn, but I have to pass on that," said Dennis. "I

left San Francisco to get away from shooting. I don't want to see any more of that stuff, ever."

Glenn glanced at me, I shook my head, and he shrugged.

After Dennis and I had washed and dried the dishes, Glenn drove his rig a mile or so to a shack beside a railroad switching yard. The sun was going down.

"Come on in," said Glenn. "Carlos is an old amigo—you'll like him."

Inside the switching shack, Carlos greeted Glenn warmly, then pulled a bottle from a drawer, along with four small terra cotta cups. From the squat brown bottle labeled *Mezcal Triunfo*, he poured a shot into each cup, waited until we had each hoisted one, and said, "¡*Salud!*"

We each tossed down the liquor. To me, it felt like I'd swallowed a wasp. After a few seconds the burning faded, and I felt a reassuring glow spread across my belly.

Evidently Carlos agreed on a price for Glenn's cargo, and he poured another round. Glenn disappeared into the camper and emerged with revolvers in boxes and a jute shopping bag full of Sony televisions. The contraband was stowed in the trunk of Carlos' Chevy.

Attack of the Vampires

GLENN DROPPED US OFF the next morning on *Camino Quince*. Dennis and I stood on the sun-baked shoulder of the road, pointing our forefingers south. "Don't stick out your thumbs to hitch, just point down the road," Glenn had told us.

It wasn't long before a pickup pulled over, and we climbed into the empty cargo bed. This ride took us south for hours, and, after being dropped off, we caught a ride in a Volkswagen Beetle. We were deposited on the beach at Mazatlan.

Across the *Avenida del Mar* stood a bus terminal with a hotel upstairs.

"Let's get a room there," I said. "We can stash our packs and go swimming..."

We didn't have much money; I had $60 and Dennis had about $100. This was supposed last us three months. The plan was to get to Guatemala City before it ran out. Dennis had an uncle who managed a paint factory there, and we had hopes of getting work.

The room turned out to be cheap enough, if we only stayed for a night. We stashed our packs in our new room. We were both happy to see a water cooler at the end of the corridor holding a five gallon glass jug of *Cristal Agua Purificada*. We filled our room's earthenware pitcher and drank up before we went back to the beach.

After a swim and a sunbath, we each bought a peeled mango on a stick, carved like a flower. The next morning we both woke up feeling sick, sick, sick.

"It must have been those mangos," said Dennis. "They probably use the same sticks over and over." He groaned from the bathroom as I looked out the window overlooking the bus yard.

As I watched, the young son of the hotel proprietor filled a *Cristal* jug from a hose bib in the parking lot.

"Or it could be something else," I said. I went over to my pack. I took out a bottle of *Halazone* tablets and dropped one into the clay pitcher and one in each of our canteens. *Too little, too late*, I told myself.

We spent the next 24 hours in the hotel room, too dizzy and wracked with stomach cramps to think about going out, or eating, or anything. We had some paperback books. I read *The Autobiography of Malcom X*, Dennis read *The Teachings of Don Juan*.

When I read about Malcom's father defending his family from the Ku Klux Klan, I thought of my Arkansas relatives who

might have been involved in white terrorism. I felt sick that
I had raised the Confederate flag daily over Goodyear School
back in Georgia. I knew that there was something wrong with
the United States that the Civil War hadn't corrected.

Sometime in the afternoon, a voice came up from the street,
through an open window.

"*Naranjas. . . naranjas.*"

I stuck my head out. Down on the street, I saw a man with
a bushel of oranges hawking them to passersby. From my
rucksack I grabbed a coil of parachute cord and tied it to the
chinstrap of my ranger hat.

Writing "*Dos naranjas, por favor*" on a scrap of paper, I stuck
the note and a few coins in the improvised bucket which I lowered towards the sidewalk.

When the hat appeared next to the vendor, he looked up
startled, smiled at me, then took some coins and replaced them
with with two big navel oranges. I drew the felt basket up and
into the room, then Dennis and I each peeled an orange. We
slowly ate them, one sweet section at a time.

The next morning we both realized we couldn't afford
to stay in a Mazatlan hotel any longer. We bought *Dexidrina*
tablets at a *farmacia*, swallowed them with chlorine-flavored
water, and humped our backpacks away from the beach towards *Camino Quince*. I felt a little shaky, but we made it to the
highway.

Before we could drop our rucksacks and point our fingers
down the road, a battered pick-up stopped for us. Two young

campesinos already sat in the cargo bed. They grinned and nodded as we tossed our packs in, then climbed aboard.

After an hour of hot wind blasting our bandana-covered faces, the pickup stopped in El Rosario, Nayarit. Dennis and I climbed off and waved a *gracias* to the driver. A palapa stood next to the highway, and we walked into the shade and sat at a table. Two grizzled farmers sat at another table nursing bottles of Pacifico beer.

A waiter emerged from the adobe hut adjoining the thatched sunshade, and he minced over to our table in high heels, a miniskirt, and a sparkly short sleeved sweater. Surprised, Dennis managed to order.

"*Dos cervezas, por favor, con frijoles y tortillas.*" This was becoming our go-to meal: cheap, filling, and available most anywhere.

The drag queen waiter said, "*Bueno,*" pursed his painted lips, and batted false eyelashes at us. He sashayed away, pausing at the farmers' table to bump and grind for them, then disappeared with a broad wink behind a beaded curtain.

Dennis and I burst into laughter, and the two farmers nodded and smiled. When the waiter returned, he vamped it up even more, encouraged by our giggles. Our beer, beans, and tortillas went down well. We had recovered from our bout with *turista.*

We had planned to follow the Rio Baluarte up into the Sierra Madre, looking for treasure or seeking enlightenment— whichever came first. We had hoped to hire a couple of saddle horses for a week—or at least a pack burro. Our waiter could speak some English, so we inquired about the possibility of renting animals. The waiter shook his curly hair, shrugged, and asked the two old farmers if they knew of any "*burros en alquiler*".

It turned out that there were plenty of burros and horses in El Rosario, many for sale, but none for rent. Our dreams of riding into *bandito* country on horseback were dashed. We had already passed up Glenn's offer of six-guns, anyway.

A dusty path led from the highway to the wide and dry riverbed. A braided stream ran between the sandbars on the south side of the *arroyo*. My partner and I paid our tiny tab, and, saluting our entertaining waiter, we shouldered our rucksacks and set off up the river.

Dennis wore a straw hat, and I had a Marine Corps drill instructor hat—a forest ranger hat, if you will. As we hiked in the burning sun, sweat poured off my face and down my chest. My pack made a slurping sound as it separated repeatedly from my soaked back, every few steps as we trudged along the bumpy trail.

"We have to find some shade," said Dennis, after an hour. "I'm burning up."

Continuing around a bend, we both spotted a lush, green thicket a few yards higher on a bench above the dry river bed. As we climbed to it, we both realized the thicket was actually a cluster of overgrown marijuana plants, with a shady clearing between the soaring stalks.

This looked like an oasis to two vagrant potheads from San Francisco, so we gratefully crawled into the scented shade. We drained the first of our four canteens of chlorinated water, which left us three quarts of the precious fluid.

The next order of business was to chop up some dried leaves and smoke them to get high. Neither Dennis nor I had smoked any pot for the past month. We found that no matter how much we toasted our lungs with the hand-rolled green cigars, all we got was a headache. There were no flowers atop the deep green foliage, so we were just smoking hemp rope.

Still, it was pleasant to relax in the shade and watch the occasional *campesino* lead his burro along the path, silhouetted against the shining waters of the desert river. Dennis and I swapped books, so I got to read *The Teachings of Don Juan*, a purported memoir of Ayahuasca visions and a spiritual quest.

The accounts of the author's hallucinations were entertaining enough, however his "spiritual journey" left me cold. Whether Baptist or Animist, any belief in souls, spirits, or religion strikes me as creepy to this day. I find it hard to believe in something I can't see, hear, touch, or taste. Preachers and witch doctors have managed to control their flocks with such nonsense for eons, but I'm not interested anymore.

Faith is NOT "the evidence of things unseen", as one New Testament writer declared. Getting people to believe in and give their lives for something for which there is zero scientific evidence is a formula for mind control.

As the sky darkened, I pulled the white gas stove from my pack and mixed a skillet of instant refried beans and treated water, which I simmered over the blue flame. After the frijoles thickened up, I set the pan aside and heated some tortillas, one by one, over the flame.

As we ate our rations, we both remarked on the number of big bats flying about the *arroyo*.

"You don't think those could be vampire bats, do you?" asked Dennis, between bites.

"No," I answered, "they are only found south of the Tropic of Cancer...." I trailed off as we looked at each other, remembering the road sign we had passed, just south of Mazatlan.

"I wish we'd brought a tent," said Dennis.

Vagabundos Mexicanos

WE SPENT THE NIGHT under the marijuana bushes, very careful to tuck the corners of our serapes tightly around us against vampire bats. Perhaps the cannabis stogies we'd puffed all afternoon had some effect after all; I only half-slept that night, constantly checking if I was exposing any skin to the leathery little demons.

After checking our arms and legs for lesions the next morning and finding none, my partner and I packed up and high-tailed it back to the highway.

Pointing our fingers, we quickly caught a ride with a salesman driving south.

San Blas, a fishing town in Nayarit, was legendary among California surfers. When we saw the exit sign along the highway, the salesman wished us well, and we hitched down the jungle road.

Riding in the bed of a pickup with some *vatos locos*, we rattled through tunnels of soaring tropical trees and hanging vines.

The pickup slowed and stopped in the main square of the old colonial town. We piled out and hit the cobblestones.

A gringo couple was walking past the municipal fountain and stopped to watch us alight.

"Welcome to paradise," said the blonde woman. "Where're you guys from?"

"San Francisco," answered Dennis.

"Far out," she said. "We're from Santa Cruz!"

The blond boyfriend smiled and threw a Shaka, the surfer hand sign for "hang loose".

"I'm Julie, and this is Sandhog," she said, gesturing at her partner. "Do you guys have a place to stay?"

I allowed that we didn't.

"Everybody stays at Maria's when they get to town," said Sandhog. "Her rooms are cheap."

"It's the pink *hacienda* on the right when you walk to the *playa*," added Julie.

Maria's place turned out to be just the thing: a square, cinder block house with a wing of rooms and a central courtyard. As Dennis and I passed through a swinging gate, two red hens squawked and ran away. Two young women, obviously Anglos, wearing cutoff jeans and embroidered blouses, sat straddling a bench, one braiding the other's hair.

"Hi," I said as we walked in. "Is Maria here?"

The one doing the braiding looked up and extended her chin towards the main house at the end of the yard. "She's in there with Dwayne. His knobs got infected."

Just inside the doorway of the main house, I could see a well-tanned surfer bending over with his trunks pulled down, exposing his white behind. A dark-haired woman in a blue dress was injecting the contents of a large hypodermic syringe into a butt cheek.

"*No surfeando por una semana,*" she said. "*Si te vuelves a infectar, la penicilina ya no funcionará. . .*"

"*Gracias,* Maria," said Dwayne, pulling up his shorts.

"*De nada, cabron,*" said Maria, as she took the glass and steel syringe apart and dropped the works into a pot of boiling water on a gas ring. Dwayne smiled sheepishly as he walked past us. Sure enough, the "knobs" beneath his knees, built up from paddling his surfboard while kneeling, were red and oozing.

Dennis asked in his best high school Spanish if she had a room to rent.

Maria replied that she had one vacant room, and we had to pay for a week up front. Since the price she named was less than the cost for one night back in Mazatlan, we paid up gladly.

The room held two metal cots with thin mattresses, a small wooden table, and a yellow painted chair. A solitary lightbulb hung on a cord. The water closets and shower stall were outside, in a lean-to against the main house.

We shoved our rucksacks under the cots and went back into the yard to get acquainted with the other roomers. Of most interest to Dennis and me were the two girls we'd seen as we arrived.

It turned out that Nannette and Lillian had hitched rides on private planes, small airport to small airport, from their homes in Vancouver, B.C. Both of us Californians were impressed, even more so when they introduced Janet, who had been with them the whole time. She was heavy with child, looking as if she might deliver any day now.

Dwayne, the afflicted surfer, occupied a cell with another surfer, Charlie. They were from San Diego, where I'd lived a few years earlier.

"The guys that were in your room got busted for drugs," said Charlie.

"What kind of drugs?" I asked.

"*Mota*, I guess. They had a kilo of Michoacán that they wanted to take back to the States."

"Bummer," said Dennis and I in unison.

"They left some tabs of acid in the room," whispered Charlie. "Dwayne and I don't want it, and the Canadian chicks couldn't care less."

"Where is it?" I asked.

"On top of the rafter right above the lightbulb," said Charlie.

Back in our room, I stood on the chair and found a small paper envelope. Inside were three Owsley purple four-ways.

The next morning, Dennis and I both woke to the triumphant crowing of a rooster just below our window. We had both slept soundly, relieved to be away from the vampire bats of the Rio Baluarte.

The packed-sand road in front of Maria's *hacienda* ran through a coconut plantation, before it ended at a broad, open beach. The coco palms soared tall in straight rows. A breeze from the Pacific rattled the stiff fronds high overhead.

In the middle of the grove we saw a table covered with huge lime green cocos, glowing in the morning sun. For a few *centavos*, Dennis and I each bought a coco.

The elderly vendor slammed an oversized nut onto a palm stump, chopped at it with a wicked sharp machete, and handed each of us a coco with a paper straw protruding from the perfectly round opening. The sweet, cool coconut water went down easy—a pint or more in each nut.

This was nothing like the sour water inside the brown, hairy coconuts I'd tasted in the States.

When we'd finished the first course, the grizzled farmer took the nut back and whacked off the top third, exposing the tender meat lining the sturdy shell. He chopped a perfectly sharp and rounded spoon from the outer husk, and stuck it into the soft layer of meat lining the shell. The tender custard bore no resemblance to the woody meat of a stateside coconut.

By the time I'd scraped and eaten the custard, I was stuffed and well-hydrated. I realized that this was the best breakfast I'd ever had, and the cheapest, as well.

We continued down the path to the beach and plopped down on the sand, just above the shore break.

"Let's eat some acid," said Dennis.

"Suits me," I said. "How much?" I pulled the envelope from a pocket and shook the three purple tablets into my palm.

"This is the most beautiful place I've ever seen," said Dennis. "Let's take it all. . ."

We each swallowed one of the tablets and split the third. This was six doses apiece of LSD-25: enough to make a bull elephant join the Hare Krishnas and wear a dhoti. We were in for a bumpy ride.

For the next eight hours I hallucinated wildly as I thrashed in the big waves crashing into the beach. After a few wipeouts in the shore break, I swam farther out and managed to catch a few waves, bodysurfing into the shallows.

Scraped and sunburned, I lay in the dappled shade of a palm and spent several hours fascinated that each grain of sand was a living insect with a beautiful soul. I then realized that my own body was actually a colony of microscopic beings. I could watch their antics when I stared closely into my hand.

The supersized dose of acid shook up my synapses much more vividly than the moderate doses I'd taken in high school. This was similar to shaking a jar of lightning bugs to make them all glow at once.

———

I started keeping a journal of my travels, about this time. Drawings, watercolors, and poems soon filled the pages. The

Canadian girls kept to themselves, preoccupied with Janet's approaching event. The surfers were always surfing and were not interested in sharing breaks or boards with a couple of hippie hodads from San Francisco. After dwelling amongst the lotus-eaters for a couple of weeks, Dennis and I were ready to move on to Guadalajara.

Duarte Garcia had been an exchange student who had lived with the McCully family during his junior year at Canyon High. Dennis had an open invitation to stay with the Garcias if he was in Mexico.

We caught a ride out of San Blas through the jungle to *Camino Quince*, where we were picked up by a student returning to the University of Guadalajara after his spring break. He let us out on a big downtown boulevard, and, with the aid of our street map, we walked for a half hour or so and found the address, which turned out to be a garishly painted Mayan temple with lush landscaping all around.

Although it looked more like Chichen Itza than a residence, Dennis stepped up and rang the bell. Señora Garcia answered the massive wooden door. After Dennis introduced himself, Mrs. Garcia exclaimed her delight and physically pulled us inside. She led us to an upstairs bedroom where we stashed our rucksacks, then introduced us to Duarte's younger brother, Juan, his sister Yvonne, and his papa, Rodrigo. Our high school friend Duarte was away in Mexico City.

Turns out that Papa Rodrigo was a professor of Mayan religion and an herbalist. While we were in his study, two gringo guys were shown in by his secretary. He gazed into one of the guys' eyes and, with a dismissive snort, pronounced a diagnosis.

"You have parasites," he said, in perfect Oxford English. Writing on a slip of paper, he said, "Buy this herb in the market. Make a tea every night for a week, then come see me again."

Later that night, Yvonne, Duarte's sister and a sophomore at the university, suggested that Dennis and I walk down the street to *Tacos de Cabeza*. Although it was close to midnight, young girls wandered the sidewalks in twos and threes, enjoying the cool night air.

The white stucco building with one big room glowed from fluorescent lights, inside and out. Inside, shiny white tile covered the ceiling, walls, and floor. Dozens of skinned and bloody animal heads stared down at us from tile ledges above.

Cabra, oveja, ternero, vaca, and *ciervo,* they were tagged. Goat, sheep, calf, cow, and deer were all on offer as taco meat, and the place was doing a land-office business.

Families with young children lined up at the hot tables, where ladies wearing hairnets scooped the steaming shredded meat into tortillas, adding chopped onions and chilis. Delicious aromas arose from the steam trays. When it was our turn, I ordered goat tacos, and Dennis ordered beef.

When I bit into my first taco, I was startled. It wasn't just good, it was wonderful. . .

Millions of lights glowed below us, as the Volkswagen descended from a mountain pass into the *Valle de México*. The driver had picked us up just outside of Guadalajara that morning, and now it was evening. He inserted a new eight-track cartridge into his dashboard tape player, and *Birthday* by the Beatles blasted over his new stereo car speakers.

More and more lights appeared as we came out of the hills and into Mexico City. The galaxies beneath us outshone the real stars above.

Elena, Duarte's mother, had given us the address of a house that rented rooms to students. The four-story building was in the old Tlatelolco district, not far from the *Plaza de las Tres Culturas*, the site of a student massacre the year before.

A mass demonstration of students and labor had gathered to protest the upcoming Olympic Games, and they began a chant: *"¡No queremos olimpiadas, queremos revolución!"* ("We don't want Olympics, we want revolution!").

Government-sponsored snipers on nearby rooftops began shooting, and, after Army helicopters dropped colored flares, the Mexican Army moved in with thousands of troops and hundreds of armored cars. The casualty figures are in dispute to this day, but thousands were killed in the plaza and more died in the house-to-house search for "radicals". Ten days later, the Olympics would open on schedule.

The "May 68" riots had already occurred in Paris, and the Kent State killings were yet to come. In those days, it seemed like the established governments were intent on quashing protest at any cost. This frightened me, but as long as baby boomers were too young to vote, I figured non-violent protest was all we could do.

We climbed the stairs to the fourth floor landing and rang the buzzer at the door. The landlady answered and, yes, she spoke English, and, yes, she had a room available. She led us up a back stairway to the roof.

The room was a small penthouse with two beds and a bathroom. This was great! The matronly landlady collected our rental deposit, then paused at the top of the stairwell.

"You boys like marijuana?" she asked, with a tilt of her head.

Dennis and I glanced at each other.

"It's alright. . ." said Dennis carefully.

The lady smiled, then said, "I'll tell my son to come up."

A few minutes later, a guy about our age came up the stairs carrying a glass decanter of red wine in his left hand and a hand-rolled cigarette between the fingers of his right.

"I am Luis," he said. "Welcome to Mexico."

Luis set the decanter down, then the three of us walked onto the rooftop terrace and looked out over the gigantic city. Luis lit the joint, and as we passed it around, we watched a thunderstorm sweep over the Valley of Mexico.

When hailstones began to clatter off the stone parapet, we retreated to the penthouse shack, and Luis demonstrated how to drink from the *porron*. The Spanish wine pitcher projects a narrow stream of wine, arcing through the air and down the drinker's throat. It's like drinking from a wineskin.

An experienced user can hold the *porron* at arm's length and swallow many times without spilling a drop. It took Dennis and me a few tries to get it right, but we finally did, and after splatters and laughter, we finished the jug. This was the first time I'd sipped Mexican wine—tasting of desert sunlight in a very good way.

Every Mexican person I'd met had been friendly and helpful, except for the Tijuana border guard. People I met hitchhiking in the States were generally friendly, too, but the police and courts seemed to be angry at young people with long hair or dark skin. I knew I could get a haircut and wear khaki pants to take off some of the pressure, but that wouldn't work for black folks. These long-simmering culture wars have grown ever more intense, up to the present day.

Luis took the decanter back to his family's quarters, and Dennis and I went down four flights of stairs to the street. We were high, a bit drunk, and hungry. Dennis pulled up the hood of his army field coat, and I buttoned up my Levi's jacket. The storm had passed and the temperature had fallen.

The pavement glistened wetly from the hailstones melting against curbs and thresholds. In the middle of the next block, a small figure sat huddled on a stool. As we approached, we saw that it was an old woman wrapped in a red blanket, a wool scarf on her head.

"*Sopes, sopes, sopes calientes,*" she called.

Two dented steel buckets sat on the sidewalk beside her, one with glowing coals inside and a blackened *plancha* wired above. The *sopes* sizzled on the griddle, small tortillas with a raised rim to hold in the shredded meat and minced chilis. We paid a few centavos and ate several as fast as our hostess could crank them out. *Delicioso* was not a strong enough word for this meal, served from a tiny sidewalk kitchen on a chilly night.

During the weeks in Mexico City, Dennis and I spent some time together, but more often spent days apart, each exploring the fantastic megalopolis on foot.

While I was admiring a marble sculpture in the National Museum of Art, I noticed a young woman studying the artwork from another angle.

"*¿Hermosa, si?*" I asked.

She looked at me and nodded. "*Si,*" she answered. "*¿Habla usted Inglés?*"

"*Si,* I mean yes," I said. Busted, I thought.

"Do you like this sculpture?" she asked, brown eyes looking directly at me.

"I like it, but it's very sad."

The marble in question depicted a nude woman lying prone on rocky ground, bound with heavy chains and trying to rise. It was labelled *Malgré Tout,* which is French for *Nevertheless.*

"But see, she is defiant. She is looking upwards. She will get up, again and again," said the dark-haired girl. "She is Mexico. . ."

Warming to her subject, the art lover continued, "When Contreras was carving this, he lost his right arm. It was cancer... Nevertheless, he learned to sculpt with his left hand only, and he finished the work."

"Thanks," I said. "My name is John."

She smiled. "My name is Maribel." She put her arm over a younger girl beside her. "This is my sister Mia."

We fell into conversation as we walked through the museum. She spoke fine English, with a lovely Spanish accent, and was an art major at the university. By the time we left, Maribel had agreed to meet me the next day at the National Museum of Anthropology, in Chapultepec Park.

I was a few minutes late as I walked into the park the next morning. I could see Maribel and a girlfriend standing beside the glass doors of the museum entryway. They idly swung their purses as they talked. When Maribel saw me she waved.

"This is my friend Nadia. She wants to see the museum too," she said, as I came up to them.

I nodded to Nadia and said, "*Buenos*."

"*Buenos*," returned Nadia, and we walked inside. I paid a low student rate, after showing my Merritt College ID card, but Maribel and Nadia got in free since they were Mexican nationals.

As we toured the monumental galleries, Maribel explained the progression of the Olmec, Mayan, Toltec, and Aztec cultures, as preserved in the calendar stones and extravagant sculptures arranged about us. Nadia spoke no English but occasionally asked Maribel a question in Spanish. I got the feeling Nadia was there more as a chaperone than anything else.

After we had walked the whole museum, we went outside and into the afternoon heat. I spied a brightly painted *helados* stand in the shade of a tree across the street. Stacks of cones in brilliant colors—green, blue, pink, and yellow—were arranged around the ice chest.

"*¿Quieres un helado?*" I asked. I had little money but I could afford three ice cream cones.

Maribel chose strawberry, Nadia wanted chocolate, and I had vanilla. Maribel wrote her address in my sketchbook and asked me to write after I returned to the States. I couldn't give her my address, because I didn't have one.

I felt pretty good about getting a date with a smart and pretty Mexican girl. There didn't seem to be much electricity between us, but just being around a girl of my age was sweet after a year of no female companionship.

I bought some masonite panels and oil paints. I made some paintings. I couldn't carry them hitchhiking. I bundled them up and took a bus to Benito Juárez International Airport. I spotted a young, hip-looking Anglo couple and persuaded them to check the bundle with their luggage on their flight to San Francisco. I sent a Western Union telegram to Arthur, back in California, and he consented to pick up and store the artwork. Such chutz-pah I had in those days!

Dennis and I bought bus tickets and rode over the shoulder of the massive snow-capped volcano, Orizaba, and down through the banana plantations and jungle forests to Puebla.

It was market day when we got to town. The sidewalks were covered with blankets of produce, handicrafts, and bloody animal parts. Brightly-clad Indian ladies sat by their wares.

The next day we hitched a ride in the cab of a semi-trailer truck. We ended up in a small village, on the lagoons just south of Veracruz, where the milkman rides a horse and delivers ladles of milk, pouring it into the customers upheld pitchers.

After more than two months together, I think Dennis and I were starting to get on each other's nerves. Dennis wanted to continue on to Guatemala City. I couldn't take the suffocating heat, and so I decided to return to the States.

It was 2,500 miles back to San Francisco. I hitchhiked alone now. I slept in ditches beside the highway, rolled in a serape. I ate whenever a driver felt sorry for me and bought me a meal. Although destitute, I felt a sense of freedom traveling through the deep jungles and vast deserts. The flip side of this freedom was loneliness.

I missed having someone to travel with. I knew that Guatemala in July would be more than I could stand, and I was eager to get back to the States, but where was home, exactly? I knew that I didn't fit back in Arkansas, and I knew that my parents' Baptist mission in Hong Kong would be unbearable. I had seen vagrants sleeping on the sidewalk in the *Zocalo* in Mexico City, subsisting on discarded cabbage leaves and fruit from the market. I figured I would probably end up like that. I didn't want to, but I doubted that the *vagabundos* did either.

———

In a few days I reached Obregon, at the edge of the Sonoran Desert, where temperatures can reach 120° during the day. Very few cars or trucks try to cross the desert in the daytime. Hitchhiking at night is no good; drivers won't stop for you.

I spent most of my remaining pesos on a bus ticket through Hermosillo to Nogales, Sonora, just below the U.S. border. Sitting in the station waiting for the night bus to Nogales, I was befriended by some college boys who noticed my French mountaineering rucksack and wanted to talk about climbing. I checked the pack with the ticket clerk, and the boys showed me around town.

Back at the station with a few minutes to spare, I handed the clerk my receipt. He claimed he couldn't find the key to the locker. The bus to Nogales was idling just outside. While the feckless clerk and his assistant searched frantically, I pulled the hinge pins from the locker door with my jackknife, retrieved my luggage, and boarded the waiting bus, cheered on by my new friends.

The bus wasn't crowded, and I got a double seat to myself. I fell asleep as the bus rattled through the desert darkness. Sometime during the night, a man sat down next to me, and I scooted over to give him some room. I was awakened again as he started caressing my shirt, and then my Levi's. I slammed an elbow into his ribs, and turned away.

Before I could fall asleep again, he was back at it. This time I stood up, grabbed his shoulders, and propelled him into the aisle. He resisted and attempted to return to the seat. I threw a right cross, hit him hard in the jaw, and he retreated, with his hands over his face, and sat down. None of the other passengers seemed to notice the incident.

At the next station, Hermosillo, some passengers got off and the driver worked his way aft, checking the tickets of remaining passengers. Suddenly a young man with longish hair grabbed a small duffel, brushed past the driver, and hurried down the aisle and off the bus. In the floodlights of the transit yard, I saw that he wore a *caballero* shirt with magic mushrooms and *mota* leaves embroidered on the yoke.

It was early morning when the bus rolled into Nogales. I claimed my pack from the bus's luggage hold. I walked a few blocks north to the international border. I didn't relish dealing with the border guards, even with my U.S. passport in my pocket. I hadn't bathed in a couple of weeks, and my clothes were tattered and stained.

I realized that the Customs agent might simply say, "No hippie in the States," and refuse to let me pass—or worse, arrest me for something, like a smidgen of pot he could plant in my pack. At this point I didn't trust anyone in uniform for anything. I could have waited until dark, hiked around the Port of Entry, and crossed the line out in the desert, but I only had a quart canteen, and dying of thirst had no appeal. I hoisted my rucksack and walked toward the chain-link fence.

The guard at the turnstile glanced at my passport, then at my clothes encrusted with months of sand and road dirt.

He escorted me into a fluorescent-lit, windowless room with a stainless steel table running the length. He ordered me to take everything out of my pack and spread it on the table. As he left, I heard him lock the door.

I complied, but it was over an hour before he returned wearing rubber gloves. He began to paw through my possessions with expressions of disgust.

He pulled my white gas stove from its sooty canvas bag. He wrinkled his nose and stuck out his tongue.

"How can you people live like this?" he asked.

"Skill and daring," I answered. He snorted, perhaps in disgust, perhaps in amusement.

He thought he'd found something when he came across a pop-top pill bottle half-full of a white powder. A rubber band held my toothbrush along the side.

"What's this?" he asked.

"Baking soda," I said. "I use it to brush my teeth."

Giving me a dubious look he pulled off the top, licked the end of his pinkie, touched it to the baking soda, and to his tongue again.

"Okay," he said. "You can go."

Down and Out in San Francisco

AFTER I CROSSED THE BORDER, I caught a ride with a very earnest Baptist pastor. He tried to give me some money as he let me off, just outside of Tucson, Arizona. I refused his offer. After all, I still had five dollars in my wallet. I must have looked gaunt and hungry to his kind, Christian eyes.

He really didn't look like a Bible-pounding evangelist. He was wearing a sport shirt instead of a sweat-soaked suit and spoke softly instead of shouting. After he dropped me off at the highway, I realized I had just committed a deadly sin: pride. I should have taken the money and thanked him. He was just a small-town pastor who wanted to help a kid that looked like he needed a meal.

I hiked for an hour or so before I found a dry ditch along a retaining wall above the interstate. The sun was going down, the golden light casting cactus shadows across the desert. I unrolled my blankets and stretched out, listening to the rumbling of my empty belly. The American border guard had confiscated my half-empty box of instant refried beans, along with a few stale tortillas.

"Regulations," he said.

The next morning I drank half my canteen of water for breakfast, then used the rest to wash my face, hands, and brush my teeth. I packed up and hiked another mile or two, until I came to a Conoco station. I filled my canteen at the radiator hose next to the gas pump.

I stood in full sun beside the highway ramp, with my thumb out. The only shade was from my ranger hat. I drank all the water in my canteen, then went back to the gas station to refill it. When I started back to the shoulder of the highway, I heard a shout.

"Hey, hippie!"

I turned around and saw the station attendant standing under the big awning.

"Stand here in the shade," he said. "You'll get sunstroke out there."

"Thanks," I said.

He shrugged and went back into his office.

Late in the afternoon, a new white Cadillac sedan pulled up to the pump. While the pump jockey filled the tank, the driver got out and approached me. She was tall, middle-aged, and wore boots, Levi's, and a pearl-snapped cowboy shirt. A white Stetson sat on her head, and short dark hair showed beneath the brim.

"I saw you hitching out here this morning," she said, "no luck, huh?"

"I guess not," I said.

She put her key into the trunk lock and popped the lid.

"Throw your bag in here and we'll take you to Redondo Beach. You can help keep me awake," she said. "You can sit in the back."

I laid my pack into the wide trunk, beside two overnight bags. As I sank into the soft seat cushions, a woman seated on the passenger side leaned over the seat top.

"Hi. I'm Nancy," she said.

"Pleased to meet you, I'm John."

The tall woman sat in the driver's seat, swung the heavy door shut, and said, "I'm Sally."

As the long Cadillac pulled onto the interstate, Nancy said, "There's some sandwiches and ginger ale in the ice box. Help yourself if you're hungry."

As I ate a sandwich and drank cold canned soda, Sally talked:

"Nancy and I are both drivers. We can drive most anything—tractors, even four-in-hand coaches. We just delivered a refrigerated truck from a dealer in Long Beach to a depot in Tucson. Since this car was waiting to go to Redondo Beach, we figured we'd drive home tonight and sleep in our own bed."

Darkness fell as we sped through the desert. Saguaro cacti reached for the stars along both sides of the road. Sally liked to talk, but she liked to listen, too. I told her about about my summer in Mexico, and she talked about hers and Nancy's adventures delivering cars, trucks, and boats all over the mountain west. Nancy mostly dozed.

It was well past midnight when we pulled into the driveway of a ranch-style house in Redondo Beach. Sally told me I could sleep in the guest room, and there were clean towels in the little bathroom.

I took the hint and took a short but satisfying shower before I hit the sack. I hadn't bathed or washed my clothes for a week and must have smelled pretty ripe.

The next morning, Nancy fixed bacon, eggs, and toast. Long Tall Sally gave me a lift to Highway 101. After I set my rucksack to the shoulder, I said, "Thanks, Sally."

"It was my pleasure," she said, and drove away.

I hitchhiked up the coast highway as far as Santa Cruz, where I was let out at a forest junction on a late afternoon. A hippie couple, my age or younger, already stood on the shoulder. The guy stood beside a green duffel, and the girl with blonde braids sat on an overnight bag made from bright Mexican blankets.

"We've been here for an hour," said the girl, "and so far the traffic has been slo-ow."

"Yeah, we have some friends in the Haight," said the guy, "and they said we could crash there tonight."

No cars came by in the next few minutes, and when a

Volkswagen with four people inside did appear, the driver shrugged and kept going. A few raindrops began to spot the pavement. Gray clouds hid the sky.

"It's getting dark; I'm going to pitch a tarp and get under it," I said. "You guys will have a better chance to get to San Francisco without me standing here."

The rain was spitting harder, and night was falling. The two kids looked at each other.

"Got room for two more?" the guy asked.

"Sure."

They followed me up an overgrown logging road, and we strung my orange nylon tarp above a level spot between two tree trunks. By the time we'd crawled under the ersatz roof, the rain had increased to a steady downpour.

My tent mates turned out to be two high school juniors who had run away when their parents forbade them to see each other.

I boiled my last envelope of dehydrated chicken soup on the white gas stove, and the girl produced some dried apple slices she'd stashed in her bag. It wasn't much, but it was something. The rain pelted the nylon all night, and we slept—warm enough, but a little damp.

By morning the rain had stopped, the sky was clear, and sunlight hit the tent.

————

In San Francisco the next day, I walked the sidewalks aimlessly for hours. I had five dollars in my wallet. I saw a card in the window of a fleabag hotel: Rooms $3.50. The unfriendly clerk took my money and showed me down a dim hall to a windowless room with rumpled sheets on a single bed.

"No visitors," the clerk said. "If you go out, I unlock the room when you get back. The sheets get changed every Tuesday."

I had just enough money left for a tiny can of chopped olives and a stack of saltine crackers at the liquor store on Turk Street. Back at the hotel, the surly clerk let me in, and I ate slowly in the seedy room.

I went out panhandling the next day, to raise enough spare change for another night's rent and maybe some food. When I returned to the fleabag, I paid the clerk $3.50, and he stuck the money in his box.

Instead of unlocking my room, he told me that since my payment was late, he had rented my room to someone else. I noticed my rucksack on the floor of his office.

"Take your shit and get out," he said.

Alone and dejected, I climbed up Telegraph Hill and camped in the junipers growing around the base of Coit Tower. I wandered around North Beach for days and read for hours in City Lights Books, where I received mail—mostly air letters from my parents in Hong Kong. I learned what time they threw out the wilted produce at Cala Foods on Nob Hill. Sometimes I walked to the panhandle of Golden Gate Park where The Diggers, an underground philanthropic group, would dish out stew and bread baked in old tin cans. At night I returned to my bum's nest.

I hitched to Berkeley, where Governor Reagan had put the city and campus under martial law in response to the Peoples Park riots. As I walked up Durant Avenue, I saw a shoulder-high sandbag wall set up on one corner, surrounding a .30 caliber belt-fed machine gun mounted on a heavy tripod. A few guardsmen wearing olive green utilities and helmets were standing inside the little fort, and I recognized one of them.

It was my journalism teacher from Canyon High. He now wore the oak leaf insignia of a major on his collar—and a .45 automatic pistol on his hip.

"Mr. Solito," I called, "what are you doing here?"

He looked at me across the sandbags, then looked away.

"I can't talk now. I'm on duty."

As I neared Sproul Plaza, I saw a heavy green helicopter flying over a mass of student demonstrators. As soon as I saw this, I turned around and hitched back to San Francisco. I had been teargassed before and did not want to experience it again.

I knew that the ostensible reason for the military occupation was the "People's Park" that had been set up on land requisitioned by the expanding university for new dormitories. The real reason was the growing rebellion against the doomed war with the Vietnamese.

Except for other outsiders and misfits, it seemed like nobody had the time of day for me anymore. I went days without talking to anyone. Schlepping around with my head down, I was becoming invisible to normal people.

Finally, loneliness started to get to me, and I panhandled a quarter to make a phone call. I had a number for Arthur Daniels, my old cohort, written on a page of my sketch journal. I dropped my coin into the slot, and laid my sketchbook on top of the pay phone.

When Arthur answered, he sounded delighted to hear from me.

"Hot damn!" he said. "I thought you were down in Guatemala or someplace. . . I got those paintings you sent from Mexico City."

When I told him I was camping on Telegraph Hill, he said, "Nell and I have an apartment on California Street. You're welcome to sleep on our floor until you find something better."

"Twist my arm," I said.

Stage Struck

WHEN ARTHUR OFFERED me a place to stay, I thanked him profusely.

"Come on over now," he said. "This'll be a blast!"

We hung up. I left the phone booth in a hurry and hiked up Telegraph Hill to get my stuff. As I retrieved my rucksack from its hiding place, I realized that I didn't have my sketch diary; I'd left it in the phone booth. When I returned, it was gone—three months of poems, drawings, and sculpture designs, as well as Maribel's address in Mexico City.

Arthur and Nell's apartment turned out to be right across the street from Cala Foods, where I'd been dumpster diving for shopworn groceries. Their windows overlooked the cable car tracks. I'd known Nell when she and Arthur were students at Washington High. It felt great to be around friends again.

I found three night's work on an assembly line in the Mission District and was able to contribute a little to the household.

One afternoon Arthur and I were sitting around smoking a joint and listening to KMPX, a North Beach radio station, when an announcement came on.

It seemed that volunteers were needed to finish the sets on a new play by Michael McClure, scheduled to open in a couple of weeks at Zellerbach Playhouse in Berkeley. I found a pencil too late to write down the address of the studio where the sets were being built.

McClure had read his poetry at the Six Gallery the same night that Allen Ginsberg had unleashed his *Howl* on the poetry world—an event that became a milestone of American literature. McClure had written *The Beard*, a play prosecuted for obscenity by the San Francisco District Attorney. The more I thought about it, the more I knew I had to be part of this.

I looked up McClure's address in the telephone directory and walked to the upper Haight. I found the house and went up the steps. I rang the bell, and the poet answered the door.

"Hi, Mr. McClure, my name is John Schnick and I'm an artist and I heard that you need help to finish the sets for your new play. . ." I said, then took a breath.

A hint of a smile appeared on his handsome Irish face, and he invited me in. I followed him to a sunny upstairs room.

"This is my wife, Joanna," he said.

An absolutely beautiful woman put down her book and stood up from the sofa she'd been curled upon.

"This is John," said McClure. "He wants to work on the sets for *The Charbroiled Chinchilla*."

"I'll fix some tea," said Joanna, and disappeared.

Michael told me about the trilogy of plays he'd written, and when Joanna returned with a pot of Oolong, I told them both about surviving the vampire bats of Nayarit. I learned that Joanna, also a poet, had been at the Six Gallery reading—the birth of the Beat movement—along with Ginsberg, Snyder, McClure, and Whalen.

After a phone call to the set designer, the playwright turned to me and said, "Welcome aboard."

———

Mike Lipsey, the set designer, had a studio south of Market. I walked downhill from the Haight-Ashbury and found the old, white-painted industrial building. In front, a guy with a wild Jewish afro was attempting to wrestle a large wooden crate into the open door of a freight elevator.

"Can you use some help?" I asked.

"I could at that," he replied.

Together we got the massive box onto the elevator deck by tipping the tall crate onto alternate corners and walking it over a curb.

"Thanks," he said. "I'm Mike."

"I'm John," I said. "I came to work on the Magic Theater production."

"McClure told me about you," he said. "Let's go."

Mike rolled the door closed and pushed an oversized button labelled "UP". A motor whirred, and the old elevator creaked up to a second story loft. Strewn about the wooden floor I saw unfinished fiberglass sculptures, huge stretched canvases, rolls of electrical wire, and cans of paint.

Mike was in the weeds. The sets and props for two of the *Gargoyle Cartoons* had been barely roughed out, and opening night was approaching relentlessly.

My first job was to attach dozens of porcelain light sockets to silver painted sheets of plywood with a power drill and screws. This took hours of simple, repetitive work. When the fixtures were all attached in swirly abstract scatterings, Mike showed me how to cut, strip, and attach the wires in parallel circuits, so that three groups of bulbs could be lit separately or together, at will.

Next I had to install dozens of 60-watt bulbs and test the whole effect. Before the electrical backdrop could be trucked over to Berkeley, I would remove each bulb and pack it in newsprint, only to reassemble the effect at Zellerbach Playhouse for the opening of the play.

Working in Mike's paint-spattered loft every day brought me back to life. The artists, actors, and costume designers coming in and out of the loft radiated the excitement of producing a new play, and I was hooked.

This is more like it, I thought. My vagabond days were over. *I'm making art with the big-time hip set. These are my kind of people. They talk to me and listen to me.*

The background flats for the first play, *Pansy,* called for a fairy tale scene with a meadow, a castle, and craggy mountain peaks. Mike had painted in the flowered foreground and the castle, but the mountains were pastel green lumps in the background.

"Can you paint some mountain peaks up there?" he asked.

"No problem."

I painted peaks and glaciers from memories of my climbs in the Sierra.

The next day, McClure showed up at the loft—along with John Lion, the long-haired and bearded director of the plays.

"This is more like it," said the playwright, when he saw my efforts. "Now we're getting somewhere."

Part of the *Pansy* set called for a big hollow log. We built a framework out of lathing and steam-curved plywood. Another volunteer, Leon, had a panel truck. He and I drove across the Golden Gate Bridge to a stand of redwoods, where we stole large, furry slabs of bark from a recently fallen tree. Back at Mike's loft, we covered the form with the ragged bark, and *presto*—the log looked real, at least from ten feet away.

The push was on, and the small crew began working into the wee hours. Mike took me home at night. I slept on a pallet on the living room floor and woke to a communal household with naked children and Mike's wife, also nude, coming down the stairs.

As opening night approached, we loaded the sets into Leon's van and a U-Haul truck. I rode across the Bay Bridge in the back of the van, careful to keep the cargo from shifting and marring our handiwork.

The manager of Zellerbach Playhouse met us on the loading dock, and we carried the flats and props into the backstage area. This is where we would be working for the next week. The theater had opened the year before, and the sight lines, raked seating, acoustics, and lighting were state of the art. There was not a bad seat in the house.

Actors, actresses, costume makers and stagehands worked side by side, in a final push to stage the play. This was *Magic Theater, for Madmen Only*. John Lion, the founder of Magic Theater, had obviously been a big fan of Hermann Hesse, and his novel *Steppenwolf.*

During rehearsals, I got to see the three plays for the first time—performed in street clothes, then in dress rehearsal, with props, lighting, costumes, and lights.

Pansy, the first play of the triptych, featured two nubile fairies, naked except for gossamer wings, dancing about in a fairy tale meadow. They delicately sniffed each other's behinds and said, "Mmm. . ."—only to be frightened by an irate bear.

The second play, *Meatball*, concerned two clueless trippers. Their costumes were made from spherical frames of hula hoops covered with old fur coats. Their bearded faces, arms, and legs protruded from the giant fur balls. They wore white tights and leotards, with white gloves and Chuck Taylor sneakers.

The scene opened with the discovery of an oversized meatball, which worries the two furballs until they finally conclude: "We are players in the greatest drama ever performed!"

The action took place against the banks of lightbulbs that I had wired. Ted, the stage manager for Magic Theater, showed me how to test the circuits and follow the hundreds of lighting cues in the script.

The third play was *Spider Rabbit*. McClure had saved the best for last. The title character, played by an extremely tall black actor, wore a costume that, from the front, was a fuzzy pink bunny. When he turned around, he became a hulking black spider.

"Hi! I'm Spider Rabbit," he said, at the beginning, with the demeanor of a children's TV host. Before the curtain fell, Spider Rabbit had electrocuted himself, sawed the skull off a hapless screaming captive, then eaten the pink brains with a spoon.

It sounds gruesome, and it was. It was also hilarious.

On opening night, it seemed impossible that the play would come off. Each rehearsal had been halted several times, and we hadn't had a clean run-through yet. As Ted and I were checking the circuits for the lighting effects, someone came into the high-tech control booth.

"Everyone's dropping tonight; have some," he said, holding out an opened palm with two large capsules filled with brown powder.

"What is it?" I asked.

"Mescaline," he replied.

Ted and I each took a cap and swallowed it with cold coffee.

Against all odds, the premiere of *The Charbroiled Chinchilla* came off without a hitch. The audience of five hundred laughed and gasped throughout the plays. The hallucinogenic writing, the surrealistic staging, and the tripping actors and stagehands had managed to produce something dazzling and wonderful. Synergy.

The successful opening at the playhouse meant the play would have a fall run at the Mandrake, a bar near the foot of University Avenue in Berkeley. We would have to reduce the sets and props to cabaret size. I stopped crashing at Arthur and Nell's San Francisco apartment and started housesitting, along with Ted, the stage manager, at John Lion's flat in Berkeley. The director was in New York, visiting his wife, working in "an Equity gig".

One day as we worked on the carpentry and painting, McClure brought a friend by the Mandrake. It was Jim Morrison, the songwriter and singer for The Doors. Several female members of the acting ensemble appeared when they heard he was in the house, and the most controversial rock star of the Sixties sat on the edge of the stage and talked with us.

I was smoking one of those black, twisted Italian cigars at the time, so I offered one to Jim.

"Man, I love these things," he said, lighting up.

As he held court with his admirers, I was struck that up close he resembled a gone-to-seed high school quarterback. This dissipated jock was a rock-and-roll Rimbaud, however.

When I mentioned that we were both Navy brats, he snorted dismissively and let me know that he had no use for the U.S.

Navy. It was years later when I realized that Admiral Morrison, who had presided over the phony Gulf of Tonkin incident, was his father.

When Jim saw me the next week, he sidled up to me and asked, "So you have any more of those Guinea Stinkers?"

One night while the play was running, I was changing the sets between acts. In the front row of the house sat Herb Caen, the journalist who had coined two lasting words: *beatnik* and *hippie*.

McClure dropped by the Mandrake another night. Jack Kerouac had just died of alcoholism, and I brought up the sad event.

The poet smiled and said, "I dreamed about Jack the other night." He paused. "He was happy."

Hard-Lovin' Loser

LIVING AT JOHN LION'S HOUSE didn't work out too well. He and his wife owned two fluffy cats who went in and out as they pleased, and Ted and I had to feed them. The run of the play at the Mandrake had come to an end, so I no longer got a share of the door—usually a few dollars after each show. It had been an exciting few weeks.

One night I came down with an intense asthma attack—even worse than the one on the night that Alice had broken up with me. I turned blue and sank to the kitchen floor. Ted called 911, and a policeman showed up. In the Emergency Room of Herrick Hospital, I was given an injection. As soon as I caught my breath, I was sent on my way.

I picked up my rucksack at the Lions' House of Cats, then hitchhiked back to San Francisco to Arthur and Nell's place on Nob Hill. When I arrived, I found five other crashers on the living room floor. Charles, Crystal, Alvin, Scott, and Dorothy were Nell's friends from her days at Reed College in Portland.

The Reedies were on winter break from the college, planning on driving across the country and visiting their families back East for Christmas. Scott and Dorothy Wilkins were fraternal twins, blond, and blue-eyed. Charles owned the VW microbus, and Crystal, a dark-haired dance major, seemed to be his girlfriend. Alvin, on his BMW motorcycle, was traveling in convoy.

Each of these kids were products of famous East Coast boarding schools: Andover, Exeter, The Hill, and so on. Although I seemingly had little in common with the preppies, we all got along great. Camping on the floor at night was an intellectual slumber party. They seemed fascinated that I had dropped out, I admired them because they had not.

Charles, Scott, and Dorothy were alpinists, trained by Outward Bound, and had made ascents on the big glaciated peaks of the Northwest. I hung on their stories of high altitude survival, and everyone wanted to hear about vagabonding in Mexico.

Besides climbing, Dorothy danced and painted. She and I both loved Abstract Expressionist painting. She was crazy about Clyfford Still. I was inspired by the action painting of Franz Kline, and we both thought Helen Frankenthaler was a genius. Dorothy unrolled her sleeping bag beside mine that night.

The next day, when the van left with its motorcycle escort, I was aboard. Arthur and Nell were likely relieved to have their apartment to themselves again, and not filled with a half-dozen pot-smoking hippies.

When our expedition got to Southern California, the papers on the newsstand were full of the Tate-LaBianca killings. Scary pictures of Charles Manson and his hippie cohorts ran above the headlines. I was so glad I wasn't hitchhiking.

None of us had any money to speak of. Gas was expensive, and there was little left over for food. Crystal had brought a ten pound sack of brown rice, so we weren't going to starve. As the sun went down, we pulled up behind a Piggly Wiggly market in Arizona.

Scott and I lifted the lid of the dumpster and gleaned some wrinkled carrots, a wilted cabbage, and a sprouted onion or two. Dorothy brushed her blonde hair, stuck her purse under an elbow, and walked through the automatic glass doors into the store.

She emerged a few minutes later and climbed proudly into the van, with a small bottle of olive oil she had purchased, as well as two cello-wrapped New York steaks tucked into the waistband of her skirt, hidden by her peasant blouse.

Back on the road, we rolled east. As darkness fell, a full moon rose. The flickering six-volt headlamps of the Volkswagen seemed feckless, and Charles turned them off. Sandy ground stretched silver in the moonlight.

After a few more miles, we parked off the highway, on a sketchy dirt road. Alvin stood his bike alongside, and Scott and I fired up our little white gas stoves. As soon as a pot of rice was boiling, I chopped up the onions, steaks, and carrots with my hunting knife, then poured some olive oil into the other pot. I browned the beef, sautéed the vegetables, then covered them with torn cabbage leaves. Turning down the flame, I let it simmer until the rice was done.

Crystal came up with a bottle of soy sauce, and six hippies ate like kings and queens, albeit sitting cross-legged on the sand in the desert.

After our supper, we all walked out into the desert among the fifty-foot Saguaro cacti that stood around us in every direction. Dorothy and I came up to an enormous green trunk. When we looked up along the furrowed flanks of the ancient succulent, we could see its icepick spines silhouetted against the blackness of space and millions of stars. We heard a desert breeze sighing through the needles.

———

The overloaded microbus couldn't make more than twenty-five or thirty miles per hour most of the time, but got up to forty or forty-five on dead-flat sections. Alvin's BMW would keep even with the driver's window for miles. Charles and Crystal in the front seat could converse with him and share slices of the bruised apples we had liberated from the dumpster. It would be a long drive to North Carolina at this rate, but we were all having fun.

Somewhere outside of Las Cruces, the van began to slow, and the steering pulled to the right. We kept slowing, and crept into a Texaco station a little after dark. The uniformed attendant listened to our plight and invited Charles to park in the garage.

After adjusting the support cleats under the vehicle, the man with the red star on his cap hoisted the van and tried to spin the right front tire—it stopped halfway through a revolution. It had to be forced around.

"You have a bad wheel bearing," he said, flipping a hydraulic control. "Mechanic won't be here 'til morning." The van settled back to the floor.

"Can we leave leave it here overnight?" asked Charles.

The attendant shrugged and said, "Sure," as he went out to fuel another customer at the pump.

Charles and Crystal pulled their sleeping bag from the van and went out to sleep behind the station, beyond a clump of greasewood. Scott pulled his mummy bag from beneath the backseat bunk.

"I want to sleep in the van tonight," said Dorothy, then looked over at me.

"Me too," I said.

Scott glanced at his sister, winked at me, then nodded. Dorothy and I climbed into the camper and rolled the side door shut. Scott smiled and pulled a hydraulic control lever. The van rose up, close to the rafters, then he left. Dorothy and I were alone in the rear bunk, a quilt pulled over us.

———

Early the next morning, the mechanic turned on the lights in the garage and was surprised to see two sleepy hippies peering out the window of the overhead microbus. He lowered the rack and we climbed out. It turned out that the bearing was shot, and installing a new one would cost some bucks that we didn't have. The mechanic suggested that we visit the blood bank a mile away. All six of us walked to the storefront clinic. We signed some forms and reclined on paper-covered couches.

A phlebotomist tapped our veins and extracted a pint of plasma apiece. They gave us each a cookie, a glass of orange juice, and a twenty-dollar bill. Everyone trooped back to to the Texaco station, and a new wheel bearing was quickly installed.

We drove into Texas and turned south towards Austin, where Scott and Dorothy's father lived. It was Wednesday—the day that Howard Johnson's advertised *"All you can eat Fish Fry $3.99"* on the lit-up signs. We pulled into the parking lot of the orange and white roadside restaurant.

Dorothy sat on a stool at the counter, and the rest of us sat to either side. Dorothy ordered the seafood dinner—the rest of us: coffee. The attractive middle-aged waitress didn't bat an eye and served us what we ordered. Embroidered on her uniform, in script, was the name "Ruby".

Dorothy took a bite, then handed out fried fish, clams, and fried potatoes wrapped in paper napkins below the counter.

When Ruby returned to top off our coffees, she replaced the seafood platter. Our benefactress repeatedly replaced Dorothy's dinner until all six of us were full of fried food and coffee.

"Well, honey, I guess that's all you can eat," Ruby said as she handed Dorothy the small check.

———

The new bearing sped the van along, and the next day we were rolling down a gravel driveway just ahead of Alvin's BMW. A two-story house with turrets and dormers stood in the dappled shade of ancient oaks. Dorothy and Scott's father, a classics professor, lived here with his second wife, April.

Dorothy was especially eager to see her half-sister, Patty, a three-year-old upon whom she doted. April appeared on the veranda holding little Patty's hand, and Dorothy ran across the lawn and scooped up the little blonde angel. April greeted everyone warmly then set about assigning sleeping quarters.

Dorothy would be sleeping in the nursery with Patty. Scott and Alvin could bunk in her son Tommy's room, and I could have a pallet on the floor of the upstairs library. Crystal and Charles would sleep in the van parked in the yard.

April cooked *Spaghetti ai Fungi* for dinner, also a romaine salad with artichokes, prosciutto, and a light garlic dressing. Everyone except little Patty drank a glass of red wine, and the room rang with happy voices and laughter. This was not the Hardshell Baptist Texas I knew from my childhood. I liked this one better.

Late that night I was sitting on my pallet, a desk lamp lighting my sketchbook as I planned a sculpture. I heard the library door open briefly, then close. Dorothy sank down beside me, brushed my cheek with her lips and slipped into my sleeping bag. I turned off the desk lamp.

When I awoke, she'd gone, leaving a warm trace of her sweet scent on the pillow.

———————

The following morning, after breakfast, stepbrother Tommy took me aside.

"Scott and Dorothy told me you were a painter," he said. "You guys will be here a week; would you like to paint something?"

"You bet!" I answered.

Tommy set me up in a garage below the main house. He showed me a box with studio tubes of oil paint, a stoneware jar of brushes, and a big can of gesso.

"Mom used to paint years ago, but now she is into cooking," he said. "She said you should use this stuff before it dries up."

There was also a fresh sheet of plywood, an electric saber saw, and stacks of fresh sandpaper.

I worked all day, cutting shapes with the saw, sanding, priming, and gluing. In the afternoon I left the glue and gesso to dry, walked through the yard, and back to the house. After washing off the sweat and sawdust with a shower, I sat with Dorothy and Patty watching a new television program, *Sesame Street*. Neither Dorothy nor I had ever heard of the show, but Patty was already a big fan.

That evening April cooked another impossibly delicious dinner. While the rest of the crew did the dishes, Doctor Wilkins summoned Scott and me into the library. He offered us each an Havana cigar, poured a finger of Cognac in each of three small snifters, and we sat across from the big console stereo.

We lit our cigars, and Scott spoke up.

"You know, Dad, how you always said that rock music was drivel," said Scott. "I've brought something that might just change your mind."

"I'm all ears, son," said the professor, taking a sip of his brandy. "Fire away."

Scott went to the stereo and picked up an album from atop the console. He extracted the disc, placed it on the spindle, and handed the cover to his father. The album was *Live Dead*, just released by The Grateful Dead. The first song on the album was *St. Stephen*.

By the time the delicate melody, medievalist lyrics, and soaring psychedelic coda was over, the professor was convinced, and Scott was vindicated. This was like the time that Arthur's dad had introduced me to Miles Davis' music, but in reverse.

I realized that I was having the time of my life: brandy, cigars, and later, blonde Dorothy.

—————

On the last full day of the visit, the Reedies, Tommy, and I all crammed into the microbus and drove to the shore of a river that fed Lake Travis. On the way, Charles passed out some tablets, and we each dropped acid.

We sat on the bank under a cottonwood, talking in subdued voices, waiting for things to go all melty. Soon the conversations became animated, and laughter pealed out from the little glade. Gradually things got quieter, as people became more contemplative. We wandered off to stare at cattails growing out of the water, or the tracery of tree branches silhouetted against a Texas winter sky.

After a sunny day of kicks and grins, the red sun dipped below the cottonwoods on the other shore, and we drove back to the Wilkins' house. Charles stuck an eight-track cartridge into his car stereo. *Hard-Loving Loser* by Richard and Mimi Fariña came on—a hard rock tune, an exception for the folk duo.

Scott and Dorothy's folks didn't seem to notice anything amiss as we sat down to another gourmet dinner: just a group of sunburned teenagers back from a day on the river. Dorothy washed the dishes, I dried them, and we mulled over our day.

She'd had a crying spell earlier, and Crystal had gone on a laughing jag, while we were peaking on the LSD. Intense emotion was usually expected on an acid trip. As we finished our chores, I tried to hug her, but she pulled away. I noticed tears welling in her blue eyes.

"I need to spend the whole night with Patty," she said quietly. "After tomorrow I won't see her for another year." I told her that I understood. She returned the hug, and went upstairs to put her little sister to bed.

Later that night, the old house was dark and quiet. I was working on a poem in my sketchbook. Feeling a draft, I looked up, and Crystal glided into the library on her bare dancer's feet.

He's got them waitin' down the stairs just to sample his affairs
And they call him a spoonful of fun. . .

The Ice Storm

LIKE DOROTHY, Crystal stole away as I slept. I awoke alone.

The van and the motorcycle left in the morning. Dorothy bid little Patty a tearful goodbye, and I tied my finished bas-relief to the roof rack, wrapped in an old tarp. Crystal sat in the front seat between Charles and Scott, and Dorothy sat beside me in the back. I had no idea if Charles or Scott knew about the game of musical beds that had gone on the last three nights. Perhaps I was Dorothy's and Crystal's dirty little secret. It was the Sixties, and we were making it up as we went along.

We drove straight through, crossing east Texas and then Louisiana and Mississippi. Somewhere in Alabama, deep into the night, we pulled over to sleep. Winter was setting in, and the night was cold.

We awoke on a deserted stretch of road. Our sleeping bags were covered with frost, as was the grass along the shoulder where we had slept. Charles and Crystal emerged from the van.

"It's colder than a well digger's ass out here," Charles announced. "Let's get going."

The rest of us climbed out of our sleeping bags into the chilly morning air. We loaded our gear into the van and climbed aboard.

Alvin mounted his bike and kicked the starter.

Charles turned the key of the Volkswagen. The starter clanked and whirred, but the engine didn't turn over.

"It's cold," said Charles.

"No shit," said Scott.

Alvin shut down his motorcycle and walked over to the van.

"Now what?" said Dorothy.

"I guess we have to wait 'til the sun warms the engine compartment," said Charles.

"That could be hours," moaned Crystal, huddled on the passenger side, a Mexican blanket wrapped around her.

"Or days," said Scott glumly.

"I have an idea," I said.

All eyes were on me.

"Let's build a fire out of sticks behind the van," I said. "When the flames die down, we can rake out the coals, and push the rig back until the engine compartment is over the heat."

Everyone looked at Charles, who shrugged.

"Why not?" he said.

I broke dead wood from the trunks of some trees, tore sheets of newsprint into wide strips, and crumpled them into a loose pile behind the van. I piled the "squaw wood" over that and held a lighted match to the halftone faces of Charles Manson and Tex Watson, from the front page of the Bakersfield newspaper we'd bought back in California.

As the dry pine caught fire, everyone squatted around the flames to catch some heat.

"I wish we had some weed," said Alvin.

We rolled the van back until the engine was over the small scatter of coals.

My harebrained scheme actually worked. When the engine had been above the glowing coals for a bit, Charles climbed back into the driver's seat, then turned the key. The motor coughed, backfired, and then ran smoothly. Charles pulled the van forward. Scott and I kicked frosted dirt over the dying coals, and we were off.

I spent Christmas in Chapel Hill with Dorothy, her sister, and her mother. Her brother, Scott, had continued on to Philadelphia with the van to see a girl, or buy a car, or something.

Dorothy's mom, Elenor, had divorced Dr. Wilkins a few years back; now she lived in Chapel Hill with Scott and Dorothy's 12-year-old sister, Clara. This was the first time I had ever met a broken family. I had heard the word "divorce" rarely growing up—usually whispered, like "adultery" or "whiskey".

Elenor and Clara were more than cordial with me, the stray that Dorothy had brought home. Elenor let me use her typewriter to write a short story. I decided to take it to New York and submit it to Grove Press.

After I delivered my manuscript, I planned on visiting the 1969 Whitney Annual and perhaps adding some painting of my own. I had visions of being recognized as a new artistic genius and breaking into the big time art world. I had stolen a pint of Chinese Red enamel and a two-inch wide brush from Elenor's shed.

Christmas night, an ice storm swept up the Eastern Seaboard. Dorothy and I walked into an orchard behind Elenor's house. Every tree, twig, and fencepost glittered as clouds swept across the face of a winter moon.

I left the next day. Dorothy had realized that I might not be Prince Charming after all. Our last try at lovemaking was less than ideal. It was time for me to go.

Before I left, Dorothy baked a pile of "Minnesota Flapjacks", a recipe learned in Outward Bound. She stirred a pound of rolled oats, a stick of butter, and a cup of sugar in a saucepan over medium heat. A little salt was stirred in, and the mix was spread over a greased cookie sheet with the back of a buttered spoon.

After baking, she pulled the tray from the oven and cut it into rectangles, before it hardened. After it cooled, she covered each bar in waxed paper and wrapped the stack with brown paper and string.

"Survival rations," she said as she handed me the parcel. "Good luck."

She drove me to the highway in her mother's Volvo sedan and let me off at an on ramp, along with my rucksack. I waited, standing on the frozen ground, with my thumb out. My first ride took me to to Highway 95, and the next let me off at a cloverleaf somewhere in Pennsylvania.

Around here, the fields were covered with white, the roads streaked with ice and blowing snow. Darkness fell, and I climbed up an embankment to a ledge just below the overpass. I stashed my rucksack and crabbed over to some ornamental junipers growing on the slope. I snapped off a dozen or so green branches, brittle from the cold, and laid them on the flat concrete. I unrolled my army surplus feather-filled mummy bag and crawled in, wearing every stitch of clothing that I owned.

I shivered, my teeth chattered, and I wolfed down two or three of Dorothy's granola bars. After swallowing half the water in my canteen, I stashed it at the bottom of the mummy bag, with my boots, to keep them from freezing during the night.

A grinding roar sounded a few feet overhead, as snowplow blades dragged across the frozen concrete roadway. The heavy iron blades made a monstrous screeching roar, and particles of snow and ice sifted down on me. After too long, my shivering subsided just enough to fall into a fitful sleep. When the shivering returned, I awoke to gray daylight.

My lips were chapped and cracked, I had a raging thirst, and I had to pee in the worst way. I wiggled around in the tight mummy bag until I could grab the canteen, then I sat up and unscrewed the cap. The water in the canteen was frozen solid.

I managed to jam my feet into my stiff leather boots and stood up to pee. The golden stream froze as it hit the concrete.

I realized I had to get out of there. I managed to roll up my ice-crusted sleeping bag and jam it into the rucksack. After skidding down the slope and stumbling through snow beside the highway for a few yards, I was away from the underpass, on the shoulder of the road. No cars had passed since I had awakened.

Everything around me was coated with crusty white: the road, the fields, the overpass, and the one vehicle I saw approaching. I stuck out my gloved thumb. As the 18-wheeler passed, I heard a popping sound like a machine gun as the driver bled off engine compression. The big rig shuddered to a stop, a hundred feet beyond me.

I ran along a shoulder littered with head-sized chunks of ice from the snowplows. I grabbed a handrail above the steel steps to the cab. Everything was crusted with white, like a Coast Guard cutter returning from iceberg patrol. The passenger side door popped open above me, and I scrambled up and into the cab.

The driver, a rawboned man of about forty, put the Freightliner into gear as soon as I slammed the hatch behind me.

"Throw your bindle in the bunk," said the driver. I complied, shoving my pack into the shelf behind, atop a canvas sleeping bag.

"Thanks," I said, "you saved my life."

"No shit," he replied.

As soon as he'd shifted gears up to cruising speed, he reached under his seat and pulled out a fifth of Smirnoff vodka.

He twisted off the cap, poured a generous slug down his throat, and extended his arm towards me.

"No thanks," I said.

I thawed out in front of the blazing cab heater. He let me off at a gas station, and I went in and filled my canteen in the restroom. I had hopes that my story would be published by Grove press, and that I might get some recognition as an artist for my planned crashing of the Whitney Museum annual show. As a nineteen-year old, I had no real idea of how things worked in art or literature, but I had vivid fantasies of success.

Since my family left the States, I had seen a side of life invisible to their middle-class eyes, and I wanted to see and do everything. Although life on the road had some unpleasant moments, there were also moments of joy and wonder. I wanted more.

––––

After several short rides and some long, cold waits, I stood beside the Jersey turnpike. A moving van slowed and stopped; I climbed into the cab.

"Where ya headed?" asked the driver.

"Manhattan."

"I have a furniture delivery on the West side," he said. "Can you help me unload the stuff?"

"You bet," I answered, warming my hands at a heater vent.

After rolling north for a few miles on the turnpike, the van pulled over at a Howard Johnson's.

"I need a cup of coffee," said the drayman, "I'll buy you one."

We sat at the counter and the driver ordered. After I took a couple of sips, the driver spoke up.

"You're drinking it black?" he asked.

"I always drink it this way," I said.

"That's stupid," he said. "It's got no food value like that."

I realized he was right. I loaded my cup with cream and sugar.

We arrived at the right address in Manhattan, and a lady dressed in black met us at the front door. We had to carry a dark wood dining suite up two flights of stairs. The table was a two-man job, as was the bulky sideboard, and there were eight dining chairs as well. We kept every piece wrapped in moving quilts until we had them in the lady's dining room, then we removed the belts and padding.

After the woman had carefully inspected the pieces for damage, she signed a paper and handed each of us a five-dollar bill. Back on the street, the driver unlocked the cab of the truck, handed me my pack, and said, "Good luck, kid."

I hoisted my pack and took out my Manhattan street map. Grove Press was in Greenwich Village, miles from here. I set out. On the way I ducked into some bars, cabarets, and stage doors of theaters and inquired about work as a stagehand or janitor. I was met by bored rebuffs or downright hostility.

As I walked through Times Square, the news ticker showed the latest headlines, the time, and temperature: 4:32 PM and -6° F.

I got to Bleecker Street, followed it south to Grove, climbed the stoop, and went into the warm office of *Evergreen Magazine*, the Grove Press periodical, just before closing time. The smartly dressed receptionist gave me a forced smile, and told me she would give my envelope to the Literary Editor. I must have looked awful, with my clothes smudged and frozen.

Back on the street, I started tramping the streets of the Village looking for a sheltered spot to sleep. It was too cold to snow. The wind whipped old snow into a ground blizzard, the particles of ice stinging my face as I searched fruitlessly for a spot out of the wind.

I suddenly remembered the long construction shed alongside the Grove Press building where I'd dropped off my manuscript earlier. I turned around and walked south on Bleecker.

The shed had a tin roof, plywood walls, and ran along the side of the building, covering the sidewalk. A chain link fence with a locked gate blocked entry. There was a gap in the fence, however, beside the steps to the office door. I squeezed through the opening and pulled my rucksack behind me. The long space was littered with construction debris and supplies. I found some partial rolls of Owens-Corning fiberglas insulation backed with foil paper. I unrolled about six feet of the pink, fluffy stuff and laid my mummy bag over it. I got in and pulled another length over me—a cozy nest among the stacks of lumber and sheetrock.

This worked pretty well, and I quickly warmed up, even in the below zero temperature. I ate two more of Dorothy's

Minnesota Flapjacks and even got to scribble in my sketchbook before I fell asleep, listening to the wind rattling the tin roof.

During the night, I was awakened twice by a night watchman making his rounds. He didn't notice me, or pretended he didn't, as he clambered over the jumbled materials. I figured I'd discovered the secret of human invisibility.

Defacing Temple Walls

I HAD BEEN TO NEW YORK only once before, in 1957, when my family was driving towards our new duty station in Newfoundland. We had taken a Gray Line bus tour and a ferry to the Statue of Liberty. I had seen a man sleeping on the sidewalk, curled around a bottle, and a woman peeing into a subway grating. That evening we attended the Billy Graham crusade in Madison Square Garden and saw thousands of people flood the aisles to accept the Lord Jesus Christ.

When I left the drafty shed, I knew I had a mission to perform. I set out north on 6th Avenue. After seventy blocks or so, I jogged a block east and found the Whitney Museum of American Art on Madison Avenue. It took about an hour and a half.

I paused on the sidewalk outside the brick cube of a museum. I took my can of Chinese Red paint from a side pocket of my rucksack and hid it in the pocket of my coat, along with a two-inch wide brush. The elegantly uniformed guard at the door told me I would have to check my backpack in the cloakroom.

"It's free," he said.

The cloakroom may have been free, but the exhibition was not—even for students, much less vagrants. I did have a five-dollar bill, but I was planning on buying something to eat with it. I explained my predicament to the lady behind the counter, and she let me in for free.

The 1969 Whitney Annual Exhibition of Contemporary American Painting was "way cool". Big paintings by Helen Frankenthaler and Roy Lichtenstein were here. A lurid *Judgement of Paris*, by John Clem Clarke, was of particular interest to me, a chronically horny teenager.

After I'd walked through the show twice, I stopped in front of a blank white wall between two sections of the gallery. I pulled my sketchbook from the pocket of my fake sheepskin coat and flipped to the page with the sketch of my next work. I took the can of paint from the other pocket. I pried the lid up with the bottle opener on my scout knife, then dipped the clean brush into the shiny paint. I felt fearful, excited, and focused.

Nobody was around me. I started painting a big sine wave on the eggshell white wall. After I'd painted two peaks and valleys, a tour group gathered around me. The funky smell of fresh oil paint and linseed oil now filled the air around us, startling in the sterile atmosphere of the museum.

The leader of the tour, a middle aged brunette in a tweed suit, came up to me.

"Tell us what you're doing," she said.

"All art is cultural vandalism," I said. "When you see a piece of art, it changes your perception without asking permission."

"That's very interesting," she said, holding her elbow with one hand, a finger beside her cheek. "Please tell my class about it while you're working. We're from Antioch College."

An audience!

While I was busy expounding my crackpot theories, a security guard wearing an immaculate grey worsted uniform, complete with peaked cap and Sam Browne belt, strode up to me and made a grab for my arm. I twisted away and held up the floppy brush loaded with Chinese Red. I grinned at him, wide-eyed. I was a feral art animal.

I called his bluff. He backed away and disappeared. I finished my piece, stood back and compared the water color in the sketchbook to my action painting on the wall.

"That's radical, dude—right on!" said one of the Antioch students, a long-haired blond guy.

I pounded the can lid closed with the butt of my jackknife. I wrapped the sticky brush in a paint rag; I was tickled to see that I hadn't dripped on the parquet floor. This was great.

A man in a black suit hurried up to me with the frightened guard in his wake.

"You'll have to come with me," he said.

"Sure," I said, handing my weapons to the guard. He took them with a doubtful look.

The Antioch students stared, and other museum goers

noticed, as the Director of Security, a scruffy artist, and a uniformed guard paraded through the galleries. The guard held my paint can and brush like an orb and sceptre.

I followed the suit into an underground passage with concrete walls, then he opened the door to a storeroom. Inside was a sturdy-looking guy wearing carpenter's jeans and a sweatshirt.

"I'll be back in a few minutes," said the security director. "Gino will keep an eye on you."

I sat on a stool across a work table from the dark-haired man. He spoke up.

"You know what I'm supposed to be doing now?"

"What?" I said.

"I'm supposed to stretch four canvases for Helen Frankenthaler today," he said. "Instead I'm babysitting you."

"I know how to stretch canvases," I said. "Can I help?"

He snorted, glowering at me. "You're lucky they didn't call the cops. They'd throw you in The Tombs. A punk like you wouldn't last long there."

When the security director returned, he thanked Gino for keeping an eye on me, and I followed him down the hall and into his office.

Looking across his desk at me, he said, "I don't quite know what to do with you."

I kept my mouth shut.

"If you promise you won't try anything like this again, I'll let you go. Here's my card," he said, holding it out to me.

I took it.

"Gino's already removing your painting. Send us some slides if you want to show us your work, okay?"

He handed me a ten dollar bill, and I took it.

"Okay." I said.

And that was how I exhibited in the '69 Whitney Annual.

———

Back on Madison Avenue, my rucksack on my back, it felt like the temperature was falling. I decided I'd had enough of New York for a while. I hiked to the entrance to the Holland Tunnel and stuck out my thumb.

I hadn't been encouraged much in my quest for artistic glory, but then again, I hadn't frozen to death yet. I had actually been planning to go on to Lowell, Massachusetts, and visit Kerouac's grave, but when I got to U.S. 95, I was drawn to the south, hoping to warm up.

Two days later, back in Chapel Hill, I called Dorothy from a phone booth and told her I was back, like *The Cat in the Hat*. She picked me up at a gas station on the highway and brought me back to her mom's place.

Elenor, Clara, and Dorothy were glad to know I hadn't frozen to death in the big ice storm. They listened to my bragging about my stunt in the Whitney Annual. Dorothy was polite with me, but not affectionate. The next morning, she and I went to the Student Union on the UNC campus and found a ride share offer on a card pinned to the cork bulletin board.

The next day we left in a Volvo sedan with Ethan, a grad student on his way to Palo Alto to finish his master's in computer science at Stanford. Ethan traded off driving with Dorothy, and I sat in the back and tried to be amusing.

When we got to Little Rock, in the middle of the night, I called my grandmother from a gas station. Grandmother had moved here after Granddad died of Hodgkins disease at the Veterans' hospital. She lived alone, on savings and Granddad's World War One pension.

Ethan, Dorothy, and I slept a few hours on the floor of Grandmother's North Little Rock apartment. We left in the morning, but not before Grandmother had cooked us breakfast: fried chicken, biscuits, and gravy. She also packed more fried chicken and some apples for us to take along with us. This was several years before she went to live in Hong Kong with my parents.

The next stop was in Beverly Hills. Ethan's parents lived here, and they put us up for the night in their dramatic Spanish Colonial style mansion. They threw a dinner party for Ethan, and I was introduced as a painter. People looked through my sketchbook and made comments about my scribblings. One of Ethan's uncles took me aside.

"All your stuff looks like dicks," he said.

"Thanks," I said.

"It wasn't meant to be a compliment." He wandered off to get his glass refilled.

Ethan dropped Dorothy and me off on the Stanford campus,

a little after dark the next day. Dorothy hoisted her pack to her shoulders.

"I'm going to stay with my friend in the dorm," she said. "Have a nice life."

She walked away, and I never saw her again.

Packing Heat

I SLEPT UNDER A BRIDGE that night. When I got to San Francisco the next day, I knew I was homeless again. Arthur and Nell had broken up, and Nell had gone back to Reed College. Arthur had taken off to Tennessee in an old school bus, with several other devotees of a new-age guru named Steve Gaskin, the model for *Saint Stephen* in the Grateful Dead song. I knew that this wasn't for me. Anything smacking of religion or "spirituality" was beginning to repulse me.

It was 1970 now. The Summer of Love was long past, and the Haight-Ashbury had become a dangerous slum full of speed freaks, ex-cons, and pimps. I squatted in a decaying Victorian in the Western Addition. A high school friend had left for the Steve Gaskin cult in Tennessee, but before he left, he'd turned me on to the vacant house—the home of his girlfriend's deceased parents. I shared it with another juvenile delinquent from the southwest, Carl, the hippie son of a famous rodeo champion.

Shouts, gunshots, and sirens sounded outside the old house at night.

I had already been robbed once, walking down Fillmore Street. I had seen the group of 12-year old-boys walking towards me on the sidewalk, but I'd ignored the alarm going off in my acid-rattled brain and hadn't crossed the street to avoid them. Our paths met in the middle of the block, away from the corner street lamps.

The kids—four of them—quickly surrounded me. A boy fell into step to my left. He grabbed my elbow with one hand and pressed the point of a knife against my side, under my jacket. As I cringed away from him, another boy grabbed my right arm and I felt another blade against the small of my back on that side.

A third boy held a can of Mace up to my eyes, and said, "Keep walking, sucker."

I moved along the dark sidewalk with the boys, and an SFPD prowl car cruised past us. The two cops in the front seat glanced at our little group, then looked away and continued on. A fourth boy started busily going through my pockets. From my Levi's, he took my wallet with my ID and sixteen dollars—all the money I had in the world. From my fake sheepskin jacket, he pulled a baggie of weed, a brass pipe, and matches.

When we got to the pool of light under the next street light, the boys backed off and faded away like smoke in the wind, each in a different direction. I was standing across the street from the Fillmore Auditorium. I felt relieved they hadn't stabbed me.

I felt in my shirt pocket. My ticket to the rock concert was still there. I went on in and met some friends. When I told them about getting mugged, they said, "Bummer, man."

I didn't enjoy the show.

Walking back to the deserted Victorian, I nervously glanced up each alley and walked quickly. This was the first time I had ever had a frightening encounter with a black person, and it freaked me out. I let myself into the derelict house without further incident.

I had explored the old house in the days I'd crashed there. The deceased residents were book hoarders, and had filled the shelves, tables, and corners with stacks of old books. I had read a California history book and a comic novel from the 1920s, and had enjoyed looking through photo albums of travel in Egypt, Italy, and South America.

Behind some moth-eaten travel guides, I had also found a nickel-plated .22 revolver. I had taken it out and handled it. It was loaded.

Back at the squat on the night of the mugging, I went straight to the bookcase. I grabbed the little pearl-handled pistol, the box of ammunition, and put them in my coat pocket.

The next day, I went down to the subbasement, set an old tin can on the dirt, and punched some holes in it from about twenty feet. If anybody heard the muffled reports, they probably thought they came from Divisadero Street a block away. Gunshots were a familiar sound in the Western Addition in the early Seventies.

Carl had hitchhiked back to Wyoming, and I was alone in a bad neighborhood. I started carrying the loaded gun jammed under my belt at the small of my back. Hauling it around with me was not as reassuring as I had hoped. The weight was a constant reminder of the lethal little tool, and I had to be careful it didn't fall out on the sidewalk as I walked. If I stretched to reach a can of chili on a high shelf in a grocery store, I had to worry if my jacket hiked up. The storekeeper might see the weapon and call the police, or, worse, shoot me in "self defense".

A week later I hitchhiked to the East Bay, where Dick Raley and Ginny, his Modoc Indian girlfriend, and her baby boy lived in a shack behind a bean field. They told me I could sleep on the floor for a while.

The three of us lived together in bohemian squalor for a few weeks; Dick painted like a madman: landscapes, still lifes, and campy nudes. I painted abstracts. We both painted on plywood scraps that we found discarded around the neighborhood. We used latex house paint instead of gesso, and combined varnish with mixing tints to make our paint.

The rent was paid from the check that Ginny received monthly from the Department of Defense. Ginny was married to Phil, who was a soldier in Vietnam. This lowlife existence came to an end when Phil was discharged and returned stateside. He moved in, and Dick and I moved out. Before that, I had traded the pistol to a pot dealer for a lid of weed.

I didn't much like the seedy life I'd fallen into. I wanted a job, a girlfriend, and a roof over my head. After being evicted from a couple of other sketchy living situations, Dick and I hit the road.

PART
THREE:

Close Calls

Freight Hopping

WE HAD EATEN the night before. With about 50¢ between us, Dick Raley and I had pooled our funds to buy a 29¢ loaf of Wonder Bread and a 10¢ Hershey bar. When you chewed the two together, it tasted like chocolate cake.

It had been a year since Dorothy had dumped me in Palo Alto. I had lived in cheap rentals in Oakland and Hayward with Dick. We had both painted, written poems, and hitchhiked back and forth to Portland. He had family there and some very cool friends.

We were hitchhiking. At least we were trying to hitchhike. Dick and I stood on a patch of scrubby grass, next to the southbound onramp of Interstate 5 in Dunsmuir, California.

Glacier-topped Mount Shasta loomed to the north of us. We had been standing in the same spot all day. Two or three cars per hour had passed, but none of the drivers had given us a second glance.

The afternoon dragged on. The last car had passed us up an hour ago. We sat glumly on our rucksacks, hoping for a ride before dark. The rumble of a train came to our ears. Below us, boxcars and flatcars rolled slowly along a southbound track.

"Want to try it?" I asked.

"Why not?" said my partner.

Shouldering our packs, we skidded down a narrow gully, boot heels scraping plumes of dust, towards the Southern Pacific tracks. Standing on the gravel ballast, inches from the moving train, we watched for a likely car to catch. A dozen locked boxcars creaked and groaned as they slowly passed.

A series of flatcars approached. Each was loaded with four immense steel I-beams: two stacks of two, held down with heavy chain. Wooden cribbing spaced the beams apart and protected the edges of the cargo where chains lashed it to the deck. The space between the beams ran the length of the load and was wide enough for two young hobos to ride in comfort, protected from view.

The next car approached. I grabbed the steel rail of the brakeman's ladder, swung my foot up to the bottom rung, and vaulted onto the deck of the flatcar. Dick followed immediately, and we both scrambled into the alley between the stacks.

As we sat on our rucksacks, we could see out between the beams and watch the trees and rocks passing. The clicking and clacking of the rails came faster and more intensely as the train picked up speed. A few minutes later, confident that we were safely out of town, we climbed up the timber cribbing and poked our heads above the top of the load.

Wind blasted my face and whipped my hair around as I looked forward towards the locomotive and backwards in the direction of the caboose. The cars disappeared around the curves in both directions. The curves became less frequent, and our speed was building.

Ringing, rattling, and rolling, the steel snake emerged from the Cascades and into the Sacramento Valley. The sun was setting. Dick and I were howling with glee, our voices drowned by the wind and the racketing roar. This was way better than standing in the heat all day waiting for a ride.

As night fell, we both withdrew to our shelter. Propping our packs against some cribbing, we could lean back, look up, and see a river of stars framed by the parallel I-beams. The rhythm of the rails soon rocked us to sleep.

Before I fell into the arms of Morpheus, I thought about how different my life was than that which my parents had wished for me. They would have wanted me to go to college, find a good job, and marry a "good Christian woman". I knew I was too lazy and stupid to go to college, but a job and a wife was starting to sound pretty good by now.

I don't know how long we slept, but we were awakened by a change of pitch in the clacking of the wheels. The train was slowing. Neither Dick nor I knew where we were. We had both heard of *Yard Bulls* or railroad detectives who had been known to beat up train hoppers that they apprehended.

As the train continued to slow, we started seeing the occasional porch light and the shapes of buildings in the darkness. We passed a white sign with black letters that spelled "Roseville". We had heard that experienced rail riders would dismount before a train came to a stop, before a freight entered the switching yard.

We saw floodlights glowing a few hundred yards ahead of the engine. We could see the gravel-covered roadbed in the moonlight. It was passing slowly enough to see the individual ballast rocks. The floodlights of the yard were getting closer by the second. We tossed our packs to the ground. Each vanished with frightening rapidity.

Taken aback, Dick and I looked at each other. I gulped. Dick smiled, shrugged, and stepped from the moving train. I followed him down the ladder to the bottom step, took a deep breath, and leapt to the ground.

My feet hit first, the impact instantly compressing my body into a ball spinning furiously along the grease, grit, and gravel of the roadbed. Head, shoulders, knees and toes, again and again, I tumbled down the embankment, until I stopped—sprawled face down in a weedy ditch. By the time I painfully sat up, the train had passed, red lantern receding as the caboose rolled into town.

Out of the darkness I heard a groan. Standing painfully, I tried my weight first on my right foot, then my left, raised my arms, then shook my head. Nothing seemed to be broken, but I was sore and smarting all over my body. I limped back along the tracks until I came upon Dick sitting on a switching box, holding his head.

"You okay?" I asked.

"Tip-top," he replied. "You?"

"Just lucky, I guess. Nothing broken anyhow."

We walked up the tracks about fifty yards and found Dick's pack, then mine, a few yards further. Leaving the railroad right of way, we found a street that continued southward into town. We followed this for a few minutes, until we passed under a streetlamp.

In the light, we stopped for a moment. Dick's tattered clothing, pack, and exposed skin was smudged black with railroad grime. Looking down, I could see that my Levi's were shredded and my suede jacket was ragged, with rips, tears, and holes crammed with greasy dirt.

After a moment of rueful laughter, we continued along the sidewalk. In the deserted hours we wandered into the center of Roseville. Growing next to the Art Deco City Hall we saw a mature hedge. Falling flat, we scuttled under the groomed boughs and found a leafy spot next to the stucco wall of the municipal building. Unrolling our GI mummy bags, we found that the feathers were leaking from dozens of tiny tears in the shell fabric. The inside of my rucksack was spattered with shards of broken glass and Heinz pickle relish, carried in the hope that we might score some hot dogs.

We slept the sleep of the exhausted or beaten. We awoke to sunlight and the sounds of a freeway already buzzing with commute traffic.

High on Jesus

DICK RALEY and I had lived together four times.

1. He slept in my closet at Canterbury House.

2. I slept on the floor of the cottage he rented with his Modoc Indian girlfriend, behind a garden of horse beans, in Hayward.

3. After my parents sent me a check for $250, I rented a two bedroom, ranch-style house in South Hayward. When the next month's rent came due, we sublet the two bedrooms to a couple of junkies and moved into the garage. Mayhem ensued and sleaze abounded.

4. We shared a Victorian flat at 22nd and Telegraph in Oakland. The rent was $85 per month.

All of these places filled up with our oil paintings, and the floors, doors, and bathtubs became stained with oil paint that we tracked around the house.

Eventually, after hitchhiking and freight hopping between Oakland, Portland, and back again, Dick decided to move back to his parents' house in Beaverton, Oregon, just outside of

Portland. Nick Albert, the banjo-playing painter from Tennyson High, took over the Oakland flat, and I hitched up to Beaverton along with Dick.

We stayed in the finished basement of the Raleys' house, and Dick's mom changed the linens on the twin beds weekly. This was the first time I'd slept between sheets in well over a year. Dick and I looked for work, and each found occasional odd jobs. Dick's parents did have one stipulation: we had to attend church every Sunday.

I had seen other baby boomers take up Hinduism, Buddhism, or follow a sleazy guru to a farm commune in Tennessee. I knew this wasn't for me. Since I was familiar with Christianity, I figured I'd give Jesus another shot. I wasn't doing real well as a hobo anyway.

I attended Maranatha, a black church in Albina, in Northeast Portland. Besides the black families, a sizable contingent of "Jesus freaks" attended—white hippies who had been saved.

I had stayed at the "House of Sonshine" commune, an ancient log cabin on the Oregon Trail. Maybe a dozen ex-hippies lived together platonically and sang every morning around the double oil drum wood stove.

> *Rise, Shine, and Give God the Glory, Glory*
> *Rise, Shine, and Give God the Glory, Glory*
> *RISE-AND-SHINE-AND-*
> *Give God the Glory Glory*
> *Children of the Lord. . .*

There was no pot or acid allowed in the commune, which was a bummer for me, but there were no junkies or speed freaks either, which was a relief. The platonic part was a deal breaker though. The young women were cute and friendly, but unavailable—more interested in Jesus than courtship.

"Yolay du lacomma, yolay de malecci!" said the girl sitting cross-legged across from me. We were seated with several other young people on an orange shag carpet, in the living room of a tract home in Beaverton, Oregon. It was late 1970 now.

"Yolay du lacomman, lacomman, lacomman! Yolay de malecca mecca heiny-ho!" The girl's dark curls fell across her closed eyes as she swayed, chanting in an unknown tongue. Her left palm was pressed against my sweating forehead, her right hand raised in the air, fingers spread, shaking to the rhythm of her voice.

"Praise God! May the Holy Spirit fill our brother John. Thank you Jesus! Thank you, Lord!"

The half-dozen other young adults sitting in the prayer circle all had their hands raised, shaking, or waving—antennas reaching out to receive the heavenly waves of the Holy Spirit.

It was getting late. This prayer meeting had started at seven. By now, after ten o'clock, everyone except me had spoken in tongues, or "received the gifts of the Spirit". It wasn't that I didn't want to be filled with the Holy Ghost; I was trying.

The other Jesus freaks had simply raised their hands, thrown back their heads, and let loose long rants in various unknown tongues. The rest of the group had laughed, cried, and shouted "Thank you, Jesus!" after each person received this "gift of the Spirit".

Craving acceptance from the others, I prayed as hard as I could, but was still unable to produce the speech in unknown tongues. From listening, I noticed that each individual made their own sounds and phrases that tended to be strung out and repeated. As the evening ground on, I came to the revelation that this could go on all night. They were going to keep praying for me to receive the anointing of the spirit until I started crying or speaking in tongues.

I decided that I had to give it a try.

"Hess foomer om belonico," I offered. "Alamantine voslipitus shogumma."

This must sound like a cross between Yiddish and Pig Latin, I thought to myself.

"Praise the Lord," said the dark-haired girl.

"Meladoray pos hemmico partollas!" I said.

They were buying it!

"Thank you, Jesus," chorused the rest of the prayer circle.

That's all it took. After congratulations all around, and a closing prayer, the meeting was over and I was free to go home. Walking alone in the dark, I thought about how easy it had been to make up the spurious speech, and how happy the others were to accept my "gift of the Spirit" as genuine.

I realized that everybody had made up their own unknown tongue in the attempt to persuade their friends, and themselves, that they also had received the gift.

Going to church and prayer meetings seemed to be the only way I could meet people. I wasn't in college, and that hadn't been too good for meeting girls anyway. At least the girls at Maranatha were polite and friendly, but none of them wanted to talk about anything except Jesus, the Holy Spirit, and the rapture. I could be part of the gang of Jesus freaks, but only as long as I sang along in church, swayed back and forth waving my open palms, and spoke in tongues.

When I talked about my doubts and lack of faith with my old friend Dick Raley, he had a ready answer. "That's Satan talking, trying to lead you astray." At this point I was having my doubts about a theistic God, and I certainly did not believe in Satan.

Dick had abandoned the Beat or bohemian lifestyle, moved back into his parents' house, and enrolled in Portland State. I was something of a lost puppy. I realized that I was too stupid for college, had too little faith for church, and no prospects to attract a woman. What I really wanted was someone to love, and someone to love me back.

I did have a love of the mountains, and I hitchhiked into the Cascades to hike, climb, and camp whenever I could.

High on the Glacier

SCOTT AND CHARLES were living in Portland, finishing their studies at Reed College. They shared the rent on a railroad flat beside the Brooklyn Yards, where Southern Pacific trains were made up. When I showed up, my friendship with Charles and Scott picked up where we had left it a year earlier. Conversation would stop, however, when the loaded rail cars would sail into each other outside the thin walls of the house. The clanging crashes happened over and over, at any hour of the day or night.

There was plenty to eat at the railroad flat, but it was simple fare. The first time I stayed for dinner, we ate brown rice, sautéed vegetables with tahini and soy sauce, and strips of fried horse meat for the carnivores among us. Portland boasted a butcher licensed to sell horse meat for human consumption, and the cost per pound was about half that of beef or pork.

Over the meal, Scott and I planned an ascent of Mount Hood. By tacit agreement we didn't talk about his sister Dorothy.

"She has a way of coming and going," was all that he would say on the subject.

Mount Hood is an 11,000-foot dormant volcano, gouged with flowing glaciers, hot sulphuric gas blasting from vents in its crater. It gleamed above Portland on rare sunny days, a tantalizing beacon for climbers and skiers.

I spent the night before our climb at the railroad flat. The sky in Portland was cloudy and spitting rain. Disappointed by the weather, we drank beer and smoked pot into the wee hours. At one o'clock in the morning we went outside and saw stars. The clouds were rapidly dissipating.

"Let's go for it!" said Scott, excitedly.

By 3 AM, Scott's VW beetle was parked at Timberline Lodge, and we were strapping on our crampons. After an interminable slog up a snow-covered moraine, we roped up, standing above the west bank of the White River Glacier. The dawn was just shining on the summit high above, and the river of ice still lay in deep shadow.

"The rabbit comes out of the hole, around the tree, and back into the hole," said Scott, "secure the end with two half-hitches." He showed me the proper way to tie a bowline. Scott then rummaged in his pack.

"Did you bring any sunscreen?" asked Scott.

"No," I answered, "I have some Chapstick though."

"That will have to do," he said.

We shared the whole tube of lipslurm, smearing it liberally over our faces, necks, and ears.

We picked our way across the glacier with ice axes and crampons, avoiding depressions in the snow which might conceal crevasses. The slopes rose steeply above the east bank, and we began to belay each other, leapfrogging leads as we climbed into brilliant spring sunlight. After crossing a dicy section of crumbly slope, high above the glacier, we made the summit.

Climbing had always fascinated me, but I hadn't really known what I was doing. Now that I'd had some solid training, the sky (or the grave) was the limit. I loved the feeling of being on the edge, with life on the right, death on the left, and ice under my crampons.

Back in Portland, I noticed that my face had turned the color of bronze, and kind of hard and glossy. In succeeding days the mask peeled off in hunks like bacon rind. With ragged strips of jerky hanging from my head, people looked away as I passed them on the street. A young mother pushing a stroller distracted her baby before the child could see me.

A week later, the bacon rind was gone, and my skin was smooth, pink, and pimple-free.

––––

Not long after my first ascent of Mount Hood, I got a phone call at the Raley's house.

"Hi, this is Susie Selkin," said the voice on the other end. "Do you remember me?"

"Sure," I said. She had been fourteen, but that was four years ago, in Hayward. She had dated Nick, my artist friend from Tennyson High.

"I just hitchhiked up from California, and you're the only person I know in Portland. I'm looking for a place to live," she said. "I'm done with Hayward."

"Would you like to go snow camping?" I asked.

"Sure," she said. "That's why I came up here."

I packed my snow camping stuff and met her in the tiny lobby of a cheap hotel on the north side of Portland. Susie was 18 now, and a "stone fox", in the East Bay vernacular. Her father was the son of a Russian Jew; her mother was San Francisco Irish. Susan was a dark-haired Jewish beauty with a turned-up Irish nose.

"John, your face looks so, so clean," she said when she saw me.

We hitchhiked to Government Camp, riding in the bed of a pickup, then caught a ride with a waitress on the way to work at Timberline Lodge. From the parking lot, we hoisted our packs and I led westward, across snow-covered moraines and gullies, until we were away from the ski slopes and the Arts and Crafts lodge.

We had been talking non-stop since we met at her hotel. We stomped out a flat sleeping platform in the crusty snow, and I stretched my orange nylon tarp over a rope strung between two tall stumps. After I laid down a waxy green groundcloth and a foam pad, Susie unrolled her thick army blanket. I spread my unzipped mummy bag over that, and we sat, side by side, admiring the view of the summit from our tent.

As I boiled Ramen noodles and a can of tuna over my *Svea* stove, it began to snow.

My homeless days were over.

Susie and I rented a charming brown shingle flat on SW Osage Street in beautiful Portland, Oregon. We had a panoramic view of Mounts St. Helens, Adams, and Rainier from the front steps.

Susie's first job was as a laundress in an orphanage across the Willamette River. She would come home at night upset, after having to wash, bleach, and press child-sized strait jackets. She was also harassed by another worker constantly trying to kiss her.

I found various odd jobs. One was digging drainage ditches with a pick and shovel; another was inflating, testing, and repairing freight balloons used to cushion bombs and rockets in transit to the ongoing war against the Vietnamese. It bothered me to be making money at the expense of innocent men, women, and children being bombed, but I was tired of going hungry and sleeping in ditches.

Soon we both found work as models for art classes at colleges and art schools in the area. This was educational for both of us. When posing nude under a skylight in the studio, you could hear the scritchy-scratchy sounds of charcoal on rough paper as the students drew the forms of your body. I imagined I could feel the crumbly charcoal defining my limbs. Occasionally the teacher would outline the muscles directly on my skin in greasy chalk to show the class.

During breaks, the model could pull on a robe, walk through the class, and see what the students had produced—often with little drawings added by the professor in the margins.

One dark and rainy day, Susie and I were posing together in an advanced life drawing class at the Portland Museum School. When the gray light from the skylight became especially dim, the teacher hauled out a slide projector and cast zebra stripes across our bodies.

"Just draw the stripes as they fall across the curves of the body," he told the class. "You won't need any outlines to define the forms."

When Susie and I donned our robes and walked among the easels, we were both amazed by the success of the new technique. Modeling was a way we could actually get paid to attend art school.

31

Rooster Rock

THE TOE OF MY BOOT felt solid on the narrow ledge, so I put my weight on it, then stretched my fingers along the rock, until I could just curl them over the knob of basalt above. As I pulled into my next stance, my face came even with a fissure in the dark rock. Inches from my eyes, a brown furry bat hung upside-down, its clawed feet wedged into a smaller crack. The animal's dark-skinned wings were folded about him, and his mouth was open. Tiny sharp teeth flashed as he screeched and scolded me. Annoyed by my noisy, clanking arrival, the bat flew away, with a few slaps of its leathery wings.

The Goldline climbing rope looped down thirty feet behind me, through an aluminum carabiner, then thirty feet more, down to Susie Selkin, who was belaying. Her upturned face, wire-rimmed glasses, and dark braids shone vividly against her red down jacket. Below her were the deep green tops of Douglas firs, growing up from the shore of the Columbia River.

Rooster Rock is a slump block of Colombia Gorge basalt, about an hour's hitchhike east of Portland, Oregon. The south face was known as a good fifth-class climb for beginners. My partner Susie was eighteen and inexperienced in climbing. I was two years older, with a little experience, and eager to share the joys of the mountains with my beautiful new girlfriend.

"How does it look?" she called up to me.

"It looks okay," I called back. I stood on a narrow ledge, less than a foot wide. A sideways shuffle of a few feet would take me to a dihedral, or open book formation, which would offer an easy scramble to the summit.

"I'll haul up the pack, then belay you up to me," I called.

Taking a coil of parachute cord from my gear sling, I uncoiled the red nylon line and hitched it to a carabiner.

"Heads up!" I called, then tossed the carabiner and a coil of the hauling line down the cliff, towards Susie. The metal ring fell freely, the rope uncoiling behind it like a scribbly crayon line in the air. It landed in the dirt, a couple of feet to the left of the young woman below. She clipped the carabiner to the metal haul-ring of our small khaki knapsack.

The pack held our lunch: sandwiches, oranges, a canteen of water, a brass stove, plus an aluminum billy, two sierra cups, and some tea bags. We were planning to have a cup of hot tea on the summit and to enjoy the spectacular view of the Columbia Gorge.

After taking up some slack, I secured my end of the line to my waist loop, then began to haul the twenty pound sack hand over hand, up the sheer face, to my stance. When it arrived, I plopped it down on the piled-up parachute cord beside me on the ledge.

"Can I come up now?" Susie called from below. "I'm getting cold."

"Just a minute," I said, as I turned toward the rock. I was beginning to feel insecure standing on this narrow ledge, sixty feet up a sheer face. I would need a piton and a carabiner above me. I could clip the belay rope into this anchor and pull down on the line to take up slack as Susie climbed, or hold her weight in case she slipped. As I fumbled in my hardware rack for a piton, I looked down, then watched, in slow motion horror, as the toe of my boot nudged the red spaghetti of the hauling line. The fully loaded knapsack rolled off the lip of the ledge and dropped like a stone, down the south face of Rooster Rock.

The heap of hauling line melted away as it was pulled by the hurtling sack. I clenched my body to brace for the impact on my waist loop. The red thread had almost run out when the last loop jammed into a narrow crack in the ledge, and the 250# test line snapped with a twang. The luggage fell free, skipped off the face, and caromed away, into the treetops below Susie.

Had the line not broken, the 250-plus pounds of force generated by the falling pack would surely have snatched me from my unprotected perch, sending me flying into the boulders sixty feet below. I should have placed an anchor before hauling anything. I felt like I might vomit.

"Are you alright?" Susie's concerned voice cut through my morbid reverie.

"Yeah, fine," I croaked. "We can get it when we go back down."

I took a deep breath, turned, and banged a soft iron piton into a horizontal crack in the face above me.

Lightbulb Coffee

I WAS ARRESTED for hitchhiking in 1970, outside of Redding, California. I was returning from a quick visit to Oakland, but Susie couldn't come since she was working full-time in Portland. My hitchhiking partner Arthur was given a ticket, but since I couldn't produce an ID, I was cuffed and stuffed. Arthur went on to Portland without me, to explain to Susie what had happened. We had no telephone at the time.

I was a skinny hippie with a rucksack. The beefy, crew cut highway patrolman, outweighing me by 100 pounds, slammed the steel handcuffs onto my wrists, behind me, with a blow from the heel of his hand. Both wrists were burning as he guided my head into the back seat of his prowl car. Buckling the seat belt over me, he grasped the strap with both hands and braced his foot against the door frame. With a violent jerk, he tightened the belt, pressing my body against my manacled arms trapped behind my back. On the drive to jail, he made a big show about accelerating over potholes and bumps. Each jolt was agonizing, the hard edges of the steel bracelets cutting into my skin. He grinned at me in the rearview mirror, obviously enjoying himself.

Nothing he did was against regulations, but the intent and effect was to torture.

Why?

Because I was in his power. I was on the other side of the law, and he was a sadist.

The officer pulled his Crown Victoria into a parking space next to a beige stuccoed office in a small strip mall. A sign hanging in the window announced "Justice of the Peace" and "Notary Public". After killing the engine and setting the brake, he hopped out, strode across the sidewalk, then let himself in through a glass door. I was left to stew in the backseat of the prowl car. By arching my back and contorting my body, I could relieve some pressure on my wrists, but my fingers were going numb.

The glass door opened, and my khaki-clad captor's brown service shoes crunched on the gravel. He opened the back door of the CHP car. He reached across and unlatched my seat belt. "Get out!" he snapped.

I scooted across the seat and stood beside the opened door. The guardian of law and order slammed the door, grabbed the chain between my manacles, and frog-walked me across the driveway, across the sidewalk, and into the office.

Inside, an older, corpulent man was just sitting down behind a desk. Smoothing his wrinkled tie, he looked up at me.

"I understand that Patrolman Crandall apprehended you trying to solicit a ride on the freeway?" the Justice asked me, looking over his reading glasses.

"I didn't know it was a freeway, sir," I answered.

"That's not my problem," he returned. "For being a pedestrian on a freeway, I'm fining you forty dollars."

"I don't have that much," I protested.

"Okay, at ten dollars a day, that will be four days in the Shasta County Jail," he spat back.

He wrote something in a ledger, then something else on a printed carbon paper form. Tearing the top sheet from the carbon pad, he handed it to the officer standing beside him.

Swiveling his chair, the fat man looked at me across his cluttered desk. I was wearing worn-out hiking boots, carpenter's jeans, a faded work shirt, and army surplus suspenders. My brown hair was shoulder length. He announced in a stern voice, "Young man, from your looks, I think you're choosing the wrong road in life: the hippie way. You'll have some time to think about it in jail."

The patrolman and the storefront judge lowered their voices to exchange a few pleasantries. A moment later I was frog-walked back to the black and white car.

I had a strange feeling that if I'd had the forty bucks, the JP would have split the money with the cop after they had cut me loose. Before this arrest I'd had only three other contacts with law enforcement: the Albuquerque policeman who picked me up after curfew, the MP who checked my arms for needle tracks in Oak Knoll Naval Hospital, and the shore patrolman in San Diego who demanded my draft card. I didn't enjoy any of the previous encounters, and this one was the worst so far. I wanted to have as little contact as possible with these guys in the future.

No matter how far I had travelled away from the conservative world of my childhood, angry right-wing types still seemed to pop up regularly in my life. I wondered if I would ever be free from these nasty people. Maybe they were just an unpleasant fact of life.

This time Patrolman Crandall didn't bother to brace his boot against the door frame, but he still pulled the belt tight. After a few miles, the patrol car turned right, into a parking lot. Driving through an open gate, we passed a tall cyclone fence, then came to a stop next to the back door of the Shasta County Jail.

I was allowed to walk into the building without being steered by the painful handcuffs. I stood in front of the booking desk. The patrolman greeted the deputy on duty, and slid the Justice of the Peace order across the Formica surface. I felt my shackles being unlocked and falling away. With relief I brought my arms around and inspected my wrists. Deep furrows with red weeping edges encircled both.

"Name?" asked a bald sheriff's deputy, who sat on a stool behind the high desk.

After I spelled out my name, date of birth, and address in Portland, a second deputy motioned me through a swinging gate that he held open. I walked through the gate and paused in front of a Formica counter. I rubbed my hands together and flexed my fingers as the circulation returned with a prickly sensation. Glancing behind me, I saw the highway patrolman carry my battered rucksack into the booking office, and set it on the counter.

"Is this all your stuff?" the desk clerk asked.

"Yes sir," I answered.

The clerk nodded at the patrolman, who touched the bill of his cap and disappeared through the door, out to the parking lot.

"Take everything out of your pockets and put it on the table," commanded the second deputy.

I complied. My wallet, house key, and a little less than a dollar in change made a small pile on the counter.

"Now take off your shoes, then stand over there with your hands on your head."

Assuming the position as instructed, I felt the lawman pat me down thoroughly. The first deputy, at the desk, was going through my wallet and spoke to me. "Hey, Schnick, where's your Draft Card?"

"I guess I lost it," I lied. I had burned my draft card in a bonfire at a peace rally in Berkeley the year before.

"I'm 4-F though," I added truthfully.

"The FBI will want to talk to you, Bud," the booking deputy said cheerily. He raked my wallet, change, and key into a tattered envelope and filed it in a gray cabinet.

The other deputy took my right hand and pressed each finger, in turn, to an ink pad, then to a printed form with empty squares. The left hand followed. Next, I was stood up against a wall painted with horizontal stripes and numbers.

"Hold this under your chin and look at me," he ordered, handing me a dark flannel-covered board with white plastic letters: SHASTA COUNTY SHERIFF'S OFFICE, the date, and a long number. I held the plaque up and a flashbulb dazzled me.

"Okay, you can put your shoes back on," the deputy said, handing me my old hiking boots after he had checked them for contraband. Sitting on a gray metal chair, I laced them up, as I watched the sergeant drag my rucksack down a short hall behind his desk.

"All set? Let's go," the deputy spoke as he unlocked a steel door. There was a wire-reinforced window about head level. He swung the door back, revealing a scuffed pastel green hallway. A third deputy was waiting for me inside, and he grasped my left arm and wordlessly guided me down the corridor. I heard a metal door clank shut behind me.

Passing several doors on the left, we ended up at the last door. Beside it was a narrow alcove with several oversized steel levers. My escort unlocked the door with a circular key and propelled me inside. Ahead of me loomed a floor-to-ceiling set of steel bars. The door behind me thumped closed. A gate in the bars clanked, then rolled to the left, propelled by the guard wielding levers in the corridor.

A potbellied Chicano of about forty stood before me. He wore a white sleeveless undershirt, a white towel around his neck, and held a Melmac cup of coffee in his hand. He seemed like he held some sort of petty authority, so I just stood there. The man looked me up and down, and in a gesture of bored amusement, pivoted towards the "tank", extending his arm into the day room.

A tall, long-haired man unfolded himself from a bench and approached me. "Welcome to D wing," he said. "My name's Edelman."

"I'm Schnick," I returned.

"What're you in for?" he asked.

"Hitchhiking," I said, looking around me. "You?"

"Shoplifting food at the Seven-Eleven."

Lowering my head, I whispered, "Why are the other guys here?"

"Drinking in public or possession of drugs, mostly," he answered. "Isn't that right, Sanchez?"

The man with the undershirt and the towel came over, sat on the steel table top, and spoke: "It's true. I was relaxing after work, and my wife was cooking supper. Two police broke down the front door. They didn't even knock. Inez screamed. She was scared. They pushed me down to the floor and handcuffed me. They found a gram of Horse that I was saving for the weekend. Shit, man, I lost my job and everything."

Maybe a dozen men lounged around the room: mostly Hispanic, with a couple of Anglos. A pastel green cinder block wall with high windows was to the right, above a long sink. The frosted glass blocked any view of the sky. A row of barred cells stood open along the left. A long steel table with benches ran down the middle of the room, bolted to the concrete floor. At the far end a raised area held a shower nozzle and a sink. Next to this stood a toilet with no seat or lid. The room reeked of sour sweat and cigarette butts.

On the smudged pastel walls around us, a library of graffiti filled any available space. There were poems, insults, rants, laments, and some surprisingly adept charcoal drawings of lightly clad women. The same artist had also drawn a mare and foal—and a guitarist bent over his instrument.

Off to the side a weekly menu was neatly penciled:

> *Monday: Beans and Dicks*
> *Tuesday: S.O.S.*
> *Wednesday: Spaghetti*
> *Thursday: Salisbury Steak*
> *Friday: Tuna Casserole*
> *Saturday: Beef Stew*
> *Sunday: Chicken Cutlet*

"What's S.O.S. ?" I asked, to no one in particular.

"Shit on a Shingle," responded several of the prisoners in unison.

I must have looked bewildered, because a rangy blond guy in a cowboy shirt laughed, then elaborated. "That's chipped beef on toast." This started a lively discussion between a few of the more well-travelled inmates.

"In Folsom we got turkey and dressing on Thanksgiving,"

said the cowboy, with a wild glint in his eye. "Christmas, too!"

"At Q we got ham and black-eyed peas on New Years," contributed one of the Chicano guys. The conversation drifted to favorite dishes from home, then gradually wound down, as the men recalled the wives, sweethearts, and mothers who had cooked for them.

With a thump, the outer door opened. All eyes turned to the sound and saw a white-clad "Trusty" (a trusted prisoner) push a bussing cart up to the inner cage wall. The outer door closed behind him, the steel gate creaked back, and the rubber-wheeled cart was rolled into the tank.

The trusty set two large, dented steel pitchers onto the table. One was steaming, full of hot coffee; the second was sweating and cold, full of red Kool-Aid. The other prisoners lined up, and the trusty handed each a pastel plastic sectioned tray.

Taking mine in turn, I followed Edelman down to the other end of the table, stepped over the bench, and sat. Just as predicted by the writing on the wall, the main section of my mess tray held a warm mass of chipped beef in a pale, starchy gravy. This had been ladled over two slices of bread more stale than toasted. The smaller sections held sad green beans, a square of fruit Jello, a pink Melmac cup, plus a cellophane envelope containing plastic cutlery, a paper napkin, and salt and pepper packets.

It had been a long day for me: arrested, tortured, tried, convicted, sentenced, and jailed—all without a bite to eat. I quickly ate everything, drank a cup of Kool-Aid—and then a cup of coffee.

As the others finished their dinners, they slid their trays into the empty slots on the mess cart, and I followed suit. One guy held a black plastic garbage bag open while another poured the leftover coffee into it. The bag was then hung from the crossbar of a cell.

A few minutes later, the Trusty returned and removed the mess cart. As soon as the outer door was closed, one of the coffee scroungers stood on the table and tied the garbage bag around an overhead lightbulb, so that the glowing bulb was immersed in the coffee. Now it would stay hot for the few hours before lights out.

When an inmate wanted another cup of joe, he could stand on the table and tip the bag to the side. Hot coffee would run into his upheld cup. It seemed a precarious arrangement, but it worked because the socket of the bulb was recessed into the ceiling, and only the glass contacted the liquid.

A few hours later, Edelman and I were seated on one of the metal benches, drinking lightbulb coffee. In front of us were a few tattered sports magazines that I listlessly flipped through. We talked about Portland where we both lived.

He was a student at Portland State. I had taken classes at the Portland Art Institute. His first name was Aaron, mine was John. I told him a little about my girlfriend Susie, who lived with me on Osage street.

Aaron leaned in a little closer, and spoke in a low voice. "You know, I never knew what it was like to be a woman until I had been penetrated by a man."

I grunted, glancing at his earnest face. "I'll take your word on that."

"Don't get me wrong, I love chicks, but, just saying. . ." Aaron trailed off, shrugging.

The daylight had faded from the high frosted windows by now, and the other jailbirds were starting to drift out of the dayroom and into the cells.

"You don't want to sleep out here," Edelman muttered. "At night the deputies shove the drunks in here. They all get sick or want to fight. The lights are on all night in the tank, but the lights go out in the cells, so it's easier to sleep. I was out there on my first night. There's too many guys in D wing for the number of bunks, but I stashed a mattress. You can crash on the floor in our cell. Sanchez won't mind," Edelman offered.

Sanchez looked up and shrugged. I glanced at the stack of thin, stained mattresses on the floor in the corner of the tank and then at the cells. Each had a toilet with a sink in the top and an upper and lower bunk along one wall. Under the bottom bunk of Edelman's cell I could see a relatively clean mattress with a pillow, no less.

"Thanks," I said, preferring the devil I knew to the one I did not. Soon, everyone who had been in the dayroom had adjourned to the cells. Some leaned against the bars, just outside the cells, and talked with others for a minute or two.

BRRAAAP! — a loud buzzer sounded in the ceiling. The loitering inmates all stepped inside their cells. A deputy watched through the window of the outer door. With a clank and a rumble, in turn, each cell door rolled shut.

Sanchez busied himself washing and shaving in the little sink atop the stainless steel toilet. He hung his white towel from the frame of the upper bunk, climbed up, and stretched out. Edelman dragged the mattress from under the lower bunk, then tossed a pillow and folded gray blanket after it.

He took a leak, made some splashing noises at the sink, wiped his hands on his trousers, then crawled into the lower berth. I washed my hands, face, and oozing wrists, drying my hands on my Levi's. I understood now why Sanchez so jealously guarded his towel. After spreading the blanket onto the mattress and removing my boots, I lay down.

BRRAAAP! – the buzzer rang again, and the cell lights all went dark. The lights in the empty day room kept burning. The steel bars cast shadows across the floor of our cell. I could hear Sanchez snoring softly in the top bunk.

Edelman spoke quietly. "You'll be okay. Four days is nothing. I've been here two weeks, and they'll let me out tomorrow. Sanchez is here for thirty days. He still has two weeks to go."

Soon Edelman too was asleep. I, however, tossed and turned. It was not my bunky's references to sodomy that kept me awake; I had no real fear of him. More likely, it was the bolted supper of salty chipped beef and lightbulb coffee that gave me the dull but persistent ache in my belly. This dyspepsia was to occur nightly while my sentence was served.

BRRAAAP! – the now-hated buzzer erupted, and I jolted awake. The overhead lights were glaring. I must have drifted off sometime during the night. Out on the dayroom floor, two new lodgers slept on mattresses. I had not heard their arrival. Now the sounds of urination and the smells of defecation wafted through the cages, as cellmates took their turns at the toilets in the back of each cell.

The buzzer heralded the cranking back of the cell doors. As each cell was opened, its inhabitants stepped out and into the dayroom. After folding my blanket and shoving the mattress under the bottom bunk, I joined them.

With a rattle and clank, the cage door rolled back. The Trusty wheeled his cart into the room. Each tray held a bowl of oatmeal, a small carton of milk, a Melmac cup, and a plastic spoon. A pitcher of coffee steamed faintly next to a pitcher of orange Tang. I tasted my oatmeal. It tasted metallic.

Edelman spoke: "They boil the oats without any salt. It tastes better with a little of this." He handed me a salt packet left over from yesterday's dinner. After sprinkling a bit on the pallid oatmeal, sure enough, it tasted ok.

After the Trusty had retrieved the breakfast trays, after the coffee crew had tied the bag of coffee onto the light fixture, a deputy opened the door from the corridor.

"Schnick, you're wanted in the Sheriff's office. Now!" he called into the day room. Then he closed the outer door, watching from the wire-reinforced window.

I stood, then walked to the gate of the cage. The other

prisoners watched, but did not seem very interested. The gate clanked back, and I stepped in. The air lock closed behind me. The deputy then swung the door back, and I joined him in the corridor.

We walked past the booking office to another door, which opened into an almost empty room. I saw a small Formica table top with a chair on each side. A man in a brown double-knit suit sat in one. An open notebook lay on the table before him. I heard the door close and lock behind me.

"Have a seat," the man intoned, gesturing towards the empty chair. I sat. After identifying himself as Agent Johnson from the FBI, he then interrogated me for half an hour, mostly about my missing draft card.

My draft classification was 4-F: "Registrant not qualified for military service". Although this was probably the most coveted designation for any draft dodger, I came by my exemption honestly, having been hospitalized with asthma more than once as a boy. Eventually satisfied that I was indeed 4F, and not subject to arrest and prosecution for draft evasion, the G-man stood, then snapped his notebook shut.

"You had better write your draft board and get a duplicate card," he announced. "Violation of the Selective Service Act is punishable with five years in a federal penitentiary." Leaning closer, he whispered, "Let this be a word to the wise."

"Yes sir. Thank you, sir," I said, trying to sound sincere.

I had no intention of contacting Selective Service. Two of my high school friends had been killed in Vietnam already. Another came back suicidally depressed. I wanted to have nothing to do with that lash up.

The brown-suited agent slid his notebook into a briefcase, turned, and knocked on the door to the main office. It was swung open by a deputy, and Agent Johnson left the room. The deputy motioned to me to stand, turn, and follow him, as he unlocked the door by which I had entered.

We left the small interrogation room and proceeded back up the corridor. As we arrived at D wing, the same Trusty that delivered the chow was waiting outside with a cart full of books and magazines. The deputy locked us through and into the day room together.

The Trusty took a seat on the steel bench, and the other captives collected the books or magazines that they had stashed in their cells. These they dropped into a bin in the bottom of the cart. Each man could then choose a book and two magazines from the library cart. I grabbed a beat-up paperback copy of *Riders of the Purple Sage* by Zane Grey, and two old issues of *Popular Mechanics*.

Each day spent in the slammer passed very much like the day before. The only thing that seemed to happen at all was the regular delivery of indigestible meals three times a day. No exercise was available, aside from pacing the length of the dayroom for hours at a time, like the slightly crazed veteran of Folsom. I had always wondered how I might react to incarceration, and now I knew. I was bored to tears.

Edelman was discharged the next day. This meant that

I got the bottom bunk but had no one to talk to. A few hours after he left, a Trusty came into the barred vestibule and called my name.

"Schnick, your bunkie dropped off some reading for you," he said, handing me two glossy new magazines through the bars: Psychology Today, and Architectural Digest. Although touched by the gesture that Edelman would steal magazines for me, I actually preferred my Zane Grey novel or reading in Popular Mechanics about an iceboat that you could build at home.

My four-day sentence passed slowly. On Friday morning, after the usual oatmeal breakfast, a deputy called my name and escorted me to the booking office. The deputy at the desk retrieved my rucksack from the storage room and handed me the reusable envelope containing my wallet and change. I put the wallet in the back pocket of my jeans, then hoisted my rucksack.

After I signed a receipt for my stuff, the desk clerk said, "Deputy Collins is going to give you a lift to the highway where you can legally thumb a ride."

Deputy Collins was silent on the five minute drive to the edge of town. I was allowed to ride in the back seat of his Ford prowl car with no handcuffs. The tires crunched in gravel as we came to a stop next to a stubbled hayfield. The lawman walked around, opened the trunk, then set my pack to the ground. After he opened my door, I stepped out, a free man.

Collins paused as he was getting back into his Sheriff's Department car, his deputy cap and sunglasses tilted towards me. "If you're smart," he said, "you'll get out of Redding and stay out!" After slamming his door, he glanced at the empty highway, made a U-turn, and drove back towards town.

I stood on the shoulder for maybe a minute, enjoying the morning sun and the light breeze. I saw a car coming and stuck out my thumb. The beat-up, orange-painted roadster slowed and stopped right next to me. The driver, a young man with blond shaggy hair and mustache, looked me over and asked, "Where you headed?"

"Portland," I responded.

"Great! I can take you as far as Eugene," he said. "Hop in."

I stowed my pack in the small luggage well behind the seats and sat in the passenger seat. As the driver let out the clutch, the old sports car coughed, backfired, and we were rolling down the highway. The driver spoke loudly, to be heard over the buffeting wind.

"Did you know? Jimi Hendrix died."

The Hogsback, Mt. Hood (U.S. Forest Service photo)

Dirtbag Honeymoon

AFTER I TURNED 21, Susie not only consented to marry me but also to climb Mt. Hood, as a sort of dirtbag honeymoon.

We asked the pastor of Maranatha Church to marry us, but he declined, saying that we would have to move apart and undergo weeks of counseling before he would do it. This didn't appeal to us one bit. Our church attendance declined drastically after that—in fact it pretty much stopped altogether.

A judge married us at Portland City Hall. Our witnesses were Dick Raley and Sissy Gnossos, the girl who had initiated me into the gifts of the spirit. After the ceremony, we had tea and sandwiches at a diner, then Susie and I hitchhiked to Mount Hood.

We camped that night on the bank of Zigzag Glacier, well out of sight of the paying guests of Timberline Lodge. Summer was upon us, and the snows of the previous winter had thawed, compacted, and refrozen into hard, glazed blue ice.

Leaving our tiny tent a little before dawn, we strapped steel crampons to our boots with leather straps. Trudging upward, our crampons crunched with each step. The summit rose five thousand feet above us. After a few hours of this, we reached the ragged, blasted crater of the dormant volcano.

To the left loomed Illumination Rock; ahead were the Hot Rocks, hoarsely exhaling their sulphur fumes, and to the right, the Hogsback. The terrain got steeper and more exposed in the caldera of the old volcano. It was time to rope up.

The sun shone upon us as I uncoiled the climbing rope. I carefully tied a bowline-on-a-bight around my bride's waist, cinching the knot. After tying the other end of the line around myself, I paced out thirty strides until the rope hung in a shallow loop between us, and we started up the looming face of the Coalman Glacier.

The trampled trail of previous climbers had frozen into a rough and ragged staircase, along the steepening "Hogsback" that ran up the center of the slope. Susie and I moved together, the rope stretched between us. Kicking our crampons into the icy track, we planted the shafts of our ice axes into the crunchy snow in three quarter time: Left, Right, Axe. . . Left, Right, Axe. . . and so on.

Near the top of the glacier, a bergschrund cut across the slope. This deep crevasse marks the division between the stationary accumulation zone, above, and the moving ice below. The bergschrund forms differently each year as accumulated ice starts flowing down the mountain. This year, the 'schrund had formed with a narrow ramp of ice bridging the two lips of the chasm, like the diagonal stroke on the letter Z.

I led on, following the trail left by other climbers. The white walls of the crevasse fell away into blue darkness on either side of the slanting slice of glacier we were ascending. A few chips of ice were dislodged by our crampons and tinkled into the gloom below. Above the bergschrund, the trail rose more steeply, a few hundred more feet, and passed between two pillars of stone that climbers call the "Pearly Gates", as they are usually coated with hoarfrost.

We kept a slow three-quarter time as we gained the final ridge, then collapsed happily on the summit rocks. Eating our sandwiches and drinking cold tea from our canteens, we chatted with a party of three that had arrived earlier. Along the horizon gleamed other peaks: Mounts Rainier, Adams, and St. Helens in the north; Jefferson and the Three Sisters to the south.

The other party began its descent, and Susie and I had the summit to ourselves. A few minutes later, it was time for us to start down. Susie went first, and I followed, about sixty feet of rope between us.

Down-climbing a slippery slope always seems more precarious than climbing up the same route. You are looking down. Each step wants to slide a little farther as you trudge down the icy lumps. You are tired, from sleeping on a rocky moraine, then hiking uphill for hours in the dark. Most climbing accidents happen on the descent.

From above, the ice bridge across the bergschrund was not as obvious as it had been on the way up. The flake of glacier peeled away from the upper lip of the big crevasse and ran at a giddy angle down to the lower lip.

We paused a few yards above the chasm, craning our necks in an effort to peer into the gloomy depths. I set to work with the adze of my axe, enlarging a sun cup. Next I drove the shaft into the crusty ice with my hammer, leaving about a foot of wooden shaft above the surface. I sat in the in the saddle-shaped dish I had carved, my legs straddling the planted axe. I faced down the fall line. After loosely coiling the slack into a pile beside me, the rope ran through my left hand, around my lower back, through my right fist, then a few feet to Susie's waist loop.

"On belay!" I said.

"Descending!" she called back.

Knees bent slightly, ankles flexed to hold her crampon points in contact with the ice, the young alpinist held her axe across her body, left hand grasping the lower shaft above the spike. Her right fist on the head of the tool, she gripped the serrated pick like a dagger—ready to be stabbed into the slope in case she started to slide. I let out line as she crabbed across the lip of the crevasse and gingerly cramponed down, onto the jammed serac that formed the ice bridge.

As the slope became steeper, Susie leaned back, away from the exposure. Then the points of her crampons broke free, and she skidded down, disappearing over the lip of the crevasse in a clatter of ice. I felt her weight come onto the rope.

"Are you okay?" I shouted.

"I hope so," her voice echoed from the depths.

Kicking her front points into the wall of ice and swinging the pick of her axe into the ice above her, her head and shoulders again became visible as I took in line. I applied some more tension to the rope. My young wife regained her footing, and was again standing on the edge of the chasm.

"Are you okay?" I asked again.

"Now I'm angry!" she said, with a rueful glance back at me.

While carefully planting her left crampon, her ice axe spike, then her right crampon into the glistening ice, small chips were dislodged by her hardware and tinkled down into the void.

"On belay," I croaked.

"Descending," she called back, as she crunched down the snow bridge, left, right, axe. I let out line as she steadily worked her way down to the lower lip of the bergschrund. Turning, she looked back up at me, then sat on the edge of the crevasse with her wool knickers, boots, and crampons jammed into the ice. She gave a yank on the rope that connected us, and called, "Slack."

I played out rope to her as she wrapped it once around her body and coiled it beside her on the glacier. When it became taut, she leaned back, looked up at me, and called, "On belay."

I was the luckiest man in the world. I had found a woman to love, and she loved me back. We trusted each other with our lives, repeatedly. I felt my super powers returning. My confidence was back, and I didn't feel invisible any more.

I wrote my parents an air letter telling them that I had gotten married. A couple of weeks later I got a letter back, wanting to know everything about her, but mostly what religious denomination she was. I guessed that with a name like Selkin, they were worried that she might be a "Jewess", which was the word my father used when referring to Hebrew females.

My mother sent a separate, air-mailed letter addressed to "Mrs. John Mark Schnick" welcoming her to the family. Susie was amused by this. She had no intention of taking my name, and I had no particular desire for her to do so. I realized that my parents' view of the world hadn't changed, but mine had.

My parents aside, I wondered if all my troubles were finally over. I hoped so.

34

"I Ditched the Joint"

SUSIE AND I had lots of friends in Portland, and we enjoyed our bohemian lifestyle: weaving for her, metal sculpture for me, hiking and climbing on weekends, and once, a scary and hilarious acid trip, with Oakland friends, driving through a Cascades blizzard in a green Hudson Hornet piloted by the intrepid Skip Strobel. He could drive while stoned on acid better than the rest of could when we were straight.

Rent was cheap, and so was food. Beans, rice, and horse meat were sold by the non-profit co-op, *Friends and Food*, at the bottom of the hill, in Cow Hollow, across the street from the freight balloon depot.

Things changed one afternoon when I came home from a modeling job at Portland State. Susie was sitting on a cushion, a teapot and two cups in front of her, her colorful skirt spread around her in a circle on the floor. She was brushing her long dark hair, which also reached the floor.

I sat facing her, and she poured me a cup of green tea.

"We're going to have a baby," she said, a slight smile on her lips.

I almost dropped my teacup. I knew this was a possibility, but here it was.

"That's great," I said. "Are you sure?"

"I'm sure," she replied. "It's been two months since I had my period, and I feel queasy in the mornings."

———

After talking over our situation for a few days, we decided to move to Oakland, where our high school friends had started a commune called "Flywheel". Plus, Susie's parents could put her on their Kaiser health plan, to cover medical expenses, since she was only 18.

On the morning we left, a friend dropped by the flat as we were closing it up.

"Sure gonna miss you guys," he said. "Here's a going away present."

He held out a bomber of a joint, made with oversized stars-and-stripes rolling paper.

"I'll take that," said Susie, tucking it into a pocket in her skirt. "If we get stopped by the heat, they might not search me."

Possession of any amount of weed was a felony at the time. I knew she would never smoke it. She wouldn't even take an aspirin, since she knew she was pregnant.

Our friend gave us a ride to Interstate 5, where we stuck

out our thumbs. We didn't have to wait too long before a car pulled over.

"I can take you to Eugene, if you don't mind flying," said the young black man behind the wheel. "My name's Nate."

We both laughed, thinking he meant that he would drive fast. When he pulled off at a small airport outside of town, we realized he was serious.

"I have to file a flight plan," said Nate. "Just wait here for a minute, then we'll walk to the plane."

When he returned to the car, Susie and I hoisted our packs and followed him across a concrete pad to a red and white Cessna 180, guyed down with steel cables. The sleek machine looked as if it was straining at its bonds, ready to leap into the sky.

Nate stowed our rucksacks in a compartment behind the rear seat, removed the guy wires, then circled the plane with a clipboard, checking fuel and hydraulic fluids.

"I've never ridden in an airplane before," said Susie, her eyes like saucers.

"You should ride up front with me," said the pilot. "I can show you how it all works, and the view is better."

We climbed into the cabin and buckled up, me in the back seat. Nate flipped some switches, checked some gauges, and stowed his checklist beside his seat.

The engine started up, then began to roar as we sped down the runway. Soon we were high above the hayfields and Douglas firs of the Willamette Valley, on a sunny spring day.

"I got my private license last month," shouted Nate over the drone of the engine. "As soon as I log enough hours, I can apply for a commercial license."

"How high are we?" asked Susie.

"Seven thousand feet," replied the young aviator.

———

We landed at a small airport outside of Eugene. This is great! I thought. Nannette, Lillian, and Janet had travelled like this from British Columbia to San Blas, and I could see why. Susie and I thanked Nate for the lift, then hiked a few hundred yards to an on-ramp for southbound Interstate 5.

Three cars passed us by, but a fourth car pulled over to the shoulder. It was a black and white Ford Crown Victoria, with *EUGENE POLICE* lettered on the side. A tall, uniformed officer emerged from the driver's side, walked back along the shoulder, and stood, arms akimbo, facing us. I didn't get the feeling that he was going to offer us a ride.

"I'm arresting both of you for hitchhiking," he said. "Please put your hands against the car."

We both assumed the position. Susie's long braid hung down as she leaned against the vehicle. He frisked me and stuffed me into the back seat, then opened the passenger side door and allowed Susie to sit in the front.

As he walked around the hood of the prowl car, Susie whispered, "I ditched the joint."

Inside the police station, we were booked, and a female officer led Susie to a room with a frosted glass window. I was searched in another room, then led to a holding cell in a back hall of the station and locked in a cage. I sat on the bare bunk and stared at the linoleum floor.

This trip started out so well, I thought.

The door to the corridor swung open, and the matron escorted Susie past the front of my cage and locked her into the next cell. A cinder block wall stood between us. We could hear each other, but couldn't see or touch.

"Are you okay?" she asked, when the matron had left.

"Tip-top," I said. "You?"

"Fine, I guess."

We didn't talk much, both of us suspecting that the fuzz could hear anything we said.

Time passed, then Susie spoke up.

"I'm hungry."

"Me, too," I responded.

As if on cue, a deputy came into the corridor and handed each of us a cellophane wrapped sandwich through a slot in the bars. We each got a Dixie cup of water as well.

More time passed, then the officer returned. "You're in luck."

"How's that?" I asked.

"The judge will see you this afternoon," he said. "Otherwise you would have to spend Memorial Day weekend in the Lane County Jail."

The jailer unlocked both of our cells, then led us through a corridor, up a stairway, and into a courtroom. A bailiff called our names, and we stood in front of a raised desk, a judge in a black robe peering down at us.

"You have been charged with standing in a roadway for purpose of procuring a ride," he said. "How do you plead?"

Susie and I looked at each other, then looked back at the judge.

"May I ask a question, Your Honor?" I said.

"Go ahead," said the judge.

"Can you tell me the legal definition of roadway?"

The judge looked amused, then opened a thick book on his desk. He flipped through it, then read silently for a moment.

"A roadway is any portion of a street or highway normally used for vehicular traffic," quoted the black-robed one. He looked at me.

"How do you plead: guilty or not guilty?"

"Not guilty, Your Honor," I said.

He turned to Susie. "And you, Miss Selkin?"

"Not guilty, Your Honor," said Susie.

After the judge had heard Officer Guth's account of the arrest, it was my turn to defend us.

"Your Honor," I said, "may I use the chalkboard?"

"Go ahead."

I stood at the board beside the desk and drew a map of the southbound on-ramp. I drew X's where Susie and I had stood, and a rectangle where the prowl car had stopped. The judge watched, while the policeman looked bored and checked his watch.

I then drew a circle around the two X's, then a much larger circle to the side. Inside the big circle I drew our feet standing behind a series of raised six-inch high curbs at the edge of the blacktop.

"Your Honor," I said, "we were standing behind a series of curbs. They were painted in black and yellow stripes. The area could not be used for vehicular traffic."

The judge now looked at the cop. "Officer Guth, do you see anything wrong with this diagram?"

The policeman walked over to the blackboard, picked up a stick of chalk, and touched it to the slate. He made a couple of light marks, then dropped the chalk back in its tray.

"No, Your Honor, I have nothing to add," he said.

"Very well," said the judge, "I find the defendants not guilty."

Looking at Susie and me he said, "You are both free to go."

Officer Guth was cheerful as he accompanied the two of us back into the station house. "You guys won this time, but if I see you hitchhiking again, I'll run you in again."

Inside the office where the cops wrote up their reports, another officer in a sports shirt spoke.

"Hey Guth, check it out." He pulled up his shirt enough to expose a shiny black leather holster with a thirty-eight caliber snub-nosed revolver nestled inside.

"Nice," said Officer Guth.

"Go ahead, try it," said the plainclothes detective.

Guth pulled the little pistol from its sheath and replaced it a couple of times. He made a light groaning sound, like a woman having sex: "Ooh, Ahh." Both of the cops laughed.

As the boys played grab ass, Susie turned away and rolled her eyes.

The cop had known darn well that we weren't breaking the law, but he had arrested us anyway. As we were released, he threatened us again with arrest, while he played with a revolver.

I thought, *What's wrong with these people, anyway? What do they have against hippies and black folks?* I still can't figure it out.

After retrieving our rucksacks, Susie and I left the cop clubhouse and stood on a sunlit sidewalk in downtown Eugene.

"How did you ditch the doobie?" I asked.

"While the cop was frisking you, he couldn't watch me," she said. "I tossed it under his car."

Neither she nor I felt too good about hitchhiking around there. From a pay phone, I made a collect call to Nick Albert, the Flywheel commune's founding father. He wired twenty dollars to the Eugene Western Union office. We rode to Oakland on a Greyhound bus and walked a couple of blocks to the house on 22nd Street, now a seething nest of our high school hippie friends.

We laid out our bedroll and joined the party.

Objective Danger

ANY HAZARD, *such as stone fall or avalanche, to which climbing skill is irrelevant, is referred to by climbers as objective danger.*

Living in Oakland, Susie's brother and I started climbing together in the Sierra. Susie was miffed that her swelling belly kept her from going with us. After climbing a few easy routes, Mike and I decided to attempt a harder climb: mixed rock and ice on a steep north face.

We kicked our crampon points into hard, frozen snow as we climbed up the Mt. Conness glacier. Darkness lay over this north side of the mountain. The first pink rays of dawn painted the granite teeth of the ridge, a thousand feet above us.

When planning this climb with my brother-in-law Mike, I knew that the morning sunlight could melt the ice in the cracks and fissures of the rock, sending rockfall down the face. We had camped on the glacier the night before, so that we could get an early start this morning. We set up the tent near a *moulin*, or glacial mill, where surface melt flowed into a crevasse. During the night we could hear a rumbling gurgle through the ice, beneath our foam pads.

I had never worn a helmet on a climb before, but for this climb we both wore construction workers' hard hats. In the lead, I carried a small rack of hardware: a few pitons, ice screws, and carabiners. We expected to encounter some mixed climbing—both rock and ice. The red nylon rope draped behind me to Mike, a hundred feet below. We continued up the slope in a three-legged gait: left crampon, right crampon, then ice-axe spike.

The slope steepened as we neared the bergschrund, the big crevasse at the top of a glacier where the moving ice separates from the static ice and snow of the headwall. Soon we stood on the lower lip of the crevasse, the upper lip rearing above us, blue ice dark in the depth below us. We coiled the rope loosely and sat on a rounded edge of ice. While Mike rummaged in his pack for some peanut butter sandwiches, I admired the view. The High Sierra stretched away to the north. Only the highest peaks and ridges were glowing above the blue valleys and canyons.

As Mike handed me my breakfast, I glanced down and noticed that the snow beneath us was peppered with pebbles and gravel. A few yards to our right, along the lip of the 'schrund, the snow was clean, with no sign of rockfall.

"Let's move over there," I said, nodding towards the cleaner area. Mike grunted his assent. We grabbed our gear and picked our way along the ice to the new spot.

As soon as we started eating, we heard a clatter, a rumble, then a shattering roar from the granite headwall above us. First gravel, then rocks and boulders shot down the face and slammed into the ledge where we had been sitting. We hunched down as rocks started rattling onto our helmets and ricocheting off the packed snow and ice. Bangety-bang, crash crash, KABOOM!

After a few seconds the roaring stopped, and the stones stopped falling. Where we had been sitting a minute earlier, the rockfall had smashed a furrow, as wide as a truck and deep as a ditch. Boulders of two feet in diameter were strewn downslope. Hundreds of smaller rocks covered the areas between. Mike and I looked sheepishly at each other. Silently, we gathered our gear and began the descent.

————

Climbing had become an obsession with me. When I wasn't climbing, I was thinking about the next excursion. Only after becoming a father did I start to realize that high-risk climbing might not be the most responsible behavior, but the peaks still drew me like a magnet.

I suspected that the "flow state" of men in battle must be similar to the feeling I had when leading a difficult pitch on a climb. My senses would focus intently on the angle of my crampon points and the pick of my ice axe as I moved up an icefall. One false move could spell death. Conversely, I never felt more alive than when I was climbing.

I realized that I didn't have to fight and kill to prove my manhood. I had conquered my own fears in the mountains. I had learned patience by hitchhiking all over North America. Soon I would be a parent, and that would bring more challenges, but I was eager to meet them.

I knew that some of my friends' fathers had never beaten their sons, yet the boys had grown up just fine. I wanted to be that kind of father, not the angry man in the starched uniform.

The Spinning Wheel

AFTER POOLING OUR RESOURCES, our group of friends was able to rent a beat-up Craftsman Bungalow in East Oakland. Susie and I had a room off the kitchen in the back—really a closed-in back porch.

Nick and Alana shared the front bedroom. I'd known Alana since we were both fourteen and picking peppers in Pleasanton as a summer job. I'd always had a crush on her, but she had gone steady with Nick in high school, and they were married now.

The remaining two bedrooms were inhabited by a changing cast of friends. Only three of us had jobs: Nick was a museum photographer, Alana a surgical nurse, and Jim, an assistant manager at a supermarket. These three were the mainstays of the commune, the rest of us being semi-employed artists and students. This was Flywheel.

Sometimes Jim would bring home sacks of expired or damaged groceries from the Lucky store, and we ate pretty well. Alana planted a garden in the back yard. One hot afternoon she removed her blouse while working in the sun. She wiped her forehead with the back of one hand, holding a basket of vegetables in the other—a smudged Demeter, in yellow sunlight.

Coleen, the folksinger from Tennyson High, was here, living with Jim, and other high school friends drifted in or out—for a week, a month, or a year.

———

One morning, as the house was just waking, the front door opened, and in swept a force of nature. She wore a silk scarf tied around the side of her head, harlequin eye makeup, a purple velvet jacket, flowing skirt, and boots. She carried a two gallon glass jar of shelled nuts under each arm. Her father ran a candy factory, and these were surplus, or something.

She certainly got my attention, and Susie's too.

Josie Jurczenia was a weaving student at the California College of Arts and Crafts, in Oakland. She and Susie immediately hit it off, excitedly talking about spinning and dyeing wool, and the advantages of the jack loom over the counterbalance loom.

Josie and Susie quickly became best friends. As Susie's belly swelled, her skin glowed and her body ripened. Josie said that she would love to photograph us together, before our baby arrived.

Josie picked us up in her yellow VW Beetle and drove to her place, an apartment close to the college. Susie and I disrobed, and Josie shot a series of photos on Tri-X film. The black and white prints that Josie made were like her: vivid, sensual, and sweet. The mark of an artist.

Jim didn't only bring home expired groceries and dented cans. One day he came home with four tickets to a concert by The Who in San Francisco. Coleen had broken up with him, and he drove Josie, Susie, and me over to the Civic Center. Susie rode in the front passenger seat, on account of her delicate condition.

The four of us sat together in the auditorium, Jim and Josie a row ahead of Susie and myself. The house lights dimmed, then Roger Daltrey, John Entwistle, Keith Moon, and Pete Townshend stepped to the stage. They set up a furious instrumental din, louder than anything any of us had ever heard.

Susie took my hand and held it to her belly. Our baby was kicking and squirming in time to the band. Perhaps the extra loud music had a permanent effect on the fetus, because our son is crazy about The Who to this day, forty-five years later.

This is my generation, baby. . .

The baby was born at Kaiser Hospital in Oakland. Susie labored mightily for a couple of hours. Every time a nurse tried to tie a gown on her, Susie would tear it off, and throw it across the labor room. She knew what she was doing, and she wanted to do it naked.

Mother and child spent the night in the hospital, as was customary in those days, and I took a bus back to Flywheel to hand out cigars.

The next day Jim drove me back to the hospital, but when Susie and the baby were discharged, we realized that we hadn't settled on a name for our offspring yet.

"That's okay," said the discharge nurse, "just get back to us in a couple of days and we can still file the name with the birth certificate."

"What happens if we don't get back to you?" I asked.

"Then he'll be Baby Boy Schnick," she said.

Jim drove us home, and we pulled a drawer from our thrift store bureau, folded a quilt in the bottom, and we laid Baby Boy in it, swaddled firmly.

The name Ezra and the name Gideon had been debated earlier. Jasper was the favorite of Josie, who was off in Connecticut visiting her parents.

"How about Ezra Gideon Schnick?" asked Susie.

"How about Ezra Icefield Schnick?" I returned.

"Icefield? Why Icefield?" she asked, puzzled.

"He was conceived on a glacier. . ." I offered.

Susie nodded, "Okay," and Ezra Icefield Schnick it was.

Life in the Flywheel commune continued. Nick and Alana moved out and got an apartment in Alameda. Susie, Ezra, and I took over the front bedroom, and Josie moved into the back sleeping porch. Susie's father delivered a cradle he'd made, with painted blessings in Hebrew and Aramaic. We moved Ezra out of the drawer, and Susie could rock the cradle with her toe as she twisted yarn on her spinning wheel.

Josie bought a Volkswagen panel van. She painted giant dancing cats on the sides. The cats carried steaming pies and were bordered by a frieze of bounding rats at the top. A checkerboard ran along the bottom: a hippie van designed by Beatrix Potter.

I started making a fiberglass sculpture in the garage, and Josie set up a counterbalance loom in the living room, next to the upright piano.

The piano was something of a distraction to Susie. It seemed like every time we had to be anywhere on time, to a Who or Bob Dylan concert, or *2001, a Space Odyssey*, Susie would be standing at the piano practicing her arrangement of *Climb Every Mountain*. We were all weirdos, including Susie. It was the Seventies.

Once, I returned from a climbing trip, and Susie came up to me with a funny little smile on her lips.

"Josie and I made love last night," she said.

I was startled, but managed to ask, "How was it?"

"Like two angels in heaven," she said, with a dreamy look.

A few days later, to nobody's great surprise, Susie, Josie, and I ended up in bed together. The experience left something to be desired, however. We each realized that such things made much better fantasy than reality. We never tried a *ménage à trois* again.

Living at Flywheel was lots of fun. A houseful of artists, we fed off each other's ideas and threw a party every weekend.

We didn't have a television, but life in the commune often resembled a situation comedy, with the additions of casual nudity and weed smoking.

———

Ezra was growing and soon learned how to crawl. The little tow-headed angel could pop up anywhere in the house—or disappear and cause general alarm. Once we had a cocktail party. We invited all our friends over for martinis. Some folks didn't really care for gin and left their unfinished drinks on the floor.

The next day, while all hands were cleaning up, Susie went into our bedroom to check on the baby.

"Ezra's gone!" said the teenage mother, with a note of panic in her voice. The rest of us ran to the front bedroom, then fanned out through the house, searching. Josie found the little tyke, curled up around a martini glass, sound asleep behind a couch.

"Just keep an eye on him," said the help nurse over the phone. "If he vomits, make sure he is breathing okay, and bring him in if you're worried."

After Ezra slept it off, Susie and I decided we should move out and get a place of our own. Jim and his new girlfriend, Irene, did the same, and Josie lit out to Montana in her hippie van. Skip Strobel came gleefully out of the closet, then moved to Rome to pursue a career in cinema. This chapter of Flywheel was over.

Susie and I found a tiny basement apartment. She and I slept in the front room, and the bedroom held Ezra's crib and a tiny bathroom. We applied for welfare and were also given food stamps. I enrolled in Laney College, at the suggestion of our social worker.

I studied design, printing, video production, and plastics. Susie stayed home in the basement and washed Ezra's diapers at the corner laundromat. Looking back, I can understand how frustrated she must have felt, trapped in a tiny basement while I went to college every day, producing video stories and print ads.

Josie had returned and lived a few blocks away. When she didn't come over to our house for dinner, Susie and I would visit her and sometimes meet guest artists visiting her college.

Josie, Susie, and Ezra set off on a road trip and spent a few weeks touring the Southwest, including the Grand Canyon. While they were gone, I found a job.

"Can you do pasteup?" asked Julie, the skinny girl that lived above our basement flat.

"Sure," I answered.

"Come to work with me tomorrow. We need a pasteup artist for the Daily Cal. Bring your book."

When I showed my portfolio to Julie's boss, a retired Navy chief, he asked, "Can you start today?"

By the time my wife, son, and our best friend had returned, I had dropped out of Laney and was working full time for a publishing company. I went to work at three in the afternoon, and got off at midnight, or the wee hours, depending if the student editors had met their deadlines or not. The boss always stocked the refrigerator with beer whenever we had to work overtime. This was better than coffee, because when we got off work during the wee hours we weren't wired and sleepless when we got home.

The typesetters, who punched out long reels of paper strips to feed into the phototypesetting machines, were all young women, except for a couple of blond, gay brothers who were the supervisors.

The tape-punching machines made a terrific racket, like strings of ladyfinger firecrackers going off continuously for hours. Julie, Sydney, and Grace would duck into the teletype room occasionally to get stoned, and I was always invited. Everybody would pull out a joint or a hash pipe and light up, passing each around the circle.

Do the math: two typesetters, two graphic artists, four joints or hash pipes. We could only take a minute or two before we had to be back in the composition room. We generally got pretty wasted, but if the Cal students had met their copy deadlines, we always got the edition to the printer on time.

Once I lingered for a moment over the Associated Press teletype machine. Its bell rang three times, then the robotic typewriter started typing, rat a tat tat.

The NASA Mars 3 orbiter is now transmitting data to Space Administration headquarters.

Rat-a-tat-tat.

Since I was bringing in a regular paycheck, Susie and I no longer received welfare payments. We could, however, continue to buy food stamps, but had to pay $80 for $100 worth of coupons. The extra twenty dollars for food came in handy.

Patricia Hearst was a Cal student, and when she was kidnapped and held for ransom by "The Symbionese Liberation Army", *The Daily Californian* was all over the story. I had pasted up stories about the group before, when they had murdered Marcus Foster, the Oakland schools' superintendent. It wasn't until years later that I realized this was a story of national importance.

An SLA associate had been a model for life drawing classes at Laney. I still have a charcoal drawing I made of her—a beautiful black woman with a fine figure. Josie's stolen Social Security card had turned up in the ashes of the Compton Avenue house in LA—the tragic last stand of the East Bay revolutionaries. FBI agents had come to the door at Flywheel, looking for leads.

Meanwhile, back at the ranch, I had problems. Susie was restless. She wanted to find herself. I realized I had to do better than leaving her alone at night while I pasted up newspapers. I typed up a new resumé and started showing my portfolio to ad agencies in the city and the East Bay.

I found a job doing packaging and collateral art for Foremost McKesson, on Post Street in San Francisco. This was the real deal: an in-house agency for a big corporation. The hefty paycheck meant that Susie and I could rent the bottom half of a Victorian house in Berkeley. The job included full medical, dental, and generous vacation time.

Things were looking up. The San Francisco Art Director's Club held their annual party on board the *Klamath*, a ferryboat that housed the Walter Landor agency. Susie and I were there. She attracted quite a bit of attention from the other admen, 19-year-old beauty that she was.

At the time, I recalled how both Alice and Dorothy had dumped me because I'd had no prospects. *This time would be different*, I thought.

At work, I drew mechanical art for prescription drug packaging in Latin America. I devised a dispenser for lineament tins. The boss, a Swiss-trained designer, decided to file a patent for the design. Our translator, a tall *Salvadoreña* named Aña, would take the crew out at lunch for pupusas in the Mission district. Aña had taken a degree at the Sorbonne, in Paris, and was a very witty woman.

By all indications, life was great, but there was trouble in paradise. Susie wasn't a bit happy finding herself the teenage mother of a rambunctious toddler, and married to a man who wore a tie and commuted to an ad agency in the city. She was a radical feminist, and this life wasn't for her. We had loud quarrels, sometimes ending in plates and saucers thrown in anger. We never hurt each other, but Ezra was terrified, crying in a corner.

Both Susie and I had been unfaithful—and not just with our friend Josie. Susie wanted out, and I was in a quandary. When I came home after work, Susie might be dressed to the nines, wearing makeup. She would be out the door immediately, and might spend the evening with her poet friends in San Francisco.

I would fix supper for Ezra and myself, and, after reading him a bedtime story, I sat up waiting for Susie's return. I ached with loneliness, and jealousy tortured me with its sickly green flames.

Back at work, the boss called me into his office.

"I like your work," he said, "but there's not room for another designer here. You need to find another job."

I felt terrible riding back to Berkeley on the bus. What would Susie say when I told her I'd been fired? I walked home from the bus stop in the dusk. When I arrived at the flat, something looked different. The window curtains flapped in the breeze, and the house was dark.

Pinned to the front door was a Dear John letter.

John and Josie in Humboldt County, 1976

37

Eyesight to the Blind

I PULLED THE NOTE from the door and went inside. I sat at the kitchen table and read the letter from Susie under the hanging bulb. She had taken Ezra and was going to stay at a girlfriend's house. She would bring him back to spend alternate weeks at my house. She would call me in the morning.

I should have felt devastated, but curiously, I felt relieved. I knew that Susie had been desperately unhappy the last few months. I had been unable to contemplate leaving my wife and child. I clung to the hope that the larger paychecks would somehow make things better.

At least I wouldn't have to tell her I was losing my job.

The next morning, back at work, I was cheered by the realization that the boss didn't care if it took me three months to find another position, and he would write a letter of introduction to any agency that I wanted. I could even go to interviews on company time. The typographer from whom I ordered typesetting offered to print 500 letterpress business cards to my design. Nobody wanted to burn any bridges.

A month after Susie left me, Josie returned from another trip to Montana. She came over to my house on a Saturday to see how I was bearing up. It turned out that she was now working for a fashion designer in North Beach. We made a date to meet for drinks after work.

This became a regular thing while we were both working in San Francisco. Sometimes we would meet at Mario's Cigar Shop, or at the Washington Square Bar and Grill, down the street. Josie had her own sense of style and would turn heads when we were out together. Once we went to El Matador, the famous jazz club on Broadway, and heard Mose Allison sing *Eye Sight to the Blind.*

You talkin' about your woman, I wish you could see mine...

————

There was a name for what we were doing: courtship. Even though we had lived together in the commune, even though we had already been to bed, we wanted to do this right.

Josie made me a cowboy shirt of red corduroy and vintage flannel. We attended an art opening, she in an outfit of her own design, me in my snazzy new shirt. A *Tribune* photographer took flash photos of us that ended up in the society pages. Josie, with her funky fashion sense and beautiful profile, was nothing if not photogenic. When I was around her, I felt beautiful, too.

We soon became lovers, this time for real. We started sleeping one night at her house, one at mine. After tiring of the back and forth, and the unnecessary expense of two houses, we decided to give up her beautiful little Spanish Colonial apartment and live together with my son in the ramshackle Victorian in Berkeley. Susie had taken a break from motherhood, seeking to "find herself", and Ezra was spending more and more time with me and Josie.

I found a new job at a boutique ad agency in Emeryville, designing packaging, corporate ID, and print ads. Susie and I had filed for a do-it-yourself no-fault divorce, which would soon become final.

Ezra and I had lived like bachelors for the past few months, and the place needed cleaning and painting in the worst way. After we read Ezra a story and put him to bed, Josie and I might stay up past midnight, painting and hanging curtains or artwork.

When I was up on the ladder with a tray of paint and a roller, I knew that I'd never felt as happy. What's more, I realized I could make Josie happy, too.

I climbed down the ladder to refill the paint tray, but set it to the drop cloth instead. Josie was hemming a new curtain at her sewing machine, pursing her lips as she concentrated.

"When do you want to get married?" I asked.

She looked up, pulled her hair back from her pretty face, and said, "June, of course."

That weekend we drove over to Miramar, on Half Moon Bay. Bob Dorough was playing at The Bach Dancing and Dynamite Society, right on the beach. We thought this might be a good spot for our wedding, and we wanted to check it out.

We got a couple of glasses of wine and found a tiny table. The jazz singer came out, sat at the piano, and a bass player perched on a stool behind him with his upright viol. Dorough played an intro on the piano, then launched into an old Ella Fitzgerald number, *I'm beginning to see the light.*

The Blizzard of '77

BARE GROUND CRUNCHED beneath our boots. In February, the trail should have been buried in deep snow. This year, however, a drought was gripping California. The snows had not come to Lake Tahoe this year. Temperatures had climbed to 65° at South Shore. David Ross and I strapped skis to our rucksacks at the Eagle Falls picnic area. We were attempting to climb Dick's Peak, a summit of just under ten thousand feet, in the Desolation Wilderness.

We leaned into our pack straps and started hiking. About a mile above the road head, we came into a clearing. Three teen-aged boys sat on a fallen log, their oversized packframes leaning next to them. They wore cotton Levi's and sneakers. Loosely tied to one pack was a shrink-wrapped, still-frozen chicken. Tied to another was a half-gallon jug of Pink Chablis.

"How you guys doing?" I asked as we dropped our rucksacks, happy to take a break after the steep hump from lake level.

"Great!" came the reply from the tallest of the lads. "We're going to camp at Velma Lakes and roast a chicken on a spit over the open fire!"

"Cool," I said, glancing at my partner. He glanced back, with raised eyebrows. "We're going to climb Dick's Peak," I ventured.

"Radical!" said the tall boy. "Maybe we'll meet up again on the way down."

"Sure," I returned. "Good Luck!"

The young threesome hoisted their packframes and tramped away, bulky rolled-up sleeping bags bobbing, lashed to the bottoms of their packs with twine. David and I saddled up and continued our approach.

Lake Tahoe dropped away behind us as we pulled past seven thousand feet, then eight thousand. As we passed the nine thousand foot contour, we reached the bottom of a mushy snowfield. Happy that we had some use for the long boards we had been packing, we spread soft klister wax on the bottom of our skis to give us traction on the soggy snow.

We skied up the slope in diagonal switchbacks linked with kick turns. At the top of the snow slope, the granite boulders and scree of the East Ridge rose towards the summit. Between the rows of boulders we found a flat area of gravel and scrubby grass, just big enough for a camp. It was Saturday night on a three-day weekend. We pitched the small nylon tent, lit the tiny brass stove, and set a dented aluminum pot full of snow on top. We leaned back in the dying sunlight, sharing sips from a pint of Scotch.

The next morning, when the first rays of dawn glowed on the tent, I awoke from the fitful sleep of a first night at altitude. Gusts of wind occasionally rattled the red nylon roof. After a cup of instant coffee and another of instant oatmeal, we crawled out into the cold air, tied the tent door closed, and set off.

Staying about fifty feet below the ridgeline above us to our left, we worked our way up the peak. The wind came stronger now, and a continuous gale was hissing, moaning, and roaring across the stacked granite slope. When our route took us onto the actual crest, it became impossible to stand on two legs; we had to crawl to make any progress upward. It was getting colder by the minute.

Huddled together at the base of a huge boulder, David and I quickly agreed that conditions were getting worse, and it was no fun being beaten up by this evil breeze. We decided that discretion was the better part of valor. We turned around. Staggering now and then in the heavier gusts, we made our way back to camp.

After descending a few hundred feet, we noticed that the wind was lighter at the lower elevation, and the sun was shining. Since Monday was a holiday, neither David nor I had to return to our advertising jobs until Tuesday. We decided to stay here for another night.

I had a chunky paperback novel, *The Far Pavilions*, to read, and David pulled a sheaf of letter-sized papers from his pack and settled down, reading happily.

Looking up from my historical novel, I asked, "What are you reading?"

"Marketing study on canned foods in the Southwest," he responded. "Did you know that 80 percent of Texas housewives think that food left in an opened can in the refrigerator can turn to poison overnight?"

"No, I didn't know that," I murmured, returning to the monsoon in India.

We read or loafed all afternoon.

The wind picked up overnight as we slept. Around midnight, I was startled awake by a blast of fine snow in my face. I groped along the icy floor of the tent next to my sleeping bag. After locating my flashlight, I clicked the switch and could see sifts of snow puffing through the small tunnel vent above the door.

Our sleeping bags and the floor of the tent were covered with a thin layer of white. I sat up in my mummy bag, drew the drawstring of the vent tight, then went back to sleep.

We awoke to dim gray light and the machine-gun flapping of the tent. Opening the drawstring on the door a few inches, we saw heavy curtains of snow sweeping sideways through our little camp. Ducking back inside, we quickly agreed that it was time to "get the hell out of Dodge", as David put it.

We quickly stuffed our damp sleeping bags, tied our foam pads to our packs, and put on every article of clothing that we had. After crawling out of the snapping tent, I got busy with the skis. I scraped off yesterday's soft wax, then rubbed on harder, cold weather wax. David struggled to take down the frozen, flapping tent and stow it in his pack.

Saddled up, skis bound to our boots, we squinted through the blowing snow at my vinyl-wrapped topo map. Our route on the mountain was marked in pencil; to get back to the Eagle Falls road head, we needed to ski north and east. The swirling snow restricted our vision to thirty feet or so. Landmarks around us were invisible in the blizzard. I placed my compass on the map and turned my body slowly until the needle of the compass lined up with the north arrow on the paper. Off we went, heading back to the Westshore Highway, State Route 89.

The snow was accumulating quickly. Already our narrow skis cut deeply into the fluffy stuff, disappearing with each stride, tips appearing again at the beginning of the next. After striding and gliding a hundred yards or so, I paused to glance at the compass. I flinched when I saw that our heading was now due west! Correcting our direction, we set off again, this time pausing after about fifty strides. The compass indicated we were more than forty-five degrees off-course.

After a couple more tries, I realized that I would have to stare at the compass continually in this whiteout. The shifting, blowing, and spiraling curtains of white made it impossible to focus my eyes anywhere but the brass compass held in my snowy mitten.

We stumbled along like this for a couple of hours, working our way down the canyon. Snow coated my wool trousers, then the seams and wrinkles of my parka. In places, the coating built up until it was over an inch thick; then it would crack from movement and fall away in chunks.

We came to a steep drop-off and stopped to huddle over the map.

"Here's where we need to turn east," I said, pointing to the right with my snow-encrusted mitten.

"No, you're wrong," said my companion. "I remember this. We have to go left. I'm sure of it."

We stood in our skis, at the edge of an abyss, arguing. We shouted to be heard over the roar of millions of snowflakes blowing against us in the gale.

Eventually, grudgingly, David said, "Okay, we'll try it your way. Let's get moving."

As we dropped below the summit plateau, the wind lessened, but the snow fell more heavily. Our skis sank deep into the drifts with each stride; the snow came up to our knees. Each step took an exaggerated effort to bring the tip and the ski back to the surface. We were expending enormous amounts of energy and were both breathing heavily from the exertion. I could feel the sweat running down my skin and dampening my clothing, even though my pants and parka were coated with white, granular ice.

As we worked our way across the deep hummocks of powder, house-sized granite boulders and heavily laden firs loomed around us. At one point, my right ski seemed to get stuck under the snow. I planted my poles firmly and kicked upwards, hard. As the wooden ski came up, both binding screws popped out, and the loose board slid to the left, disappearing down the steep slope. Dumbfounded, I scrambled clumsily after it, the boot with the missing ski flailing in the bottomless powder.

Before I could reach the lip of the cliff, Jonathan skied to the edge, threw his skis into a hockey stop, and peered down.

"I can see it!" he shouted into the wind.

I crabbed over to his stance and looked down the steep windswept slope. Lodged against a lone fir tree was the skinny red ski, its pointed tip stopped against the trunk.

"I'll get it," muttered my partner, as he dropped his rucksack to the side. Both skis across the fall line, he sideslipped a few feet at a time down the incline, as I watched helplessly. Grabbing the derelict ski, he sidestepped back up and handed it me.

BOOM! An explosion sounded, quickly followed by another, louder one.

The reports seem to come to come from nowhere or everywhere, not short and sharp like a hunting rifle, but long and rumbling, like distant cannon fire.

Avalanche! the thought came to my mind. Neither of us spoke.

The stainless steel binding screws had vanished into the soft snow.

"You lead," I barked hoarsely. I couldn't break trail with one ski, but perhaps I could follow in David's compressed track.

After following for a few yards, it became clear that I could make very little progress through the deep powder.

"I've got to fix my ski somehow," I called. A few yards ahead, I could barely see a house-sized boulder through the billowing curtains of wheeling flakes. "Let's set up the tent in the lee of that rock."

At the base of the granite block we tramped down the snow with our skis and then boots. Spreading the stiffly frozen tent on the lumpy platform, we held it down with our bodies as we pushed the aluminum stakes into the snow.

We inserted the poles, then tightened the guy lines until the walls stretched. We threw our foam pads and packs inside and burrowed into the tiny, crooked shelter. I pulled the wayward ski and binding in after me and set to work.

After pulling off my mittens, I took out my Swiss Army knife. I twisted the awl blade repeatedly in each empty screw hole until it went completely through the ski. From the top flap of my pack, I took a small roll of baling wire. I passed the end of the wire down through the right hole in the toe plate, through the ski, and up, out of the left hole in the plate. After repeating this twice, I pulled the wires tight and twisted them together with the small pliers on the knife. It might hold, I thought.

Outside the tent, we heard the storm raging through the trees and the creaking and groaning of limbs and trunks battered by the wind. More muffled explosions came to our ears, and then *BAROOM!* came another—much louder, much closer. The sandblast of snow on nylon tent walls was continuous. Although only 3:00 PM Pacific Standard Time, the light was dim and getting darker.

Neither of us relished heading out in this weather, so we

grimly settled down to spend an uncomfortable night. When we attempted to fluff up our sleeping bags, we found that the goose down insulation had frozen in clumps. The brand-new Optimus stove would not burn more than a minute before the flame would die, and it had to be pumped up to pressure again. Some time passed before we were able to melt enough snow to drink a cup of water apiece.

By the time we took a few sips of melt water and ate some cheese and pilot bread, night had fallen. The candle lantern sent shadows flickering crazily across the heaving tent walls. I blew out the candle. We lay side by side spooning as tightly as possible. The two sleeping bags could not zip together. Avalanches roared in the darkness.

Neither of us spoke much as we shivered, each lost in his own morbid thoughts. I do remember David musing, "You know, I don't think this sport will ever become real popular." Another loud boom sounded somewhere off in the darkness. Things didn't look good.

I was overcome with melancholy: *if I die tonight I won't be able to marry Josie this June! I won't get to see my son Ezra grow up! Bummer!* I thought. I wasn't frightened, but more than a little sad. I lay shivering in the darkness, thinking of Josie and the way she pursed her lips to one side when she concentrated on a sewing project. I was wearing a hand-knit turtleneck sweater she had given me, the warmest garment that I had, since the down gear was damp and frozen.

Somehow, David and I both fell asleep that night.

We woke simultaneously; it was quiet! The ridgeline of the tent was glowing bright orange.

David loosened the drawstring and opened the tunnel door to a blank wall of white. Fortunately, we had brought the short aluminum snow shovel into the tent with us, and David quickly dug out the top of the drift. We saw clear blue sky through the hole. Overjoyed, we enlarged the opening and clambered out to stand in full sunlight beside the buried tent. There was not a breath of wind.

Below us, to the east, we could see the deep blue of Lake Tahoe. To the west, behind us, we could see a towering wall of boiling gray snow clouds.

Moving as quickly as we could, we broke camp and hastily stuffed the frozen gear into our sacks. Clamping our boots to our skis, I stamped a few times to test my ersatz binding, then we set off down the hill.

We could see again!

We could ski again!

Coming to a broad, open slope, I was in the lead. Trying to get some speed going, I broke into my best diagonal stride. The soft surface would only give up a short glide at the end of each stride, but my funky repair seemed to be holding.

As I moved along, I realized that the snow was breaking loose under my skis as I passed over it, triggering an avalanche. If I paused in one spot, my skis would start sliding down too. This was like running from danger in a dream with your feet mired in sticky mud.

The nightmare was repeated a few more times as we crossed unstable slopes, but finally we skied across the Eagle Falls picnic area to David's buried Toyota. We dug out the little car, threw the rucksacks into the back, and clamped our skis and poles to the roof rack. The car started right up, and we made it just onto Highway 89, where the vehicle became firmly stuck. We held a quick council of war and decided to set up our tent yet again. We hung up our damp gear to dry.

"We can wait for a snowplow and follow it down to South Shore," said David.

After pitching the tent and hanging the sleeping bags in the bright sunlight, I started gathering firewood. If we had to spend another night in the open, we needed to have a fire for cooking. As I snapped dead branches hanging from the trunks of the firs, I heard, then saw, a dark green pickup with oversized tractor tires coming down the snowed up highway. The big truck pitched and wallowed through the drifts as it approached. David and I "post-holed" to the edge of the buried road as the rig stopped. A young man wearing a green baseball cap with a bear silhouette on the front stuck his head out. "Are you guys okay?"

"Yes, but we seem to be stuck," David answered.

"That storm caught everyone by surprise," said the ranger, climbing down from the cab. "I work at D. L. Bliss State Park. Have you seen three high school kids back there?" he asked, inclining his head towards our ski tracks where they emerged from the forest.

We told him that we had talked to them on Saturday, that they told us they were going to camp at Velma Lakes, and that we had not seen them since. Taking a memo pad from the pocket of his khaki wool shirt, he wrote something down. "Could I have your names, please?"

Just as I was spelling out my last name, a gray Seahawk helicopter appeared over a snowy ridge, its rotors thumping the air loudly. NAVY was painted in big black letters on its side. A huge, white cloud of dry powder snow boiled up in the brilliant sunlight, as the clattering machine settled to the unplowed parking lot. As its turbines started to wind down, our interrogator stuffed his pad and ballpoint back in his pocket and ran towards the craft.

The side door slid back, a helmeted crewman crouching in the doorway. Our new friend had covered the 50 yard distance by this time, and he went up to the open hatch and spoke to the aviator. The ranger drew back, and the airman began heaving large duffel bags out of the copter and onto the snow.

The crewman slammed the side door closed, and the turbines and rotors of the big machine began to wind up. Ducking away from the rotor blast, the ranger retraced his footsteps back to his monster truck. After the airship roared off in another cloud of white, he told us what he'd learned.

"They found those three kids up by Velma Lakes and landed next to their camp. One of the kids is dead, and the other two are in bad shape. The helicopter couldn't lift out all three at that altitude, so they came here to unload their sea rescue stuff," he paused. "They want to get out before the back half of the storm arrives."

Silent, we all looked westward, where the wall of gray cloud seemed closer.

"I'm going to try going down to Camp Richardson," the young ranger said. "If you guys want to get out of here, pack up your gear and come with me. This road won't be plowed for another week or so, until the avalanche danger has gone down."

Without hesitation we both said, "Thanks!" and scrambled to stuff and stow our drying tent and mummy bags. Five minutes later, the state park truck was pitching and rolling through the drifts, our packs, skis, and poles stowed in the back.

In another hour night had fallen. The big truck came to a stop under a streetlight in South Lake Tahoe. We could see a glowing Motel 6 sign and, next door, a Mexican restaurant. Pulling our gear from the cargo bed, we thanked our rescue ranger again.

"Your tax dollars at work," he said as he pulled away. "Take care!" The truck disappeared into the night. It began to snow.

Before David and I got a room, before we had tacos and beer, I had a phone call to make. On the corner stood a glowing telephone booth, snowflakes swirling out of the dark around it. Dropping a couple of quarters into the slot, I dialed my home number.

"Hello?" came Josie's voice.

"We're okay," I said.

———

I realized what a close call that had been. Luck, grit, or providence had spared me.

In a way, I was living on borrowed time. I intended to make it count.

Now I Get It

AFTER ALL MY ADVENTURES on the road, lightbulbs were clicking on. I had begun to figure out a few things. I knew that authorities couldn't always be believed. Back in Arkansas, I had been taught that black folks were lazy, stupid, and dirty. After seeing how hard the Cooney family had to work, and how clever Robert was with mechanical things, I knew that lazy or stupid they were not.

As far as dirty was concerned, indoor plumbing would have cured that easily. Black sharecroppers simply couldn't afford showers, toilets, or water heaters. The federal government had made some progress in civil rights, but this was far too little, and much too late, to improve the lives of the sharecroppers or Pueblo Indians that I had known.

I had learned that the government could not be blindly trusted. When the State of Arkansas condemned and destroyed our dairy herd, our family trusted that it was necessary to stop the spread of brucellosis. The government later admitted that not one of our cows had been infected. Uncle Sugar fooled us again when the Vietnam war was cooked up. My parents' generation dutifully supported the effort—my generation less so.

Experiences with various police departments left me with an abiding mistrust of people with badges. I had been rousted, arrested, shackled, teargassed, tortured, and jailed by officers without any real reason except for my long hair. When I started getting haircuts again, after I began working at an advertising agency, the harassment stopped. It's not that easy for young black or Latino men. As I write this in the twenty-first century, darker-skinned people are stopped, jailed, and executed unjustly, at a much higher rate than their light-skinned brethren.

A society that doesn't evolve will stagnate, wither, and die. The Old South was destroyed by its hidebound devotion to slavery, a medieval practice both cruel and outmoded. The luxurious lifestyle of the white slaveowners was doomed, because slave labor was less efficient and productive than the free enterprise system of the North.

These days, forces are angrily trying to roll back the calendar to some imaginary "golden era" of racism and imperial wars. Idiots proudly wave Confederate flags in violent demonstrations, and angry men try to dictate what goes on in a woman's private parts. I knew that Skip Strobel, my old pal from high school, was gay—and more than happy about it. Linda and Lucy, Alice's lesbian friends, were in love and excited about spending their lives together. I don't think anyone can choose who they love, and it's nobody else's business, anyway. Society is now starting to recognize that gay people are integral to human life—not dangerous criminals.

After my family had been raptured off to Hong Kong by the Foreign Mission Board, I'd been left to sort life out on my own. When I had gone on the road to homelessness, I missed food, shelter, and most of all, companionship.

I knew I was a hopeless romantic. My friendships with girls were easygoing and sweet, with none of the roughness and competition I felt around other males. I was as irresistibly attracted to women as I was to breaking waves or mountain peaks.

I knew, down deep inside, that I wanted and needed to marry and have children with Josie, my own true love.

Married on the beach at Half Moon Bay, June 11th. 1977

Epilogue

DAVID ROSS and I stood on the sand of Miramar beach. My father stood behind us, holding a black book. Walking towards us across the sand, a bagpiper skirled a wedding march. Here came Josie on her father's arm, with a hundred friends, relatives, and children in loose ranks behind. Even Susie, my former wife, showed up.

My folks had returned from Hong Kong, so my family and Josie's were there. Ezra and his five-year-old cronies hoisted goldfish kites on bamboo poles.

The bride wore a simple, white gauze gown by *Gunne Sax*, a garland of flowers on her head. My dad said an invocation in his big Baptist preacher's voice, then Josie and I read the vows we had written a few days before. Ezra, wearing a sailor suit, held up a pillow with two rings tied on top. I slid one onto Josie's finger and she put the other on mine.

"By the authority vested in me by God and the State of California, I now pronounce you husband and wife," said my father.

Josie and I put our arms around each other and kissed. We held hands as we walked up the beach. The piper struck up *Bonaparte's Retreat*, and the surf roared.

We've been holding hands for over forty years now.

Acknowledgments

I OWE A DEBT OF GRATITUDE to the people that encouraged me to write these chapters, and to those who patiently listened when I read aloud from my first attempts.

John Coate, a long-haul trucker, musician, and Internet pioneer kept me honest and contributed a blurb to my previous volume, *Cold 'Coon & Collards*.

Ruth Ganong, Anna Hobbet, and Ginny Holmes-Hobbet said they enjoyed the stories—and asked for more.

Peggy Vincent gave me some expert coaching at the beginning. She had been either the nurse, midwife, or Lamaze instructor for the birth of each of my children. For the birth of my memoir, she shared her experiences and methods for writing and publishing her own memoir, *Baby Catcher: Chronicles of a Modern Midwife*.

My Berkeley neighbor, Emily Hancock, started a memoir writers group. She, Sarah Liu, Jane Harada, and I met weekly and read copies of each other's work, marked them up, then discussed the latest chapters. Two of these women have PhDs. Two are retired magazine editors, and one is a published author. As a high school dropout, I listened closely to these brilliant women. They never steered me wrong. I only hope my observations helped their work as well.

David Hazard of *Ascent* writers services coached me in developing my written scenes into two coherent books: *Cold 'Coon and Collards* and *Lightbulb Coffee*. His experience in writing and publishing gave me prompts and techniques invaluable for this first-time author.

My old friend and ceramic art mentor Christa Assad put on her proofreader's hat and cleaned up my messy punctuation and occasional faulty sentence structure in preparation for publication.

My sister, Polly Schnick Aftreth, contributed memories that helped me greatly, and provided the photos in the book.

My biggest debt is to Josie Jurczenia, my dear wife and partner in crime. She put up with my daily disappearance into my writing studio and gamely sat through countless readings. Only because of her steady encouragement and sage criticism have I been able to pull this off.

John Mark Schnick

Berkeley, California, 2020

CPSIA information can be obtained
at www.ICGtesting.com
Printed in the USA
FSHW010826131120
75758FS